CW00823164

Conversations with Octavia Butle

Literary Conversations Series
Peggy Whitman Prenshaw
General Editor

Conversations with Octavia Butler

Edited by
Conseula Francis

University Press of Mississippi
Jackson

www.upress.state.ms.us

The University Press of Mississippi is a member of the Association of American University Presses.

Copyright © 2010 by University Press of Mississippi
All rights reserved
Manufactured in the United States of America

First printing 2010
∞
Library of Congress Cataloging-in-Publication Data

Butler, Octavia E.
    Conversations with Octavia Butler / edited by Conseula Francis.
        p. cm. — (Literary conversations series)
    Includes index.
    ISBN 978-1-60473-275-7 (alk. paper) — ISBN 978-1-60473-276-4 (pbk. : alk. paper)
1. Butler, Octavia E.—Interviews. 2. Authors, American—20th century—Interviews.
3. African American authors—Interviews. 4. Science fiction—Authorship. I. Francis,
Conseula. II. Title.
    PS3552.U827Z46 2010
    813'.54—dc22
    [B]

                                                                      2009019222

British Library Cataloging-in-Publication Data available

Books by Octavia Butler

Patternmaster (Doubleday, 1976)
Mind of My Mind (Doubleday, 1977)
Survivor (Doubleday, 1978)
Kindred (Doubleday, 1979)
Wild Seed (Doubleday, 1980)
Clay's Ark (St. Martins, 1984)
Dawn (Warner Books, 1987)
Adulthood Rites (Warner Books, 1988)
Imago (Warner Books, 1989)
Parable of the Sower (Four Walls Eight Windows, 1993)
Bloodchild and Other Stories (Four Walls Eight Windows, 1995)
Parable of the Talents (Seven Stories Press,1998)
Fledgling (Seven Stories Press, 2005)

Contents

Introduction

"When I began writing science fiction, when I began reading, heck, I wasn't in any of this stuff I read. The only black people you found were occasional characters or characters who were so feeble-witted that they couldn't manage anything, anyway. I wrote myself in, since I'm me and I'm here and I'm writing."

—Octavia Butler, *New York Times*, 2000

Octavia Butler was born on June 22, 1947, in Pasadena, California. After her shoe-shiner father died when she was very young, Butler (nicknamed Junie) was raised by her mother, who supported the family by working as a maid. Painfully shy and awkward as a child, Butler, in the manner of shy and awkward kids everywhere, used reading and writing to combat loneliness and boredom. So begins the standard introduction interviewers use when talking about Octavia Butler: native Californian, raised by a single mother, loner as a child, science fiction fan turned Nebula and Hugo award–winning science fiction author, recipient of a MacArthur "genius" grant, the only black woman (for a time) working in a decidedly white, male genre. All of these things are true. Yet, none of them even begins to scratch the surface of what makes Octavia Butler such a fascinating figure in American letters. The interviews gathered here, beginning early in her career before the publication of the novels that would bring her great fame and ending with an interview conducted shortly before her death, help us begin to assess what Butler's literary legacy will be.

Butler and her work are often linked to the work of fellow African American science fiction writer Samuel R. Delany. In some respects, this coupling makes sense. Both Butler and Delany are black writers working in a genre with very few black writers, or characters. Both write stories that explore and challenge our notions of race, gender, sexuality, and humanity. But while Delany dedicates a great deal of his work to challenging our notions of human desire and human consciousness, Butler focuses on reshaping traditional science fiction subgenres, like the alien abduction story or the dystopian novel. And where Delany is often more than forthcoming in his interviews about his personal life, especially his sexual life, Butler tells interviewers very few intimate details. Whether interviewers are too focused on her work to care about who she was dating or sensed that certain questions were off-limits, the interviews collected here reveal a woman who seemed to accept her public role as a writer, and who was also very good at maintaining the boundaries of that public role.

Butler is also often compared to other female science fiction writers like Ursula K. Le Guin, Anne McCaffrey, and Andre Norton. Again, at first blush these comparisons make sense. Butler peopled her novels with strong, complex, capable female characters who challenged conventional science fiction notions of gender. Rather than women existing only as appendages to men or who retreat happily to Stone Age gender roles at the first sign of a crack in the social order, Butler instead offers women through whom the reader explores questions of the essential elements of human nature and the most effective way to organize human society. Yet, while Butler was a feminist, her feminism, as with her blackness, serve as a backdrop to her writing. As she "wrote [her]self" she did so without a particular feminist or racial agenda. Instead she grounded her work in truths based in her understanding of her self as black and female. She felt it important to acknowledge that her black, female existence produced different experiences than those typically found in science fiction. She tried to write stories rooted in those experiences.

The interviews collected here reflect the three audiences Butler always claimed she had: science fiction fans, black readers, and feminists. And after she is awarded the MacArthur Fellowship in 1995, the interviews begin to reflect a literary fiction audience as well. Despite the wide array of places she was interviewed, however, there are number of consistencies in the interviews.

First, there is Butler's sense of her own writing project. She repeatedly tells reviewers that she is interested in social power and that she understands humans to be hierarchical by nature. She tells interviewers that she aimed to challenge the conventions of the science fiction of her youth and tried to write about the world as she knew it, a world which included few white swashbuckling men and happily, inexplicably submissive women. In these interviews we get a strong sense that Butler remained committed to a vision all her own throughout her career.

We also see in these interviews Butler being quite savvy about the identity categories most often attached to her. She was well aware of the marketing benefit of touting her as the "only black female science fiction writer" and of continuing to label her work science fiction even when it ceased to have anything to do with science at all. She seemed to get what was seductive about the narrative of a poor black girl turned award-winning science fiction legend. Yet, we also see in the interviews Butler resisting these identity categories. The interviewer from *Crisis* insists on comparing her work to Richard Wright's *Native Son*, and Butler's impatience with the narrative the interviewer is trying to construct, that of a lone black literary voice railing against the American system, is clear. And as much as she understood publishers' need to market her work, she tells the interviewer of SciFiDimensions.com that she finds questions about her identity "tiresome." The interviews gathered here reveal that Butler worked very hard at making clear distinctions between the person created by publishers to sell books and the person she understood herself to be. She insisted that interviewers make this distinction as well.

When asked to describe herself, Butler often fell back on the self-penned description included in many of her books: "I'm comfortably asocial—a hermit in the middle of Seattle—a pessimist if I'm not careful, a feminist, a black, a former Baptist, an oil-and-water combination of ambition, laziness, insecurity, certainty and drive." While this is certainly as much a construction as the marketable "only black female writing science fiction" Octavia Butler, it was, at least, her own construction. Every once in a while, though, the interviews reveal a piece of Butler outside the construction. For instance, from the 2000 *Seattle Times* interview we find out to what she attributes her early persistence in writing despite the lack of any success or encouragement: "I just didn't have any sense," she says. In the 1980 *Equal Opportunity Forum Magazine* interview, we learn that she was addicted to TV talk shows; and the 1990 Larry McCaffery interview reveals that she collected comic books.

The interviews also reveal a writer who was incredibly generous with her time, sitting down for interviews with major publications (*Publishers Weekly*), independent newspapers (*San Francisco Bay Guardian*), and individual fans (Jelani Cobb). And while she seemed happy to entertain questions and discuss the particulars of her work in depth, she was not above correcting people she thought had misread her. This is particularly true of those interviewers who insist on citing slavery as a central theme in her work. Her response to Randall Kenan's insistence that the story "Bloodchild" is about slavery, that it is, in fact, a story about "paying the rent," is a classic in Butler lore. And while she seemed to have little problem with differences in critical opinion about her work, she rejected wholly any attributions to her subconscious some reviewers insisted on. The interview with Marilyn Mehaffy and AnaLouise Keating is fascinating in this regard.

But mostly what we get in these interviews is that Octavia Butler is serious about her work and serious about what her work reveals about society and humans and our future. The post-apocalyptic future of the Parable stories, the inability of humans to assimilate change and difference in the Xenogenesis books, the destructive sense of superiority in the Patternist series—these were not simply interesting fiction for Butler. Keeping with the tradition of the best science fiction, Butler holds up a mirror, reflecting back to us what is beautiful and corrupt and worthwhile and damning about the world we live in. And while her vision of us is often dark and violent, it is also, always, hopeful.

Butler speaks often in interviews of her three audiences: science fiction fans, feminists, and African American readers. Both Butler and her interviewers treat these three audiences as if they were mutually exclusive, meeting only in the readerly space created by Butler's work. But there I was, an avid reader and English major, often the only black student in my literature classes, just discovering science fiction; coming to my own feminist consciousness, in the manner of many young women in college; and navigating the shifting boundaries of black identity, my college years coinciding, as they did, with the neo-black nationalism of the early 1990s. Though I didn't know it when I read that first Butler novel, *Dawn*, I was all of Butler's readers rolled into one. What struck me about that book was that it didn't speak to me as black person, though I think her work falls solidly within the African American literary tradition; or a feminist, though, of course, her work is guided by a decidedly feminist politics; or as a science fiction fan. Here was a black woman writing about black women without defining for me womanhood or blackness. A writer creating worlds shaped by feminist politics who didn't dictate to me what my feminism should look like. She defied my expectations of what science fiction, women's writing, and African American literature could be, and in defying those expectations showed me new (intellectual, literary, personal) possibilities. Her work, as much as the author herself, resisted labels.

What readers will find in these interviews, and in her work, is a writer who consistently resisted labels and challenged expectations. We want her to be deeply interested in protesting racism because she is a black writer. We want her to create female utopias because she is a feminist writer. We want her to charm us with surprising details about her life because that's what writers do. But Butler refuses all of these expectations. In the end, as the interviews reveals, the only expectations she tried to live up to were her own.

When I first proposed collecting Octavia Butler's interviews for University Press of Mississippi's Literary Conversation series, her last novel, *Fledgling*, had just been released and seemed poised to be the first in a series of stories set in a world as engaging and provocative as the worlds she created for the Patternist, Xenogenesis, and Parable series. I hoped this collection would include an interview of my own, a second chance at meeting Butler, this time as a scholar rather than as a fan awash in the fog of new motherhood. I imagined asking her the questions I wished I'd asked the first time I met her, at a bookstore in Seattle: did she believe that art had the power to affect change? Does she feel a particular responsibility after winning the MacArthur "genius" grant? What character from her books did she most identify with? What did she find so compelling about the issue of social power? Does she see her work as part of the African American literary tradition? I won't ever get to interview her, but I believe her inclination would be to respond to my questions by directing me back to her work. For, if a collection like this, particularly one put together after an author's death, is an attempt at shaping a legacy, surely what Butler's interviews reveal is that her legacy lies within the novels and stories that she's left us.

This book would have been impossible without the indefatigable assistance of Teresa Hooper and Edward Lenahan, the wit and camaraderie of the Super Ninja Writing Force, and, as always, the patience of Brian McCann. My many thanks to them all.

CF

Chronology

1947 Octavia Estelle Butler is born in Pasadena, California, on June 22, 1947 to Laurice and Octavia M. Butler. Her father, a shoeshine man, dies when Butler is very young. Her mother supports Octavia, her only child, with domestic work.

1959–60 Butler sees the science fiction film *Devil Girl from Mars* on television and decides that she can write a better story.

1968 Earns an associate's degree from Pasadena City College.

1969 Enrolls in the Screen Writers Guild Open Door Program at Cal State, Los Angeles. There she meets science fiction writer Harlan Ellison who encourages her to attend the Clarion workshop.

1970 Attends Clarion Science Fiction and Fantasy Writing Workshop.

1971 Publishes first story, "Crossover," in Clarion anthology.

1976 Publishes first novel, *Patternmaster*; uses book advance to take a Greyhound Ameripass Tour around the country; visits Seattle for the first time.

1977 Publishes *Mind of My Mind*.

1978 Publishes *Survivor*.

1979 Publishes *Kindred*.

1980 Publishes *Wild Seed*.

1984 Publishes *Clay's Ark*, which wins a James Tiptree Award; her short story "Speech Sounds" wins a Hugo award and another story, "Bloodchild," wins a Nebula.

1985 "Bloodchild" wins a Hugo.

1987 Publishes *Dawn*, the first book in the Xenogenesis series.

1988 Publishes *Adulthood Rites*.

1989 Publishes *Imago*.

1993 Publishes *Parable of the Sower*, the first of the Parable books; the book is a Nebula finalist.

1995 Wins the MacArthur "genius grant," which comes with a $295,000

prize; publishes a collection of short stories, *Bloodchild and Other
Stories.*

1998   Publishes *Parable of the Talents*; the book wins a Nebula.

2000   Moves to Seattle, Washington.

2005   Publishes final novel, *Fledgling.*

2006   Dies in Washington on February 24, 2006, after a fall outside her home.

Conversations with Octavia Butler

Sci-Fi Visions: An Interview with Octavia Butler

Rosalie G. Harrison/1980

From *Equal Opportunity Forum Magazine*, November 1980.

RGH: How did you become interested in science fiction (s.f.) writing?

OB: I have always read sci fi. I enjoyed it when I was young although I didn't realize it was a separate genre. As a child I wrote many stories about horses; I was crazy about horses. One day, when I was twelve, I was writing one of my horse stories and watching television when I noticed that I was watching a really terrible science fiction movie. I thought, "I can do better than that." So, I turned off the TV and I wrote a s.f. story. Reading or watching a dreadful s.f. story has been the impetus for a lot of science fiction writers.

RGH: What were your early writing years like?

OB: Frustrating. Frustrating. During those years I collected lots of frustration and rejection slips.

RGH: Because you wrote science fiction?

OB: No. Because I didn't know what I was doing and I didn't really have anyone to help me. If I had a chance to write a little fiction for a class it would always be s.f. My teachers would read it and insist that I had copied it from somewhere or that someone had written it for me because it sounded stranger than anything they knew about.

English teachers were people I had to escape from. I learned to write one way for English teachers and another way for myself. When I enrolled in a class—"Writing for Publication"—I discovered that there is one kind of writing that does not go over well with publishers and that was the kind English teachers seem to like.

RGH: What kept you writing despite the rejection slips and the frustration?

OB: People. People who were willing to listen to me even when I was rolling in rejection slips . . . somebody who would listen and not say, "You're crazy; why don't you do something else?"

The people who have had the most influence on me are people that I've never met. Writers, mostly. They wrote books—corny, self-help books. Not the seventies type which say "Get them before they get you." I'm talking about books like *The Magic of Thinking Big.* They are incredibly corny but they gave me the kind of push that I needed and that nobody among my family or friends could give me. These books helped give me the ability to persist. I would go and read them almost the way some people read the Bible. They would help me go on despite feelings of absolute worthlessness.

I had one very good teacher who is also a writer, Harlan Ellison. He gave me a lot of help and a hard push or two when I needed them. It so happens that he writes a lot of fantasy and science fiction and was able to give me the kind of help I wouldn't have received from some English teacher.

RGH: Will you ever work in other genres?
OB: There's always going to be something a little strange about my books or characters. For instance, the novel *Kindred* did not come out of s.f. It's fantasy. But that is probably as far as I'm going to get from s.f.

Right now I'm working on a novel about a woman who develops a cancer somewhere around her pituitary gland. She is very reluctant to have any kind of surgery because one of her relatives died in surgery and her father shot himself because he had cancer. So she lets it go and lets it go, and it slowly develops that she's growing a new gland. She is a kind of mutation.

RGH: What do you find most beneficial about writing science fiction?
OB: The main benefit for me is the freedom. For instance, I'm planning a novel that will take place in ancient Egypt and it will have the Doro character from *Wild Seed* going back to his origins. I've written a novel that takes place in the distant future and one that takes place in the present. I have written two novels about early America—one in colonial times and one in pre-Civil War days. In s.f. you can go into any sociological or technological problem and extrapolate from there.

RGH: What sets sci fi readers apart from the general reader?
OB: I think science fiction writers are a little bit more willing to use their minds. They want different things to think about. They don't want to read about things as they are. They're bored with the present. Maybe they want to escape from the present. A lot of science fiction readers start out as the weird kid, the out kid in junior high or grade school. When I went to the Clarion Science Fiction Writers

Workshop, I was surprised to find myself surrounded by the out kids. People who are, or were, rejects.

Science fiction in America began with a lot of young people, the weirdos, who were interested in science and technology. Their interest in people was not always encouraged by their social circumstances.

RGH: Let's talk about the writers for a moment. How many successful black writers are in science fiction?

OB: I know of three who are actually living off their work. I'm one. Steve Barnes who also lives in L.A. is another. And Samuel R. Delany who lives in New York City is the third.

RGH: You're the only black woman science fiction writer.

OB: Yes. That's true. It makes me the smallest minority in science fiction. At this moment, at least.

RGH: Blacks don't seem to read a lot of science fiction. Why is that do you think?

OB: I think it's a kind of circular problem. I think blacks don't like to read about a universe that is either green or all white.

RGH: What do you mean? Martians and white people?

OB: You have your aliens, extraterrestrial beings, and white humans in most science fiction stories. I think the only way to remedy that is to have more black science fiction writers. Unfortunately, s.f. writers come from s.f. readers and since not very many blacks have been attracted to s.f., we have very few black science fiction writers.

At my first s.f. convention in 1970 there was one other black person there. I went to a convention in Boston this year and there were a large number of black people. I do see a slow growth in the black s.f. readership.

RGH: Science fiction movies have been big box office hits in the last two or three years. The big one, *Star Wars*, excluded minorities, but in the sequel, *The Empire Strikes Back*, Billie Dee Williams is one of the main characters. Do you think we'll see more minorities in s.f. now?

OB: Well, let me put it this way: if it's okay to include human beings, I think it's okay to include minorities. As far as Williams is concerned, I don't really know. I was glad he was there, but watching Billie Dee Williams play that role was like watching *Jesus Christ Superstar* and realizing that we'd finally made it into Biblical films: we could play Judas. Some book I read made the observation that they finally gave us a black character in *Star Trek* and they made her a telephone operator.

I guess I don't like taking what I'm given. That's why I'm hoping there will be more black s.f. writers, more black writers period. Any minority group needs people who can speak from the group's perspective, maybe not speak for the whole group, but at least from a certain point of view and experience.

RGH: You speak of minorities and their place, or lack of place, in science fiction. What are your feelings about the view that a black character should not be introduced unless his or her blackness is in some way significant to the story?
OB: What it really means is that to be black is to be abnormal. The norm is white, apparently, in the view of people who see things in that way. For them the only reason you would introduce a black character is to introduce this kind of abnormality. Usually, it's because you're telling a story about racism or at least about race.

I've agreed to do an anthology with another writer. It's supposed to be an anthology about and by black people. He sent me six stories that he thought would possibly be worth including. But . . . they were not stories about black people. Except for one, they were all stories about racism. I wrote back to him about something I feel very strongly: racism is only one facet or aspect of black existence. A lot of white writers (and some black writers) see it as the totality of black existence. What I want to do is pull in some good black writers who will write about black people and not just about how terrible it is to be hated.

RGH: How can science fiction's influence be used in a positive way in regard to minorities and women?
OB: I see science fiction as a way of disseminating the fact that we don't have only one kind of people, namely white males, in this world. They are not the only ones who are here; not the only ones who count. It's very easy for a person who lives in a segregated neighborhood, either black or white, who works at a job with only one kind of people, who goes to movies and watches TV (which is pretty white) to forget this fact. It's easy for a person, if it's a white person, to get the idea that they are really the only ones who matter. They may not think of it quite that way, but that is the impression they internalize because of all that's around them. I think it is a writer's duty to write about human differences, all human differences, and help make them acceptable. I think s.f. writers can do this if they want to. In my opinion, they are a lot more likely to have a social conscience than other kinds of writers.

Science fiction writers like to think of themselves as progressive. They like to think of themselves as open-minded and it's possible in some cases to show them that they are lying to themselves when they portray the world as all white or the universe as all white.

RGH: There seems to be a widespread opinion that blacks have had their day. Do you see the same happening to the women's movements?
OB: Well, America is a country of fads. I don't think that it will happen to the women's movement. But it seems to me that the media is advertising the death of the women's movement. A vast majority of states have ratified the ERA but those few left are preventing the ERA from being added to the Constitution. I keep hearing, on TV talk shows (something I'm becoming addicted to), the attitude that somehow ERA is not what people want. If it is what the people wanted, then it would have passed. These people often don't realize how many of the states have already ratified it. I don't mean to imply that there is some organized media campaign against the ERA, but since we're so faddish, and since the ERA is kind of old news, in a sense, it is being helped to die.

RGH: *Omni* magazine recently quoted Dr. Sabin, developer of the live virus oral vaccine for polio, as saying: "It may sound like a paradox, but my hope is that in the future we may die, ultimately, in good health." When I read this, I thought of your character, Anyanwu, in *Wild Seed*, who is able to look inside her body and detect which organ is malfunctioning and repair or correct it. Does this lend some credence to the idea that s.f. is prophetic?
OB: Science fiction can be prophetic although I hadn't really intended Anyanwu to be prophetic. I find myself in agreement with Sabin, although I wonder how one would die of good health. Why wouldn't one just linger until senility or dis-integration?

I was surprised to read an article, not too long ago, by a doctor who said it was really kind of silly to try to get rid of some of these diseases because, after all, we have to die from something. That might sound all right if you are hardened to watching people die, but I watched one person die of cancer and that was enough to start me thinking about characters like Anyanwu.

RGH: And yet, at one point in the novel, Anyanwu decided to shut herself off.
OB: Yes. She had that much control over her body.

RGH: If we reach a point where people no longer die of physical diseases, what do you think will cause death?
OB: Probably boredom.

It is actually possible to die of boredom. Anyanwu had a different reason for dying. Actually she and Doro (main characters in *Mind of My Mind* and *Wild Seed* with chameleon-like qualities) are different versions of what immortality could be. Doro is immortal and destructive. Anyanwu is immortal and creative. Her whole reason for deciding to die was being unable to tolerate Doro any longer although she was also unable to get along without him.

RGH: What changes have you seen in s.f. in the last ten years?
OB: Science fiction is becoming a lot more human. We have a lot more women writers now. It really is remarkable how well the woman characters have developed. Earlier s.f. tended to portray women as little dolls who were rewards for their heroes, or they were bitches . . . In other words, non-people. In a way I suppose that this is similar to the stage black people are going through; although I do find a lot more women who are interested in writing s.f. and who are doing it.

RGH: If indeed, science fiction is prophetic, do you, as a science fiction writer, have any prophecies to share? What kind of future do you see for humanity?
OB: I am pessimistic about our real future. I see so many books about the future, both science fiction and popular science, telling us about the wonderful technological breakthroughs that will make our lives so much better. But I never see anything about the sociological aspects of our future lives. Some science fiction people are thinking in terms of ecological problems, but the attitude in popular science seems to be, "Oh, we'll solve these problems; we always have."

For instance, there is the question of the nuclear waste from power plants. I'm not saying that it is going to destroy us all. It's just that I think it is a little dangerous to decide we will go ahead and make this stuff that is going to take more time than we have been civilized to deteriorate. But we assume that somehow, someday, someone will find a way to take care of it. I don't think people are paying enough attention to the long-term aspects of what we are doing to the earth. We are shortsighted. Especially in this country. I'm afraid that we are so used to having it good that what we want to do is find another way to have it just as good as we have always had it.

RGH: What do you see as the difference between the future as science fiction writers see it, and certain religious beliefs that say we are coming to our last days?
OB: My mother is very religious so I'm very much aware of the attitude that these are the last days. But, let's face it, no matter where we have been in history, whoever has existed has been living in the last days . . . their own. When each of us dies the world ends for us. Not too long ago, I was at a science fiction convention and we had a panel on religion. One of the topics was the fact that s.f. tends

not to deal with religion, and when it does deal with it, it's with contempt. Science fiction seems more interested in machines than in people. It tends to dismiss religion.

I don't think that's wise because religion has played such a large part in the lives of human beings throughout human history. In some ways, I wish we could outgrow it; I think at this point it does a lot of harm. But then, I'm fairly sure that if we do outgrow it we'll find other reasons to kill and persecute each other. I wish we were able to depend on ethical systems that did not involve the Big Policeman in the sky. But I don't think this will happen. I'm not sure about the meaning of the Born Again movement. It could be positive but it could also be very destructive.

I see religion as something that really isn't controlling people and helping to channel their energy away from destruction. Sometimes it becomes destructive itself. It scares me. I was raised a Born Again Baptist and I remember a minister from a different church coming to our church. He was really spewing out prejudice against the Jews and Catholics and anyone else who disagreed with him. Just as telling, he didn't get the kind of congregational feedback that you would expect from people who worshipped the Prince of Peace. The kind of religion that I'm seeing now is not the religion of love and it scares me. We need to outgrow it.

What we've done is create for ourselves the massive power of a Big Policeman in the sky. It would be nice if we would police ourselves. I think that in one way or another we will do ourselves in. Sooner or later the generation that says "we're living in our last days" really will be. But not because somebody strikes us from heaven. We'll do it to ourselves. And, to the future.

An Interview with Octavia E. Butler

Larry McCaffery and Jim McMenamin/1988

From *Across the Wounded Galaxies: Interviews with Contemporary American Science Fiction Writers*, edited by Larry McCaffery. Urbana: University of Illinois Press, 1990. Copyright © 1990 by Board of Trustees of the University of Illinois. Used with permission of the University of Illinois Press.

Although labels distort what is unique about an author's work, to say that Octavia Butler is a "black feminist science fiction writer from Southern California" serves to open up a discussion of her work, rather than to narrowly pigeonhole it. As Butler herself puts it, "I really have three fairly distinct audiences: feminists, SF fans, and black readers." The way her work weaves these three strands into a provocative whole is what makes her fiction so unusual and compelling.

Butler made these observations to Jim McMenamin and me at her home, a modest duplex in a middle-class, primarily black neighborhood located near the absolute center (if such a point exists) of Los Angeles. It was a glorious July afternoon in 1988, and although we conducted most of the interview on a park bench overlooking the La Brea Tar Pits, our brief interlude at her home provided numerous clues about the seemingly paradoxical elements of her intellectual and literary sensibility. While Butler was signing some of her books for us, we busied ourselves examining her bookcases, which contained (in addition to the expected rows of SF novels) a revealing selection of scientific texts, anthropology books, volumes devoted to black history, albums (jazz, rock, blues), and an impressive number of cassette tapes, which turned out to be mostly National Public Radio selections that she listens to on her Walkman, mainly while riding the bus or walking. (Like Ray Bradbury, Butler does not drive a car.)

Octavia Butler has been publishing SF novels since the mid-1970s. Her early work received excellent critical notices and reviews, but only during the past several years has she begun to attract significant attention from outside SF's insular community. Her fiction has its roots in her experiences as a black woman growing up in a society dominated by white people, particularly white men. With the publication of her Patternist novels, she immediately signaled her interest in anthropological, racial, and political themes.

Given her background, we might naturally expect Butler to focus specifically on racial and sexual issues—and to use science fiction to suggest alternatives to our own society's sexual and racial structures. On one level her works do exactly that. For example, two of her most expansive and provocative novels, *Kindred* (1979) and *Wild Seed* (1980) employ time-travel premises that permit strong black heroines to roam through prior historical periods; Butler uses these confrontations with actual historical circumstances to create fresh, revealing perspectives about past and present racial and sexual biases. In *Kindred*, a strong, adaptable black woman is cast back to the early days of slavery in pre–Civil War America—a wonderfully simple but suggestive vehicle for developing juxtapositions between our own age's assumptions and those of earlier eras. Such interactions are further developed in *Wild Seed*, which moves across two continents and spans over two hundred years. *Wild Seed* traces the evolution of an unlikely love affair between Anyanwu (an African sorceress and shape-shifter) and Doro, a vampirish figure who is intent on establishing a superhuman race by selectively breeding individuals who possess "special" traits. Part of the success of *Wild Seed* is due to Butler's meticulously detailed and vivid renderings of the various environments through which Anyanwu passes. Each of these cultures—a neolithic African village, a slave ship, eighteenth-century New England, and antebellum Louisiana— provides her with an opportunity to examine societal and personal attitudes that not only gave rise to slavery and gender stereotyping but also contribute to contemporary prejudices.

What gradually becomes clear in both *Kindred* and *Wild Seed*, however, is that the dilemmas facing the heroines arise not only from specific, locatable sources of racial and sexual oppression but also from larger political, economic, and psychological forces. The struggle for power, control, and individual dominance/mastery over other creatures and the natural environment is a primal struggle common to all creatures—and it is in this sense that Butler's best work, for all its vivid particularities and subtle treatment of psychological issues, transcends narrow categorization as "black" or "feminist." Anyanwu is probably Butler's most complex and fully realized character to date, possessing the inner strength and nurturing tendencies we associate with many recent feminist authors; she is also a fierce and violent woman who is not reducible to familiar stereotypes. Butler uses race and gender to explore the universal issues of human isolation and our mutual desire for power and transcendence—and the longing for means to bridge this isolation via community, family, and sexual union.

These issues are developed throughout Butler's Patternist novels, including *Patternmaster* (1976), *Mind of My Mind* (1977), and *Survivor* (1978), which move backward and forward through past and future histories on Earth and in outer space. The unifying motif in all these works is the linking of minds through telepathy; but unlike most of the notable previous treatments of mental telepathy (for instance, Theodore Sturgeon's *More Than Human* or Arthur C. Clarke's *Childhood's End*), Butler's communities are racked by internal conflicts and are portrayed in distinctly ambivalent terms.

Most recently, Butler has been expanding similar themes in her Xenogenesis trilogy. *Dawn* (1987), *Adulthood Rites* (1988), and the recently completed *Imago* (1989) examine a postholocaust humanity that has been sterilized and genetically altered by the alien Oankali. Rescued from an ecologically devastated Earth and forced to accept alien intervention in order to procreate, Butler's humans face the ultimate confrontation with the Other. The impetus of these novels is the human's xenophobic fear of the Oankali, who provide the only hope for survival—through mutation and an acceptance of a broader interpretation of the designation "human."

Larry McCaffery: In one way or another, all your books seem to explore different forms of slavery or domination.

Octavia Butler: I know some people think that, but I don't agree, although this may depend on what we mean by "slavery." In the story "Bloodchild," for example, some people assume I'm talking about slavery when what I'm really talking about is *symbiosis*. That's not to say that I haven't dealt with slavery or that I don't think about it—*Kindred* and *Wild Seed* deal very directly with slavery. Let me tell you an anecdote about slavery. When I was about thirteen, I found out on a visceral level what slavery was; before that I hadn't understood why the slaves had not simply run away, because that's what I assumed I would have done. But when I was around thirteen, we moved into a house with another house in the back, and in that other house lived people who beat their children. Not only could you hear the kids screaming, you could actually hear the blows landing. This was naturally terrifying to me, and I used to ask my mother if there wasn't something she could do or somebody we could call, like the police. My mother's attitude was that those children belonged to their parents and they had the right to do what they wanted to with their own children. I realized that those kids really had nowhere to go— they were about my age and younger, and if they had tried to run away they would have been sent right back to their parents, who would probably treat them a lot worse for having tried to run away. *That*, I realized, was slavery—humans being treated as if they were possessions. I stored that away in the back of my mind, without realizing I was doing it, until at a certain point in my work I needed to call it up. The nice thing about being a writer is that anything that doesn't kill or dismember you is typewriter fodder. Whatever it is, no matter how terrible, can be used later.

Jim McMenamin: Even books like *Wild Seed* and *Kindred*, in which you investigate aspects of black experience, seem to suggest something that transcends specific racial or cultural situations.

OEB: I hope so. When I put together my characters, it doesn't occur to me to make them all black or all white or whatever. I never went to a segregated school or lived in a segregated neighborhood, so I never had the notion that black people, or any other ethnic or cultural type, made up the world. When I write, I'm very comfortable not seeing things in terms of black or white. If I feel self-conscious about something, I don't write about it; I *write it out*—that is, I write about it and think about it until it is so familiar that it becomes second nature—not like some of the early SF writers who include a black character to make a point about racism, or the absence of racism. I want to get to the point where these things can be in the story but are incidental to it.

LM: What has drawn you to writing SF?

OEB: SF is what I like to read, and I think you should write about what you enjoy reading or you'll bore yourself and everyone else. I started writing SF when I was twelve. I was already reading SF, but I hadn't thought of writing it—I was writing fantasy and romance, both of which you know a lot about at ten or eleven, right? What happened to me sounds like a cliché but it's true: I was watching a movie on television, *Devil Girl from Mars*, and I thought, I can write a better story than that. So I turned off the TV and started writing what was actually an early version of one of my Patternist stories. The short stories I submitted for publication when I was thirteen had nothing to do with anything I cared about. I wrote the kind of thing I saw being published—stories about thirty-year-old white men who drank and smoked too much. They were pretty awful.

LM: Joanna Russ told me the same thing—that when she was in high school she thought if she didn't write about men going off to war or hunting big game then she didn't have anything significant to say.

OEB: Right. And a slightly different problem was that everything I read that *was* intended for women seemed boring as hell—basically, "Finding Mr. Right": marriage, family, and that's the end of that. I didn't know how to write about women doing anything because while they were waiting for Mr. Right they weren't doing anything, they were just waiting to be done unto. Since I didn't know what else to do, in those early Patternist stories I more or less copied the boys' books. I eventually got very comfortable with that approach, but there are stories that were written in the mid-1970s where the strain really shows.

JM: In *Patternmaster* Amber says, "When I meet a woman who attracts me, I prefer women . . . and when I meet a man who attracts me, I prefer men." Talk a bit about the sources of this openness.

OEB: Because of the way I looked, when I was growing up, I was called various and sundry unsavory names by people who thought I was gay (though at the time nobody used that word). I eventually wondered if they might not be right, so I called the Gay and Lesbian Services Center and asked if they had meetings where people could talk about such things. I wound up going down there twice, at which point I realized, Nope, this ain't it. I also realized, once I thought it over, that I'm a hermit. I enjoy my own company more than I enjoy most other people's—and going to parties or trying to meet Mr. or Ms. Right or whatever simply doesn't appeal to me. At any rate, I was intrigued by gay sexuality, enough so that I wanted to play around with it in my imagination and in my work. That's one of the things I do in my writing: either I find out certain things about myself or I write to create some context in which I can explore what I want to be. You can see how this works in the way I created Mary, in *Mind of My Mind.* I wanted to become a bit more forward, not so much to take charge (although sometimes it comes to that) but to take responsibility for what happens to me. I made Mary an extremely feisty, not very pleasant woman and then inhabited her life so I could see how it felt. I even had her live in my old Pasadena neighborhood, in the house my best friend lived in.

JM: Do you transpose these specific biographical elements into your work on a regular basis?

OEB: I use actual details only when I feel they'll *work.* For example, all the street names in *Mind of My Mind* parallel Pasadena street names, some in English and some in Spanish, though reversed. I really enjoy doing this sort of thing—along with going back and winning some of the battles I actually lost.

LM: Your father died when you were a baby and you were raised by your mother and grandmother. Did that experience affect your work in any direct way? In *Patternmaster,* for example, the kids are raised elsewhere, protected from their parents.

OEB: Growing up without a father influenced my life and, undoubtedly, my work because I didn't have that one male person around to show me what it means to be male; instead, I would watch my uncles and wonder why they did things the way they did, which may be why I later became interested in anthropology. Certainly, though, my childhood had something to do with the way I sometimes present parents as not being able to raise their own children. In *Mind of My Mind*, the parents can't stand being close to their children and hearing all that undisciplined mental shrieking. And in *Patternmaster* you have a society formed by a psychotic individual who is doing the best he can with what he has. He's not a good person—among other things, he sees the rest of humanity as food—and the daughter he raises is not a good person. But how can she be? She wouldn't survive if she were "good."

JM: Throughout the Patternist series you have different hierarchies yet the same kinds of control mechanisms we see around us.
OEB: No, they're *worse*, because the mutes don't know what's happening to them. If you know that you've been completely taken over, if you're aware of this happening, you might be able to fight it. But if you don't know about it, you don't have a chance.

LM: The idea of control being exercised through mind operations that the victims are unaware of has its parallel in our own society—you go out to buy a Bud Light or a Toyota without being aware that you've been programmed to do it.
OEB: Exactly. And even if you are aware of these forces, they can still possess or control you because you're not necessarily aware of exactly what they're doing when they're doing it. I remember going through a period in my teens when I was very depressed about my writing. I had no siblings—I was basically a solitary person anyway—so I would spend hours watching old movies and whatever series was on TV. After a while, it seemed that everything I'd ever wanted to write about had already been condensed and trivialized on television. I couldn't articulate this at the time, of course; nor could I write much of anything, at least not that I'd show to anyone.

LM: What sorts of SF did you read while you were growing up?
OEB: Until I was fourteen, I was restricted to a section of the library called the "Peter Pan Room." That had the effect of stopping me from going to the library much, because after a while I felt insulted by the juvenile books. Before I got into SF, I read a lot of horse stories, and before that fairy tales. For some reason I didn't read Asimov until later, but I did read Heinlein and the Winston juveniles (with those fantastic inside pictures of all sorts of wonderful things that

never happened in the book). My first experience with adult SF came through the magazines at the grocery store. Whenever I could afford them I'd buy copies of *Amazing* and *Fantastic*; later I discovered *Fantasy and Science Fiction* and eventually *Galaxy*. After I got out of the Peter Pan Room, the first writer I latched onto was Zenna Henderson, who wrote about telepathy and other things I was interested in, from the point of view of young women. I'd go down to the Salvation Army bookstore and buy copies of *Pilgrimage* for a nickel and hand them out to people because I wanted someone to talk to about the book. Later I discovered John Brunner and Theodore Sturgeon. I can remember depending on people like Eric Frank Russell and J. T. Macintosh to give me a good, comfortable read, to tell me a story. Whether they told me anything I didn't know or hadn't thought about or read someplace else was another matter. Later I read all of Marion Zimmer Bradley's Darkover books. I especially liked Ursula Le Guin's *Dispossessed*, and the original *Dune* by Frank Herbert was another favorite of mine. I read Harlan Ellison's stories and also John Wyndham, Arthur C. Clarke, A. E. Van Vogt, Isaac Asimov—all the SF classics, whatever I got my hands on.

LM: I remember being drawn to a certain kind of SF that seemed very different from what I was used to—works by people like Robert Sheckley and Alfred Bester, for example.
OEB: I think they were writing a sort of humorous, satirical SF that I felt totally alienated from, probably because I had little sense of humor as a kid. The stuff I was writing was incredibly grim—so grim that teachers would accuse me of having copied it from somewhere.

JM: What about the books that Samuel Delany was writing back in the sixties?
OEB: No. I didn't even know he was black until I was at Clarion. I got *Nova* when I was a member of the Science Fiction Book Club in my early teens, but I couldn't get into it. I did read some of his stories but none of his recent work, except his autobiography, *The Motion of Light in Water*.

JM: Were you into other types of reading when you were growing up—comic books or *Mad* magazine, that sort of thing?
OEB: I didn't discover *Mad* until 1962 or 1963, when my mother brought home a couple of issues that someone at work had given to her. She didn't have any idea what they were, even after she leafed through them, but she gave them to me anyway. I got hooked on *Mad* but from an emotional distance—since I didn't really want to write anything funny, I thought I shouldn't enjoy reading anything funny. From the sixties through the early seventies I was also very much

into comic books—the Superman DC comic books first, then Marvel, and so on. I went around to all the secondhand stores and bought up the back issues as fast as I could. I was living in a world of my own then—or, I should say, in the worlds of other people—and I had no one to talk to about what I was interested in. I don't think I would have enjoyed being involved in a network of SF fans— I've noticed that people heavily into fandom have a lot of little squabbles, which eats up valuable time and energy and doesn't accomplish anything, so I'm glad I wasn't involved with it back then. What I *would* have enjoyed was having one or two people to talk to about all the strange things I was reading and writing about.

LM: I spoke with Delany about the relationship of black culture to science and SF and why there aren't more blacks writing SF. He said that in some ways it's very obvious.

OEB: He's right. Writers come from readers, and for a long time there simply weren't that many black SF readers. I got used to reading books in which everyone was white, but a lot of blacks didn't—they just stopped reading or read books they were told were realistic, like historical romances, spy stories, detective novels. For some reason they didn't get into SF, although they later got sucked in by the *Star Wars* and *Star Trek* movies. I remember talking to a young black student at a conference in Michigan who told me she had thought about writing SF but didn't because she had never heard of any black SF writers. It never occurred to me to ask, If no one else is doing it, do I dare to do it? But I realize that a lot of people think if there's no model, then maybe there's some reason not to do something.

LM: You said that when you were starting out, your work consisted of versions of the Patternist series.

OEB: For one thing, I never wrote anything "normal"; I never really wanted to. I was fascinated with telepathy and psionic powers and eventually stumbled upon some old J. B. Rhine books, as well as other, more fantastic stories that announced, "You, too, can develop ESP!" I fell in love with that kind of material. About the only genre I never cared for was the ghost story, probably because I stopped believing in the afterlife when I was around twelve—although I didn't get up the courage to tell my mother until I was seventeen or eighteen. What set me off, I think, was going to church one Sunday—I was raised a born-again Baptist—and hearing the minister read a passage from the Bible and then say, "I don't know what this means, but I believe it." Somehow you're supposed to believe and have faith but not worry about having any *evidence* to support that belief and faith. That just doesn't work for me, and I never went back.

LM: Although a lot of your work is about immortality, then, it's not so much about life after death as about finding a way to be immortal while you're still alive.

OEB: You're right. When I was in my teens, a group of us used to talk about our hopes and dreams, and someone would always ask, "If you could do anything you wanted to do, no holds barred, what would you do?" I'd answer that I wanted to live forever and breed people—which didn't go over all that well with my friends. In a sense, that desire is what drives Doro in *Wild Seed* and *Mind of My Mind*. At least I made him a bad guy!

LM: What was it that drew you so strongly to the idea of breeding people? Was it the ideal of being able to control the direction of life?

OEB: Basically, yes. I didn't really understand the direction of my thoughts on this topic until sociobiology became popular and unpopular at the same time. I kept reading things like, "The purpose of such-and-such a behavior is so-and-so"—in other words, the assumption that every behavior has a purpose important to survival. Let's face it, some behaviors don't; if they're genetic at all, they only have to stay out of the way of survival to continue. Then, just a year or so ago, I read one of Stephen Jay Gould's books in which he says much the same thing. I was relieved to see a biologist write that some things—physical characteristics or behaviors—don't kill you or save you; they may be riding along with some important genetic characteristic, though they don't have to be. Also, to whatever degree human behavior is genetically determined, it often isn't determined *specifically*; in other words, no one is programmed to do such-and-such.

JM: Could you talk about how your Xenogenesis trilogy deals with the downside, with the possible dangers of sociobiology?

OEB: What scares me now is the direction genetic engineering is taking. I don't mean creating monsters and other terrible things—although that might happen— but the idea that "familiarity breeds contempt." I deal with this in *Imago*, where the genetic engineer talks about the fact that it can't mate within its own kinship area because it thinks "familiarity breeds mistakes." I'm concerned that once humans feel more comfortable with genetic engineering, we're not going to exercise that caution and we'll be more likely to do terrible things just because someone isn't paying attention.

LM: Of course, this immediately raises the question of the purpose of these experiments by whom, and for whose benefit?

OEB: They're going to be put to whatever purpose appears to make the most money at the time. Right now we seem to be operating on the principle that we'll realize something is going terribly wrong before it's too late. But when you're confronted with toxic and nuclear waste problems, the destruction of the Amazon rain forest, the depletion of the ozone layer, and so on, it should be obvious that it may already be too late.

LM: You seem to be interested in exploring the issue of where intelligence fits into the scheme of species evolution. In my view, we may be getting too intellectually advanced for our own good—that is, our intellects have evolved more rapidly than our ability to emotionally deal with what we're uncovering in areas like nuclear power and genetic engineering.

OEB: Intelligence may indeed be a short-term adaptation, something that works well now but will eventually prove to be a kind of destructive overspecialization that destroys us. What I'm exploring in my Xenogenesis series is the idea of two competing or conflicting characteristics: intelligence being one of them and hierarchical behavior, simple one-upmanship, the other. Since the tendency toward hierarchical behavior is older and more entrenched—you can trace it all through the animal species of this planet and into the plants, too, in some ways—hierarchical behavior is self-sustaining and more in charge of the intellect than it should be. Whenever we look at the degree to which our behavior is predetermined genetically—and this is where sociobiology comes into play—we get hung up on who's got the biggest or the best or the most, on who's inferior and who's superior. We might be able to stop ourselves from behaving in certain ways if we could learn to curb some of our biological urges.

LM: We see this with birth control, for example.

OEB: Yes, and also in our everyday behavior. If you become angry with me, you probably won't pull out a gun and shoot me or reach across the table and grab me (although some people will). Yet a politician may become angry and say, "I'm not going to let this bill go through, even though it will help millions of people, because you didn't respect my authority, my personal power." Of course, politicians never actually say that, but we know it happens. The same kind of destructive struggle for domination occurs in some doctor/patient relationships, where patients wind up suffering.

LM: That seems to be one of the underlying concepts in *Dawn*—that we are biologically programmed for self-destruction.

OEB: It's less a matter of being programmed for self-destruction than it is that self-destruction occurs because we're not willing to go beyond that principle of who's got the biggest or the best or the most. We can; in fact we do, individually. And if we know we are like that, we ought to be able to go beyond it. In *Adulthood Rites*, the aliens say, "We know you are not going to make it, but we are going to give you a second chance anyway." The constructs (that is, the new generation of mixed children) convince their alien relatives to give humans another chance at simply being human.

LM: In all of your work there is a complex balance between the need for beneficial change versus the feeling that such change will produce a loss of humanity.
OEB: There are a lot of people (unfortunately, some of them are writers and editors) who seem to see things strictly in terms of good and evil: the aliens either come to help us get our poor heads straightened out or they come to destroy us. What I hope to wind up with in my work are a series of shadings that correspond to the way concepts like "good" and "evil" enter into the real world—never absolute, always by degrees. In my novels, generally, everybody wins and loses something—*Wild Seed* is probably the best illustration of that—because as I see it, that's pretty much the way the world is.

LM: What was your original conception for the Patternist series? I know, for example, that they weren't published in the order in which you wrote them. Did you have an outline for the whole series?
OEB: No, they were in my head for so many years that I didn't need an outline. I conceived of the first three books dealing with three different eras: *Mind of My Mind* takes place in the present, *Patternmaster* is set on Earth in the distant future, and *Survivor*, which occurs in the nearer future, deals with those who got away but who didn't fare well because they were so strong in their religion that they couldn't consider self-preservation. "Bloodchild" is also a survivor story, though the characters react differently: they survive as a species, but not unchanged. This idea of change seems to me to be one of the biggest challenges I face as a writer—and the inability to face this is a big problem in a lot of SF. Some kind of important change is pretty much what SF is about.

JM: When you actually started to work on this series, did the books take shape independent of one another?
OEB: No, they were all going at once and for a long time I couldn't finish any of them. I had been able to finish some short stories, which were about twenty pages long, and I finally decided to try writing twenty-page chapters until I finished each novel. Of course, the chapters all ended up being different lengths, but having that goal helped me trick myself into completing the first novel.

LM: You seemed to have developed a fairly elaborate overall concept before you completed the first book.

OEB: I enjoy working with the effects of difficult human situations. The complexity of the Patternist series resulted from the fact that I'd been in that universe, in my mind, for so long. At the time I was writing *Wild Seed,* for example, all I had to do was see that the numbers and dates were accurate—to make sure that Anyanwu and Doro weren't the wrong ages, that sort of thing. I felt I could do almost anything because I was so comfortable in that realm. But I had problems in the Xenogenesis universe because I hadn't inhabited that world, imaginatively, long enough. I had to look back to see what I had said and to make sure everything held together and wasn't contradictory.

LM: The disease described in *Clay's Ark* seems oddly prophetic, given what has happened with AIDS. Had you heard of AIDS when you wrote that book?

OEB: No, I didn't hear of AIDS until later. The disease I wrote about was based on rabies, which I had read about in an old book of mine. I was fascinated by the fact that one of the side effects of rabies is a briefly heightened sensitivity. I always thought it would be great to contract a disease that was both contagious and a real physical boost. So in *Clay's Ark* I wrote about a disease that would be great for you—if you survived.

JM: *Kindred* seems like a very conscious break from what you were doing in the Patternist series.

OEB: Actually, *Kindred* was supposed to be part of the series but it didn't seem to fit, probably because I wanted to be more realistic than I had been in the earlier books. In fact, *Kindred* grew out of something I heard when I was in college, during the mid-1960s. I was a member of a black student union, along with this guy who had been interested in black history before it became fashionable. He was considered quite knowledgeable, but his attitude about slavery was very much like the attitude I had held when I was thirteen—that is, he felt that the older generation should have rebelled. He once commented, "I wish I could kill off all these old people who have been holding us back for so long, but I can't because I would have to start with my own parents." This man knew a great deal more than I did about black history, but he didn't feel it in his gut. In *Kindred,* I wanted to take somebody with this guy's upbringing—he was pretty much a middle-class black—and put him in the antebellum South to see how well he stood up. But I couldn't sustain the character. Everything about him was wrong: his body language, the way he looked at white people, even the fact that he looked at white people at all. I realized that, unless I wanted to turn *Kindred* into a wish-fulfillment fantasy, I simply couldn't make the main character a male. So I developed an abused female character who was dangerous but who wasn't perceived as being so dangerous that she would have to be killed.

LM: It's interesting that *Kindred* was published as non-SF.
OEB: Yes, and that was one of the things reviewers complained about. The idea of time travel disturbed them. Their attitude seemed to be that only in the "lower genre" of SF could you get away with such nonsense, that if you're going to be "realistic," then you must be *completely* realistic. Yet readers will accept what someone like García Márquez is doing without complaining. I remember hearing Mark Helprin being interviewed on the radio about *Winter's Tale.* When the interviewer referred to it as fantasy, Helprin became upset and said that he didn't think of his work in those terms, in spite of the flying horse and all the other fantastic elements. The implication was that if a work is fantasy or SF, it can't be any good.

LM: Like Márquez, Toni Morrison uses seemingly fantastic elements in some of her work—flying, magic, ghosts—yet her stories are considered realistic.
OEB: Realism in Morrison's work is blurred. There's a scene in *Sula* where two little girls accidentally drown a much younger child and don't tell anybody about it. That's grotesque, maybe even fantastic, but I believed every word. I don't think it's at all unlikely that the girls would try to "Who, *us?*" their way out of it. There are several other things Morrison does in the book that are equally strange, but they rang absolutely true.

LM: At the opposite extreme, we have the "hard SF" party line, which argues that relying on any fantasy elements is a cop-out.
OEB: What's usually important to the hard SF people is the logic of what they're dealing with; as a result, some of them fail to develop their characters—I call this the "wonderful machine school of storytelling" approach. Why can't writers play around with actual science and still develop good characters? I think I accomplished that in "The Evening and the Morning and the Night," which is the most carefully developed story I've written from a hard SF standpoint. It deals with medicine—I used three existing diseases as the basis of the disease in the story. A doctor I know called to tell me how much she liked it, which is probably the nicest compliment I could have received.

JM: What was the origin of *Wild Seed?*
OEB: I had a lingering sense that *Kindred*, which I'd just finished writing, had once been a different sort of novel that somehow involved Doro and Anyanwu in

early America. But neither character appears in *Kindred* because *Kindred* didn't really belong in the Patternist universe—it was too realistic. Because of the nature of the research—slave narratives and history—*Kindred* was a depressing book for me to write. By contrast, I thoroughly enjoyed writing *Wild Seed*. In terms of research, it's one of the hardest novels I've written, because I initially thought that dealing with the Ibo would only involve one people and one language—I didn't realize how many dialects there were. I found a huge ethnography about the Onitsha Ibo that was very useful; and before somebody torched the L.A. Public Library, I also found a book called *The Ibo Word List*, with words in five different dialects. It was a wonderful old book, shabby and falling apart, and it helped me get the language I needed.

LM: How did your conception of *Wild Seed*'s main female character take shape?
OEB: For a while I didn't know how I was going to relate Anyanwu to the Ibo. The solution came from a footnote about a woman named Atagbusi in a book called *The King in Every Man*, by Richard N. Henderson. Atagbusi was a shape-shifter who had spent her whole life helping her people, and when she died, a market gate was dedicated to her and later became a symbol of protection. I thought to myself, This woman's description is perfect—who said she had to die? and I had Anyanwu give "Atagbusi" as one of her names. I gave Doro his name without knowing anything about his background, but later on I looked up "doro" in a very old, very tattered Nubian-English dictionary and discovered that it means "the direction from which the sun comes"—which worked perfectly with what I was trying to do. And Anyanwu ties into that, since "anyanwu" means "sun."

LM: What inspired you to develop the Xenogenesis series?
OEB: I tell people that Ronald Reagan inspired Xenogenesis—and that it was the only thing he inspired in me that I actually approve of. When his first term was beginning, his people were talking about a "winnable" nuclear war, a "limited" nuclear war, the idea that more and more nuclear "weapons" would make us safer. That's when I began to think about human beings having the two conflicting characteristics of intelligence and a tendency toward hierarchical behavior—and that hierarchical behavior is too much in charge, too self-sustaining. The aliens in the Xenogenesis series say the humans have no way out, that they're programmed to self-destruct. The humans say, "That's none of your business and probably not true." The construct character says that, whether the humans are self-destructive or not, they should be allowed to follow their own particular destiny. The idea is that Mars is such a harsh planet—and so much terra-forming has

to be done by the people who are living there (even though they get some support from the outside)—that perhaps it will absorb whatever hostilities and problems of dominance arise. It ain't necessarily so, but at least it was something to hope for.

LM: When you decide to use, say, Mars as the backdrop for one of your books, do you actually research the planet?
OEB: In this case, no, since none of the scenes take place on Mars—all I really did was check on the Martian environment, to see if the aliens, who work with biological tools, could do what I wanted them to do. I decided that I could write about them doing it without actually *showing* them doing it because that process is not what the novel is about.

Another idea I wanted to examine in the Xenogenesis trilogy (and elsewhere) was the notion of cancer as a tool—though I am certainly not the first person to do that. As a disease, cancer is hideous, but it's also intriguing because cancer cells are immortal unless you deliberately kill them. They could be the key to our immortality. They could be used to replace plastic surgery—that is, instead of growing scar tissue or grafting something from your thigh or somewhere else, you could actually grow what you need, if you knew how to reprogram the cells. I use this idea in the third Xenogenesis novel, but I haven't really done what I want to with it. Probably it's going to evolve the way shape-shifting did from *Wild Seed* to *Imago*. I'll do something more with it.

LM: How much of the Xenogenesis series do you have worked out in advance?
OEB: I have the ending worked out, not that it will necessarily stay that way. I find that when I begin to write I need two things: a title and an ending. If I don't have those things I just don't have enough. Sid Stebel, one of the teachers with the Writers' Guild, would make us state the premise of a story in one sentence—"This is the story of a person who does such-and-such?" It's important to me that my stories are about people who *do* such-and-such, rather than about people who *are* such-and-such—the latter can make for a very static story that is all describing and explaining and doesn't really go anywhere. When I write, I sometimes put huge signs on the wall: Action, Struggle, Goal. I tend to be too nice to my characters, and if I'm not careful, nothing particular will happen that taxes them in any way. That doesn't make for as good a story.

JM: The Bible seems to provide an underpinning to your work. Is that because you see it as a compendium of fantasy?
OEB: I've always loved the Bible for the quotable things I could borrow from it. All the subtitles in *Wild Seed* are biblical, and in *Dawn* I name one of the charac-

ters Lilith, who according to mythology was Adam's first wife and who was un-
satisfactory because she wouldn't obey him. *Brewer's Dictionary of Phrase and
Fable* defines "Lilith" first as a Babylonian monster. I wonder whether her terrible
reputation results from her refusal to take Adam's orders. So yes, I have a lot of
fun with names and references; I like to use names that work with who my characters are. For instance, according to its roots, Blake suggests "white" or "black";
and Maslin is a "mingling." Until I've settled on a character's name—and I frequently use name books to help me—I can't really work with that character. Some
of this probably comes from being taken to the cemetery a lot as a kid. Half my
relatives are buried in Altadena, and my mother used to take me with her when
she went there to leave flowers. I remember running around copying names off
headstones—somehow, having those names made me feel connected to those
people.

JM: Do you think of your work as a self-conscious attempt to break down the
white-male-oriented traditions and biases of most SF?
OEB: My work has never been traditional, at least not since I stopped writing
those terrible stories about thirty-year-old white men who drank and smoked
too much. It's interesting that you use the word "self-conscious," though—I don't
think I'm self-conscious in the way that you're suggesting. I write about what
I'm interested in, not what I feel self-conscious about. Often, that means writing about a world that seems a bit like the one I inhabit. Let's face it, people who
write about whole universes filled with American whites probably can't deal with
the real world, let alone alien worlds. I remember walking down a street in Cuzco,
Peru—I went there with a UCLA study group—with a blonde woman about my
height. Everybody around us was brown and stocky, about a foot shorter, with
straight black hair. The two of us agreed that this was probably one of the few
places in the universe where we looked equally alien.

LM: SF would seem to be a useful area for feminists and people from other cultures to explore, in order to explode some of the biases.
OEB: True, but there's a trap. Fiction writers can't be too pedagogical or too po-
lemical. If people want to be lectured to, they'll take a class; if they want to hear
a sermon, they'll go to church. But if they want to read a story, then it had better
be a fairly good story, one that holds their attention *as a story*. It's got to compete
with TV, movies, sports, and other forms of entertainment, not to mention vast
amounts of fiction.

LM: There has been a lot of SF in the last, say, fifteen years, by feminists working
with utopian models.

OEB: Yes, and I have some major problems with that—personally, I find utopias ridiculous. We're not going to have a perfect human society until we get a few perfect humans, and that seems unlikely. Besides, any true utopia would almost certainly be incredibly boring, and it would be so overspecialized that any change we might introduce would probably destroy the whole system. As bad as we humans are sometimes, I have a feeling that we'll never have that problem with the current system.

LM: Have you received any response from radical feminists criticizing the way the masculine and the feminine in your works seem to be trying to find ways to coexist? I'm thinking specifically of Sally Gearhart, who says that we must do something very radical—like completely getting rid of males—if the planet is to survive.

OEB: No, I haven't—but does she really think that? Getting rid of all males (except for breeding purposes) or totally emphasizing the feminine won't solve our problems. If females did manage to take over, through violence or some other means, that would make us a lot like what we already are—it would wind up being self-defeating. I think we humans need to *grow up*, and the best thing we can do for the species is to go out into space. I was very happy to read that it's unlikely there's life on Mars or anywhere else in this solar system. That means, if we survive, we have a whole solar system to grow up in. And we can use the stresses of learning to travel in space and live elsewhere—stresses that will harness our energies until we've had time to mature. Not that we won't continue to do terrible things, but we'll be doing them to ourselves rather than to some unfortunate aliens. Of course, we probably won't get to the nearest stars for quite a long time. I like the idea.

An Interview with Octavia E. Butler

Randall Kenan/1990

From *Callaloo* 14.2 (1991), 495–504. © Charles H. Rowell. Reprinted with permission of The Johns Hopkins University Press.

Octavia E. Butler is something of a phenomenon. Since 1976 she has published nine novels, more than any other black woman in North America, and even more amazing: She writes science fiction. Having won all the major SF awards, (a Nebula and two Hugos), she has gained a substantial cult following, as well as critical acclaim, particularly for her 1979 novel, *Kindred*, reissued in 1988 in the prestigious Beacon Black Women Writers Series. *Kindred* is the tale of Dana Franklin, a black woman from an interracial marriage in LA in 1976, who is mysteriously plucked back in time on a number of occasions to 1824 Maryland and to a moral dilemma involving her white ancestor. A book often compared to *Metamorphosis* for its uncannily successful blend of fact and fantasy, it is considered by many to be a modern classic. Butler manages to use the conventions of science fiction to subvert many long held assumptions about race, gender, and power; in her hands these devices become adept metaphors for reinterpreting and reconsidering our world. Strong women, multiracial societies, and aliens who challenge humanity's penchant for destruction inform her work and lift it beyond genre.

Her works include: *Patternmaster* (1976); *Mind of My Mind* (1977); *Survivor*, (1978); *Wild Seed* (1980); *Clay's Ark* (1984); and the Xenogenesis trilogy: *Dawn* (1987); *Adulthood Rites* (1988); and *Imago* (1989). Butler has also published a number of short stories and novellas, including the award-winning, "Bloodchild" in 1984. She is working on the first book in a new series.

Octavia Butler lives in Los Angeles. This phone interview took place on November 3, 1990.

Kenan: Do you prefer to call your work speculative fiction, as opposed to science fiction or fantasy?

Butler: No, actually I don't. Most of what I do is science fiction. Some of the things I do are fantasy. I don't like the labels, they're marketing tools, and I certainly don't worry about them when I'm writing. They are also inhibiting factors;

you wind up not getting read by certain people, or not getting sold to certain people because they think they know what you write. You say science fiction and everybody thinks *Star Wars* or *Star Trek*.

Kenan: But the kind of constructs you use, like time travel for example in *Kindred*, or ...

Butler: *Kindred* is fantasy. I mean literally, it is fantasy. There's no science in *Kindred*. I mean, if I was told that something was science fiction I would expect to find something dealing with science in it. For instance, *Wild Seed* is more science fiction than most people realize. The main character is dealing with medical science, but she just doesn't know how to talk about it. With *Kindred* there's absolutely no science involved. Not even the time travel. I don't use a time machine or anything like that. Time travel is just a device for getting the character back to confront where she came from.

Kenan: In earlier interviews you mentioned that there's an interesting parallel between your perception of your mother's life and some of the themes you explore in your work. You spoke of how in your growing-up you saw her in an invisible role in her relationship with the larger society. How have certain ideas about your mother's life consciously or unconsciously affected your work?

Butler: My mother did domestic work and I was around sometimes when people talked about her as if she were not there, and I got to watch her going in back doors and generally being treated in a way that made me ... I spent a lot of my childhood being ashamed of what she did, and I think one of the reasons I wrote *Kindred* was to resolve my feelings, because after all, I ate because of what she did ... *Kindred* was a kind of reaction to some of the things going on during the sixties when people were feeling ashamed of, or more strongly, angry with their parents for not having improved things faster, and I wanted to take a person from today and send that person back to slavery. My mother was born in 1914 and spent her early childhood on a sugar plantation in Louisiana. From what she's told me of it, it wasn't that far removed from slavery, the only difference was they could leave, which eventually they did.

Kenan: I was also curious about the amount of research that you do when you're working on a book.

Butler: It varies greatly. With *Kindred*, I did go to Maryland and spend some time. Well, I mostly spent my time at the Enoch Pratt Free Library in Baltimore and at the Maryland Historical Society. I also went to the Eastern Shore to Talbot County, to Easton actually, and just walked around, wandered the streets and probably looked fairly disreputable. I didn't have any money at the time, so I did all my traveling by Greyhound and Trailways and I stayed at a horrible dirty little hotel . . . it was kind of frightening really . . . I didn't know what I was doing . . . I had missed the tours of the old houses for that year, I didn't realize that they were not ongoing but seasonal. Anyway, I went down to Washington, D.C., and took a Grayline bus tour of Mount Vernon and that was as close as I could get to a plantation. Back then they had not rebuilt the slave cabins and the tour guide did not refer to slaves but to "servants" and there was all this very carefully orchestrated dancing around the fact that it had been a slave plantation. But still I could get the layout, I could actually see things, you know, the tools used, the cabins that had been used for working. That, I guess, was the extent of my away from home research on *Kindred.* I did a lot more at the libraries.

Kenan: I'm assuming that entailed slave narratives and . . .

Butler: Yes, yes. Very much so. It was not fun . . . It's not pleasure reading. As a matter of fact, one of the things I realized when I was reading the slave narrative—I think I had gotten to one by a man who was explaining how he had been sold to a doctor who used him for medical experiments—was that I was not going to be able to come anywhere near presenting slavery as it was. I was going to have to do a somewhat cleaned-up version of slavery, or no one would be willing to read it. I think that's what most fiction writers do. They almost have to.

Kenan: But at the same time, I think you address the problem of accuracy and distance with amazing intelligence and depth. In place of visceral immediacy you give us a new understanding of how far removed we are from manumission. For example, the scene where Dana in *Kindred* witnesses the patrollers catching the runaway, you address this issue straight on; how she was unprepared to bear witness to such horror. So at the same time, you are making the reader aware of how brutal it all is, was, and doubly, how much we're separated from that past reality and how television and movies have prejudiced us or in some cases blinded us to that fact.

Butler: The strange thing is with television and movies, I mean, they've made violence so cartoonishly acceptable . . . I was talking to a friend of mine the other day about the fact that some kids around the L.A. area, on Halloween, kids around fourteen and fifteen, found a younger child with Halloween candy and they shot him and took it away from him . . . Now when I was a kid, I knew bullies who beat up little kids and took away their candy, but it would not have occurred to them to go out with a knife or gun to do that, you know. This is a totally different subject, but it's one that interests me right now. Just what in the world is to be done, to bring back a sense of proportion of respect for life?

Kenan: But another thing that makes *Kindred* so painful and artful is the way that you translate the moral complexity and the choices that have to be made between Dana and her white husband and not only in the past but in the present.
Butler: I gave her that husband to complicate her life.

Kenan: And even though the roles in many ways are more affixed by society in the past, she has to make similar choices in the present; so it's almost as though time were an illusion.
Butler: Well, as I said, I was really dealing with some 1960s feelings when I wrote this book. So I'm not surprised that it strikes you that way, as a matter of fact I'm glad. I meant it to be complicated.

Kenan: Violence also seems to be a part of the fabric of your *oeuvre*, in a sense. The fact that Dana loses her arm, in *Kindred*, which is inexplicable on one level . . .
Butler: I couldn't really let her come all the way back. I couldn't let her return to what she was, I couldn't let her come back whole and that, I think, really symbolizes her not coming back whole. Antebellum slavery didn't leave people quite whole.

Kenan: But also, for instance, in "Bloodchild." I mean, the idea that sacrifice has to be . . .
Butler: Not sacrifice. No, no . . .

Kenan: You wouldn't call it sacrifice? Cutting people open?
Butler: No, no . . . "Bloodchild" is very interesting in that men tend to see a horrible case of slavery, and women tend to see that, oh well, they had caesarians, big deal. [*Laughter*].

Kenan: So really, you wouldn't characterize that as being violent?
Butler: Not anymore than . . . well, remember during the Middle Ages in Europe, I don't know what it was like in Africa, if a woman died giving birth, they would try to save the baby.

Kenan: Over the woman?
Butler: In this case, they were trying to save both of them and, I mean, it's not

some horrible thing that I made up in that sense. In earlier science fiction there tended to be a lot of conquest: you land on another planet and you set up a colony and the natives have their quarters some place and they come in and work for you. There was a lot of that, and it was, you know, let's do Europe and Africa and South America all over again. And I thought no, no, if we do get to another world inhabited by intelligent beings, in the first place we're going to be at the end of a very, very, very, long transport line. It isn't likely that people are going to be coming and going, you know, not even the way they did between England and this country, for instance. It would be a matter of a lifetime or more, the coming and going. So you couldn't depend on help from home. Even if you had help coming, it wouldn't help you. It might help your kids, if you survived to have any, but on the other hand it might not. So you are going to have to make some kind of deal with the locals: in effect, you're going to have to pay the rent. And that's pretty much what those people have done in "Bloodchild." They have made a deal. Yes, they can stay there but they are going to have to pay for it. And I don't see the slavery, and I don't see this as particularly barbaric. I mean if human beings were able to make that good a deal with another species, I think it would be miraculous. [*Laughs*] Actually, I think it would be immensely more difficult than that.

Kenan: Fascinating and faultlessly logical. But at the same time—again with the idea of violence—the relationship between Doro and Anyanwu in *Wild Seed*. That takes on a different paradigm. They are extremely violent to one another.
Butler: That's just men and women!

Kenan: [*Laughs*] But particularly in their various metamorphoses, when she becomes a leopard, or the sheer number of people Doro kills. It's a sort of natural violence. Or a violence of survival, I should say . . .
Butler: It's not something I put there to titillate people, if that's what you mean. [*Laughs*] I don't do that. As a matter of fact, I guess the worse violence is not between the two of them, but it's around them, it's what's happening to the people around them who are not nearly so powerful.

Kenan: In your work it does seem to be a given that this is a violent universe and you don't romanticize it in any respect.
Butler: I hope not, I haven't tried to. I think probably the most violent of my books were the early ones. A friend brought this to my attention the other day because she was just reading some of my stuff. She said that she was surprised at the amount of violence in *Patternmaster* and casual violence at that. I said it

probably comes from how young I was when I wrote it. I think that it is a lot easier to not necessarily romanticize it, but to accept it without comment when you're younger. I think that men and women are more likely to be violent when they are younger.

Kenan: You have mentioned the African myths and lore that you used in *Wild Seed.* Can you talk more about that? I didn't realize that you had gone to such pains.

Butler: I used in particular, the myth of Atagbusi, who was an Onitsha Ibo woman. She was a shape-shifter who benefited her people while she was alive and when she died a market-gate was named after her, a gate at the Onitsha market. It was believed that whoever used this market-gate was under her protection . . .

Doro comes from an adolescent fantasy of mine to live forever and breed people. And when I began to get a little more sense, I guess you could say, and started to work with Doro, I decided that he was going to be a Nubian, because I wanted him to be somehow associated with ancient Egypt. And by then his name was already Doro, and it would have been very difficult to change it. So I went to the library and got this poor, dog-eared, ragged Nubian-English dictionary. I looked up the word Doro, and the word existed and it meant: *the direction from which the sun comes; the east.* That was perfect, especially since I had pretty much gotten Emma Daniels, who came before the name Anyanwu, but I had been looking through names for her, Igbo names, and I found a myth having to do with the sun and the moon. Anyway the problem with that is: I lost it. I didn't write it down and I never found it again and all I had was one of the names: Anyanwu, meaning the sun. That worked out perfectly with Doro, the East. So I wound up putting them together.

Kenan: Such rich etymological and cultural resonance. It's almost as if the African lore itself is using you as a medium.

Which leads me to a slightly different, but related topic. You seem to be exploring the idea of miscegenation on many different levels throughout your work. In Xenoenesis it seems to reach a new peak. Over the years you've been dealing with sex, race, gender; but here you're able to raise it yet another complicated step.

Butler: [*Laughter*]

Kenan: Seriously. In *Kindred* miscegenation is quite literal. But in *Dawn, Adult Rites,* and *Imago,* genetics put an odd twist on an old idea.

Butler: One of the things that I was most embarrassed about in my novel *Survi-*

vor is my human characters going off to another planet and finding other people they could immediately start having children with. Later I thought, oh well, you can't really erase embarrassing early work, but you don't have to repeat it. So I thought if I were going to bring people together from other worlds again, I was at least going to give them trouble. So I made sure they didn't have compatible sex organs, not to mention their other serious differences. And of course there are still a lot of biological problems that I ignore.

Kenan: How many other black science fiction writers do you know personally?
Butler: I know two others personally. [Steve Barnes and Samuel R. Delaney]

Kenan: Any other black women?
Butler: I don't know any black women who write science fiction. Lots of white women, but I don't know any black women—which is not to say there aren't any. But I don't know any.

Kenan: I couldn't compare you to other winners of the Nebula and the Hugo Awards. When you interact with your fans, how do they react to your being black and a woman? Is there a great deal of interest in the novelty of your being practically *the* only black women sci-fi writer?
Butler: No. If they're curious about that, they tend not to tell me and I'm just as happy to have it that way. No, I've been in SF for a long time and I know people. I go to SF conventions and no matter where I go in the country, I generally see someone I know. SF is kind of a small town and there is no problem with enjoying yourself. Obviously in some places you will meet with some nastiness, but it isn't general. The only place I was ever called "nigger," had someone scream nigger at me in public, was in *Boston*, for goodness sakes. It wasn't a person going to a conference, it was just a stranger who happened to see me standing, waiting for a traffic light with other SF people who were headed toward the convention.

Kenan: In light of that question, how do your readers react to the fact that most of your main protagonists are women and more often black? Does that ever come up?
Butler: Yes, as a matter of fact it came up more before I was visible. I wrote three books before anybody knew who I was, aside from a few people here in L.A. And I got a few letters asking why? The kind of letters that hedge around wondering why I write about black people; but there were few such letters. People who are bigots probably don't want to talk to me. I hear signs of bigotry every now and then when someone slips up, someone's manners fail, or something slips out. But there isn't a lot of that kind of thing.

Kenan: Speaking of women in science fiction, a lot of black women writers whom I've been in contact with lately speak of the ongoing debate between black women and feminism. I'm sure the feminist debate is ongoing within science fiction. Do you find yourself at all caught up within that debate?

Butler: Actually it isn't very much. That flared up big during the seventies and now it's a foregone conclusion. Not that somebody is particularly a feminist, but if somebody is it's their business . . . I was on a little early Sunday morning TV show a while back, and the hostess was a black woman and there were two other black women writers, a poet and a playwright and me. And the hostess asked as a near final question how we felt about feminism and the other two women said they didn't think much of it, they assumed it was for white people. I said that I thought it was just as important to have equal rights for women as it was to have equal rights for black people and so I felt myself to be very much a feminist.

Kenan: And you feel your works then actively reflect feminist ideals?

Butler: Well, they do in a sense that women do pretty much what they want to do. One of the things that I wanted to deal with in the Xenogenesis books, especially the first one, was some of the old SF myths that kind of winked out during the seventies but were really prevalent before the seventies. Myths where, for instance, people crash land on some other planet and all of a sudden they go back to "Me Tarzan, you Jane," and the women seem to accept this perfectly as all right, you know. We get given away like chattel and we get treated like . . . well, you get the picture. I thought I'd do something different.

Kenan: There seems to be a movement in your work from a view of continuance to a view of apocalypse. For instance in *Clay's Ark* the civilization has been attacked by a microorganism. But in Xenogenesis there is a postapocalyptic scenario. Has your thinking about that changed? I understand there is a huge debate in science fiction now about writers who tend to wipe the population clean and start over again, as opposed to writers like William Gibson and the other cyberpunk writers, who take as a given that we are going to survive somehow, someway, and then extrapolate from that assumption.

Butler: I don't think we are more likely to survive than any other species especially considering that we have overspecialized ourselves into an interesting corner. But on the other hand, my new book isn't a postapocalyptic type of book. I'm not really talking about an earth that has been wiped clean of most people. As a matter of fact earth is as populated as ever and in fact more so because it takes place in the future. The greenhouse effect has intensified and there has been a certain amount of starvation and agricultural displacement. There are real problems. Some of our prime agricultural land won't be able to produce the crops that it's been producing and Canada will have the climate, but on the other hand Canada caught the brunt of the last few ice ages and has lost a lot of top soil, which wound up down here. These are big problems and they are not sexy as problems so they are not the prime problems in the series that I am working on, but they're in the background. It's not a postapocalyptic book, it's a book in which society has undergone severe changes, but continues.

Kenan: I am really impressed by the way your characters often speak, almost epigrammatically, not to say that it is stiff dialogue, but you achieve a sort of majesty, particularly when you're talking about the human species; how we interact with one another. There is a lot of wisdom in what you have your characters say, without sounding didactic. What are your literary influences to that effect, both science fiction and non-science fiction, what writers?

Butler: All sorts of things influence me. I let things influence me. If they catch my interests, I let them take hold. When I was growing up, I read mostly science fiction. I remember getting into Harlan Ellison's class and at one point having him say, science fiction fans read too much science fiction; and he was no doubt right, but as an adolescent that was all I read except for school work. I guess the people that I learned the most from were not necessarily the best writers (although Theodore Sturgeon was one of them and I think he was definitely one of the best writers). They were people who impressed me with their ideas. I didn't know what good writing was frankly, and I didn't have any particular talent for writing so I copied a lot of the old pulp writers in the way I told a story. Gradually I learned that that wasn't the way I wanted to write.

But as for what influences me now, well, for instance I was reading a book about Antarctica . . . It was a kind of a difficult book to read because it involved so much suffering. Antarctica is probably as close to another planet as we've got on this earth . . . I thought what if I had a bunch of outcasts who had to go live in a very uncertain area and I made it a parched, devastated part of future southern California because there are areas here where the hills fall into the canyons and cliffs crumble off into the sea even without earthquakes to help them along. My characters go to this ruined place as though it were another world and the people they meet there are adapted to their new environment. They won't be savages crawling through the hills. I wanted them to have found some other way to cope because obviously some people would have to. Not everybody would go ape or become members of gangs and go around killing people. There would be some people who would try to put together a decent life, whatever their problems were . . .

Really, I think that's what I mean about something influencing me. The book I read didn't influence me to write about Antarctica but it influenced me to take a piece of the earth as we know it and see what it could become without playing a lot of special effects games.

Kenan: Are there other literary or nonliterary sources that you see consciously or unconsciously affected your work?
Butler: Every place I've lived is a nonliterary influence, every place and every person who has impressed me enough to keep my attention for a while. If something attracts my attention I am perfectly willing to follow that interest. I can remember when I was writing *Clay's Ark*, I would be listening to the news and I would hear something and it would be immediately woven into the novel. As a matter of fact some of the things that I found out after I finished *Clay's Ark* were even more interesting. Down in El Salvador, I guess about a year after I finished *Clay's Ark*, I read that it was the habit of many of the rich people to armor-plate Jeep Wagoneers and use them as family cars and that's exactly the vehicle that my character was using and I was glad I had chosen well.

Kenan: Science fiction writers—with a few notable exceptions like Samuel Delaney—are often slapped about the wrists because people feel that their writing styles are wooden and are merely there to get the plot across. Your writing has almost biblical overtones at times. Have you consciously striven for such a style?
Butler: I've developed my love for words late in life really. I guess it was when I realized that I was writing pulp early on. I realized I didn't want to. I read some of my own writing, which is a very painful thing to do, and I could see what was the matter with it, having gotten some distance in time from it. And I realized that there were things that I would have to learn even before that. Back during the 1960 election and the Kennedy Administration, that was when I began to develop into a news junkie. I was very interested in Kennedy and I would listen to his speeches and I guess I was about thirteen when he was elected, and I realized that half the time I couldn't figure out what he was saying and I felt really, really bad about that. I felt stupid. Although I didn't know it at the time, I'm a bit dyslexic. I realized that there was so much more to learn. You're always realizing there is so much out there that you don't know. That's when I began to teach myself as opposed to just showing up at school. I think that there comes a time when you just have to do that, when things have to start to come together for you or you

don't really become an educated person. I suspect that has been the case for a lot of people, they just never start to put it all together.

Kenan: Obviously, you write beautifully. So is it all organic in the sense that all these disparate ideas and themes fit together, that your interests coincided?
Butler: No, it's work. [*Laughs*] But you mean style. Yes, and it's something I can't talk about. It's very, very intimate. I make signs. The wall next to my desk is covered in signs and maps. The signs are to remind myself sometimes of things. For instance, a sign from a book called *The Art of Dramatic Writing* by Lagos Egri, it's a kind of a paraphrasing really; tension and conflict can be achieved through uncompromising characters in a death struggle. And just having signs on my wall to remind me of certain things that I need to remember to do in the writing; signs in black indelible ink. That sort of thing, it's kind of juvenile but it really helps me. But there are some things about the writing that are just so personal that you can't even talk about them.

Kenan: I should ask in closing: Do you have any advice for young writers?
Butler: I have advice in just a few words. The first, of course, is to read. It's surprising how many people think they want to be writers but they don't really like to read books.

Kenan: AMEN!!!!
Butler: And the second is to write, every day, whether you like it or not. Screw inspiration. The third is to forget about talent, whether or not you have any. Because it doesn't really matter. I mean, I have a relative who is extremely gifted musically, but chooses not to play music for a living. It is her pleasure, but it is not her living. And it could have been. She's gifted; she's been doing it ever since she was a small child and everyone has always been impressed with her. On the other hand, I don't feel that I have any particular literary talent at all. It was what I wanted to do, and I followed what I wanted to do, as opposed to getting a job doing something that would make more money, but it would make me miserable. This is the advice that I generally give to people who are thinking about becoming writers.

Kenan: [*Laughing*] I don't know if I would agree that you have no literary talent. But that's your personal feeling.
Butler: It's certainly not a matter of sitting there and having things fall from the sky.

PW Interviews: Octavia E. Butler

Lisa See/1993

From *Publishers Weekly*, December 13, 1993. Reprinted with permission of *Publishers Weekly*.

Octavia E. Butler has made a reputation for herself as the only African American woman in the science fiction field. She has won back-to-back Hugos and a Nebula, science fiction's most prestigious prizes, and so far has published ten books, including the highly successful Patternmaster and Xenogenesis series. Feeling, however, that the conventional labels attached to her name—African American, woman, feminist, SF writer—have been a hindrance as well as a blessing, she decided to place her latest book, *The Parable of the Sower*, with Four Walls Eight Windows with the express purpose of reaching a broad general audience. In its marketing materials, the publishing company and Butler's editor Dan Simon have tried to position Butler differently, comparing *The Parable of the Sower* to the "speculative fiction" of Toni Morrison's *Beloved* and Toni Cade Bambara's *The Salt Eaters*.

Butler lives in Pasadena, close to where she grew up, in an old-fashioned California court. On the day *PW* comes to visit, a brush fire is raging in the hills behind her bungalow. Perhaps for this reason, Butler has the shades drawn in the small living room where books and magazines stand in floor-to-ceiling shelves, in piles, in boxes. In what might have been a breakfast nook, Butler has her work area: a typewriter, notes jammed up on the wall, and more piles of books and papers.

At six feet tall, Butler cuts an imposing presence. She speaks with a deep, strong voice. "I'm black. I'm solitary. I've always been an outsider," she says. Like many writers, Butler daydreamed as a child, as a way to escape real life: her father died when she was a baby, her mother worked as a maid. Reading became a solace as she worked her way through the children's section of the Pasadena Library. When she found she had to be fourteen to gain admittance to the adult section, she discovered science fiction magazines and fell in love with the genre. At age twelve, inspired by the movie *Devil Girl from Mars*, Butler began writing what would become the first version of her Patternmaster series. The following year, she began submitting stories to magazines.

During her first semester at Pasadena City College, Butler won a short-story contest, but then there was a long dry spell before she received any other recognition for her work. She moved on to Cal State–L.A. where she "took everything but nursing classes. I'm a little bit dyslexic and worried about killing people," she says. (For this reason, Butler doesn't drive a car.)

In 1969, Butler was admitted to the Open Door Program of the Screen Writers' Guild, where she took a class from Harlan Ellison. He suggested she enroll in the Clarion Science Fiction Writers' Workshop, a "science fiction boot camp," which was then held in Pennsylvania. Butler's mother loaned her the money, and the twenty-eight-year-old Butler spent six weeks immersed in science fiction. At Clarion she found "another twenty-five outsiders. The first thing I did was hide and sleep in my room. The woman next door did the same thing. But then we emerged. We were all social retards, but we seemed to get along with each other."

She pauses. "I can't *think* how *that* will go over," she says, then lets out a big, deep, rolling laugh. "But to write science fiction you do have to be kind of a loner, live in your head, and, at the same time, have a love for talking. Clarion was a good place for that."

As luck would have it, Butler sold her first two pieces while she was still at the workshop: one to the Clarion anthology, the other to a projected Ellison collection that was never published. Then she didn't sell a word for the next five years.

To support herself, she took menial jobs: washing dishes, sweeping floors, doing warehouse inventory, sorting potato chips, all the while getting up at two or three in the morning to write. When she was laid off from a telephone solicitation job two weeks before Christmas, 1974, she decided it was time to fish or cut bait.

Earlier attempts to write a novel had been frustrated because Butler had been intimidated by the length. Determined now to look at each chapter as a short story, and finding inspiration in her earliest stories, she was able to produce *Patternmaster* in a matter of months. The book chronicles a future where humanity is divided into "Patternists," the ruling class who are joined together through telepathy, mute humans who serve the Patternists, and "Clayarks," mutant human/griffin creatures who've been contaminated by a disease brought back from outer space.

With information gleaned from *Writer's Market*, Butler mailed her manuscript to Doubleday. By return mail, Doubleday editor Sharon Jarvis voiced her interest in buying the novel, albeit with the changes she outlined in a three-page, single-spaced letter. Elated, Butler complied, and she continued writing; by the end of the year, she had written *Mind of My Mind* and more than half of *Survivor*. Beginning in 1976, Doubleday began releasing the first four books in the Patternmaster series. (In 1984, St. Martin's published a fifth, *Clay's Ark*.)

Midway through the series, Butler realized she had the need to write another kind of book. It was *Kindred*, in which an African American woman is transported from Southern California back through time to the antebellum South and the plantation of the man who is her ancestor. Doubleday published it as mainstream fiction in 1979; Butler herself calls it "a grim fantasy."

"I had this generation gap with my mother. She was a maid and I wished she wasn't. I didn't like seeing her go through back doors. . . . I also had this friend who could recite history but didn't feel it. One day he said, 'I wish I could kill all these old black people who are holding us back, but I'd have to start with my own parents.' He hadn't sorted out yet what the older generation had gone through. He thought they should have fought back. Well, it's easy to fight back when it's not your neck on the line."

Butler, on the other hand, had already made her peace with the past and what African Americans—including her own mother—had done in order to survive. "If my mother hadn't put up with those humiliations, I wouldn't have eaten very well or lived very comfortably," she explains. "So I wanted to write a novel that would make others feel the history: the pain and fear that black people had to live through in order to endure."

Since Butler had already been pigeon-holed as a science fiction writer, *Kindred* was, in many ways, a breakout novel. Later, it was the first of Butler's many titles to be reissued (by Beacon Press as part of its Black Women Writer Series) and is now often used in African American Studies classes. Still, the SF label stuck. Coming off the SF awards, Butler's agent, Merrilee Heifetz, negotiated a three-book deal with Warner Books for the Xenogenesis series, for which Butler drew heavily from the world around her.

"I'm a news junkie," Butler has explained in her author bio. "Science fiction fascinates me. Mythology interests me. Medicine sends my imagination all sorts of places. Whatever doesn't interest me today may very well interest me tomorrow." In person, she elaborates, "I started the series at a time when Reagan was saying we could have winnable nuclear wars and how we'd all be safer if we had more nuclear weapons. I thought if people believed this, then there must be something wrong with us as human beings."

These thoughts, combined with other news about captive breeding projects, prompted Butler to pursue a theory in which human intelligence is put at the service of hierarchical behavior. Through the mid-eighties, Butler buried herself in the story of a post-nuclear earth and the aliens who offer salvation to the handful of human survivors by altering their negative genetic structure through interbreeding with the anemone-like aliens. The result: *Dawn* (1987), *Adulthood Rites* (1988), and *Imago* (1989).

What followed was what Butler calls on good days a "literary metamorphosis" and on bad days a "literary menopause," more commonly known as writer's block "I knew that I wanted my next book to be about a woman who starts a religion, but everything I wrote seemed like garbage," she says. Over four years, Butler composed the first seventy-five pages several times. Reflecting back, she sees the problems as being threefold: "I was bored with what I was doing. I was trying to rewrite Xenogenesis. I also had this deep-seated feeling that wanting power, seeking power, was evil."

Poetry finally broke the block. "I'm the kind of person who looks for a complex way to say something," she explains. "Poetry simplifies it. When I started to write poetry, I was forced to pay attention word by word, line by line." (Poetry appears in *The Parable of the Sower* in the form of excerpts from "Earthseed: The Books of the Living," the holy works written by the protagonist, Lauren Oya Olamina.) Butler still faced the problems of creating a religion she herself could believe in. "I didn't want to make fun of religion. Lauren's father, a Baptist minister, is neither a fool nor a hypocrite. He's a decent man who can't cope with the situation he's in. Lauren feels about religion the way I feel about writing. For her it's a positive obsession, even while she realizes it's ridiculous and impossible."

Lauren's "Earthseed" religion is centered around the idea that God is change. "I think one of our worst problems as human beings is our lack of foresight and our denial. Educated people behave this way so they can keep their jobs. Uneducated people do it by doing drugs and taking too much alcohol. I used to think that we'd all die from nuclear war. Now I see that we're not going to do that, but it wouldn't be much different than drinking ourselves to death. So for the book I looked around for a force that nothing could escape. One of the first poems I wrote sounded like a nursery rhyme. It begins: God is power, and goes on to: God is malleable. This concept gave me what I needed."

In her writing Butler has probed science fiction's three premises: what if, if only, and if this goes on. In *The Parable of the Sower* she pursues the and-if-this-goes-on category, once again drawing from the news—smart pills, gangs, global warming, drought, sociopathic behavior, the swallowing up of American companies by foreign conglomerates—to create a story that takes place in a desperately dry twenty-first-century Southern California, a place of walled enclaves and drugged-out arsonists, where people murder for water, food, and jobs. Lauren is a "sharer," one who suffers from a congenital trait: her mother took a "smart" drug while pregnant, and Lauren feels other people's physical pain as well as her own. "This is a rough disability for her time," Butler concedes. "Lauren's ability is perceived as a problem, not a power."

Most of Butler's female characters, including Lauren, appear almost incidentally to be black. "The fact that they're black is not the most important thing on my mind," she says. "I'm just interested in telling a story, hopefully a good one." Nevertheless, she concedes that she offers a unique voice in a field dominated by white men. "I'm the only black woman writing science fiction today *because* I'm the only black woman writing science fiction," she explains. "I don't mean to be facetious, but it's true."

White women have already prospered in the genre, of course, and Butler herself has been influenced by many of them. At the Clarion workshop, she was encouraged by Joanna Russ to stop using her initials, a then-common practice for women who wanted to write science fiction. In addition to Ursula Le Guin and Kate Wilhelm, Butler has also been inspired by Marion Zimmer Bradley and Zena Henderson. "But for me the greatest influences were the early pulp magazine writers. I loved the story by Ray Bradbury and Leigh Brackett [she was one of the best-known early women science fiction writers] called 'Lorelei of the Red Mist.' Its central idea was having a private eye on Venus instead of on Main Street."

As time goes on, Butler hopes to shuck off all her labels. "I write about things that interest me, and I'm not the most unique person on earth," she concludes. "So I figure what will interest me will interest other people."

Sci-Fi Tales from Octavia E. Butler

H. Jerome Jackson/1994

From *Crisis* (April 1994). The author wishes to thank the Crisis Publishing Co., Inc., the publisher of the magazine of the National Association for the Advancement of Colored People, for the use of this material first published in the April 1994 issue of *The Crisis*.

The tales of science fiction by Octavia E. Butler have entertained readers for two decades. Her characters are strong, African ancestry, often women who perform extraordinary feats to overcome extraordinary struggles. But mainly, her people—and creatures—are internal and involve strength of character and complicated personalities facing problems that often are strikingly similar to those we face in reality—or could face. Her skillful weavings have generated her three audiences: blacks, feminists and science fiction fans.

Her latest effort, *Parable of the Sower*, is a foray into futuristic America. A family lives in an America where the schisms between rich and poor have become stark. Walls separate enclaves of economic difference. Complicating the matter is a new devil drug that has a heinous side effect. Users like to watch things burn.

When the poor people and aggressive addicts encroach on the affluent settlement, the inhabitants must flee to search for something that they will seek on the other side of the continent in Washington, D.C. The story is seen through the eyes of a young woman who is wrestling with life, trying to come of age in America of 2025 where for some, death is a preferable alternative.

When *The Crisis* first spoke to Ms. Butler, she had just completed her daily four-mile run and was about to tackle her next effort *Parable of the Talents*. Following is a compression of two conversations.

The Crisis: A reviewer in St. Louis compared you to Richard Wright.

Butler: He was much more stern and realistic than I tend to be. I'm not unrealistic, except in the sense that some things are so unpleasant I need to alter them a bit. When I wrote *Kindred*, for instance, I started out writing a lot of slave narratives and I realized quickly that nobody was going to want to read the real thing. So that meant that I had to soften it a bit—what I call clean slavery, as opposed to the real thing. That's what I mean. There are limits to what people will put up with when they're reading a novel.

The Crisis: What's your job as an author?
Butler: My first effort is to tell a good story. I'm not out to preach to people in the usual sense. I do preach to them, but I first have to hook them with a good story, otherwise they won't be around for the preaching. . . . I recognize the reality that I have a lot of competition out there. I'm in competition with the television set, and the video games and the basketball court and whatever else is out there— one's friends. It would be silly of me not to take that into consideration.

The Crisis: So what is your emphasis? In *Parable of the Sower*, were you trying to make a point?
Butler: The *Parable of the Sower* was probably more serious than anything I've written since *Kindred*. It was an "If this goes on . . ." story. And, frankly, there isn't anything in there that can't happen if we keep on going as we have been. That's pretty frightening when you think about it. And the horrible thing is some of them are happening already anyway. . . . Even the things you try not to think about as part of American life. Slavery, for instance. Every now and then, it will come out that people have been held against their will and forced to work after having been seduced by lies about good salaries and that sort of thing. In this part of the country they're usually Hispanic. I've heard of the same sort of thing happening to black people in the South. It's already happening. I'm talking about people who can't even leave. If they try, they're beaten or killed.

The opposite of slavery is also in evidence now: throw-away labor. I think the [American factories] in Mexico were the best examples of it. American companies going down there to take advantage of cheap labor and unenforced environmental regulations. It's what was going on before NAFTA. One of the things they do down there, they employ people and make no provision for safety. They may be poisoned with chemicals, hurt in equipment foul-ups, that kind of thing. Or they may just have to live in horrible shacks because there's nothing nearby. There's no plumbing, open sewers, drinking polluted water; not really enough money to sustain life, so they have to put the whole family to work. These are American companies down there taking as much advantage as they can get. And people tend to get used up after a certain time. So if you're a thirty-five-year-old woman who's been working in a luggage factory or something like that for ten years, you probably have enough things wrong with you that they don't want you any more. And they're perfectly happy to go get the twenty-year-old who's perfectly happy to think they're going to make it, then use her up.

The Crisis: This sounds like it rattles you.
Butler: It shouldn't be happening!

The Crisis: But these are Hispanics. Don't black folks have enough problems?
Butler: (Long pause) I recognize that you're asking that only because you want to get a reaction. But if you only pay attention to what's happening to your own folk, by the time you notice, then it's creeping into your people too; and very well entrenched.

The Crisis: What's your role . . . as a science fiction novelist?
Butler: First, as I said, to tell a good story. If I don't do that, it doesn't matter what else I'm doing. No one is going to pay any attention. And second, to say what I feel is true. Obviously, I mean verisimilitude as well as the literal truth. But also, I mean, for instance, if I see things going as they have been for the past several years, and us taking many paths to disaster, I almost have to say something about it. I was surprised to find myself back in the pre-NAFTA days reading a lot about the [American factories in Mexico]. I was surprised to find myself getting very political when I made speeches. I hadn't been doing that. I had gotten political in the sense of how the races got along and how blacks were treated and that sort of thing, especially if I was speaking to a group that . . .

The Crisis: What makes a good story?
Butler: It has to be entertaining. And you're going to ask what's entertaining.

The Crisis: Thanks for your help. It's been a long day.
Butler: People are happier reading about good and evil, but I don't tend to give them that, because I find it boring. It's difficult to go out and find causes and find people who are 100 percent good or 100 percent evil. I think that's why Hitler is so popular, because he's so easily hate-able. But I tend to write about the struggles that people have between themselves, toward something or away from something, the struggle to grow up or deal with some change. Tension. Not so much that people want to get away from you and rest, but enough so they're kept reading. My stories are not as fast-moving as some—I notice that a lot of popular stuff tends to be very fast moving.

The Crisis: You say you like to portray the struggles.
Butler: I like to write about human struggles, people who are clearly needing to do something or be something or reach something, people struggling with each other. I have a kind of slogan to remind myself what I'm to be doing: The chase, the game, the quest, the test.

My first novel was a chase story. It's easy to hold your own in a chase story. You have one character or group of characters and another group behind them that's not going to be kind to them if they catch them.

The game? I love reading game stories. Two characters pitted against one another, not fist fights, but the kind where they're using their minds—the kind where they really are doing a human chess game.

The quest: In a sense, the *Parable of the Sower*, the second part is a quest. Although they don't know until near the end where they're going. They know what direction they're going in, but they don't know when to stop.

The test: is natural for a coming of age story. *Parable of the Sower* is a coming of age story. She undergoes quite a test towards the middle of the book. If she didn't pass it, it could end right there.

The Crisis: The symbolism of the walled neighborhood. A cul-de-sac with a few homes on it. In *Native Son*, Bigger Thomas found himself walled in by forces from the outside. In *Parable of the Sower*, they . . .
Butler: A walled cul-de-sac is loaded with symbolism. People are walled in but they're clearly going nowhere, in spite of the fact that they're surviving as long as they do.

Their way of life is going nowhere. What they're doing is trying to hold on until the good-old-days come back. Even though they're decent people, that's what we would do, because we wouldn't know what else to do. And the people who pick it up and carry on from there are the kids. Because it doesn't occur to them that they don't know what good-old-days they're talking about because they weren't around for them.

The parents of my main character, they're waiting for the times of plenty to come back; in the beginning at the second part of the dream. It's in two parts, something when she was a little girl; and they're living in a rather early twenty-first-century way.

The Crisis: You're so perceptive about the state of society and where it's going.
Butler: I'm a news junky. I need to know or think I know that I imagine I know what's going on.

The Crisis: But some of the issues you tackle are things that many people use to stand on boxes in the middle of the street and run for office.
Butler: I'm a writer; I'm a loner, very solitary; this is what I do. I've been writing since I was ten years old; since my mother let me know it was possible to be a writer. I was writing before that I didn't know there was a future in it.

The Crisis: In your work, you don't seem to treat capitalism kindly.

Butler: . . . I don't believe in pure good or pure evil characters. Well I don't believe in pure systems either; or pure anything. There are good aspects of capitalism and there are really rotten aspects. The worst aspects are the [American factories on the border in Mexico], and they're going to creep here. For instance, if you can get labor for a dollar an hour or eighty cents an hour, then, even if you don't move down there, you're going to be able to lower wages where you are by threatening to move down there. And if you can spew filth into the rivers down there, you can always threaten to move down there if the environmental regulations get a little tight up here.

And remember the Reagan attitude—and they didn't put it quite this way—but that it was OK to kill people as long as you didn't kill too many and you made a profit at it, and they were already born. . . . The worst aspects of capitalism are pretty nasty. I've spent some time in the Soviet Union, when there was a Soviet Union. And I stayed in a brand new hotel that was crumbling. And the worst aspects of socialism or communism are obvious too.

So what I see is a system that takes in the best aspects of any system out there. Change is difficult for people and people want to find something and adhere to it very narrowly; it becomes almost like a religion. I got the impression that for the extreme right during the Reagan administration, capitalism was definitely a religion. So if you said anything against capitalism, it's as if you were cursing God or a preacher or something.

The Crisis: What gave you this keen sense of perception?

Butler: I pay attention. And I care. One of the horrifying things I'm noticing is that the younger kids, especially the ones who are raised in poverty, they're raised with a great contempt for caring. My God, look how they have to live. By the time they're old enough to get a gun and shoot somebody with it, they've seen enough so that's nothing.

The Crisis: Do you see women having a special place in the future?

Butler: No more so than men. . . . One of the things I recognized when I wrote *Kindred*, there wasn't any other time that I would go back to. Because women were treated so badly. I don't necessarily mean beaten or tortured. It's just that women had this very narrow niche that they were to fit into whether they fit or not. I would never have fit. Just being a solitary individual would be enough. In school it was enough to get me beaten up until I grew past everybody. I recognized life would be hell for me any other time in the past. It would be hell for most people, especially for women. The better a society is treating women, the better the society is likely to be. The societies that separate women from one another, where the man visits the woman from time to time . . . those tend to be the most violent societies because men encourage each other to violence. And their behavior toward women is generally awful.

The Crisis: Do you have any specific problems because you're a black woman?
Butler: There are problems that don't involve the writing itself. For instance, I can remember doing signings in general bookstores. I like signing in one of the three kinds of specialty book stores that I mentioned, science fiction, feminist, or black. At least when I get there I decide that they're interested in something and they decide I must be interested in it too or I wouldn't be there. But in a general bookstore, they tend to walk past me if I'm doing a signing there and they say, Oh well, she's black, so no white people stop. I've been known to call out to them and corral them. They're courteous and they don't stomp away. Sometimes they stop and now and then buy something, and maybe surprise themselves for having done it. So in that sense there's a problem. People think they know what you write and never really find out. I think I did more damage by being classified as a science fiction writer than I did being classified as a black woman writer. People think it's stuff for kids, high-class comic books, and not that high class. And they've grown out of that. Anything science fiction couldn't possibly be good.

Interview with Octavia Butler

Jelani Cobb/1994

From JelaniCobb.com, http://jelanicobb.com/ (site accessed in 2005). Copyright © 1994 Jelani Cobb. Reprinted with permission of Jelani Cobb.

JC: Like I said, the first set of questions is kinda loosely based on writing and how you got the impulse to write and developed, and the last part deals with your work itself.

OB: If you could talk a little louder it would help too.

JC: Okay. How did you start writing?

OB: Well, I began writing when I was ten and the thing is, I had begun telling myself stories when I was about four so it was almost a natural progression to write them down—eventually. I just got the idea when I was ten to start writing them down because I was forgetting some of them. And I enjoyed it so much I kept doing it.

JC: What kind of things did you read as a child?

OB: Oh, anything I could put my hands on. I especially liked animal stories, fairy tales, mythology, that sort of thing, but truth to tell, I would read anything I could get a hold of—including some things my mother definitely did not want me reading.

JC: I read something I thought was interesting. You said your mother or your grandmother would bring home books . . .

OB: My mother . . .

JC: I interviewed Baraka about two weeks ago and he said the same thing . . .

OB: Yeah . . .

JC: His grandmother worked for some white people and she would bring home books. Anything she could find that, especially that was intended for children, but she really didn't stop it there. I mean, if they threw away old magazines, she'd stop and bring them home, you know? Who actually influenced you as a writer in terms of developing your craft and style and sensibilities?

OB: Influenced? Define.

JC: O.K., well . . .
OB: Do you want to know who encouraged me?

JC: Who encouraged you and—
OB: Nobody.

JC: Really?
OB: My mother was less annoyed by it than most people. I mean, most of my family just assumed that it was a good thing because it kept me out of trouble, but they didn't think that it could actually lead to anything—because they didn't know that there were any Black writers. In fact, my aunt assured me that there weren't any and that I couldn't be one.

JC: That's interesting—
OB: My mother helped me out economically. For instance, when I stupidly, well, I was a kid, what did I know, but I got involved with an agent who charged a reading fee. She scraped up the reading fee which was more than our monthly rent at the time. She tried to help me, you know. But she even felt that it was kind of silly and it was good for me to stay out of trouble and she hoped I would be a secretary or something.

JC: So what kept you going as a writer? What kept you pursuing that goal?
OB: Writing is all I really ever wanted to do. Once I discovered it, I found that I enjoyed it and my mother just made a remark accidentally when I was about ten. She saw me writing and I told her I was writing a story and she said "Well, maybe you'll be a writer." And at that point I had not realized that there were such things as writers and it had not occurred to me how books and stories got written somehow. And in that little sentence, I mean, it was like in the cartoons where the light goes on over the guy's head. I suddenly realized that yes, there are such things as writers. People can be writers. I want to be a writer.

JC: The other part of that influence question was have you ever had an experience where you read someone's work and it clearly outlined to you the way fiction was supposed to work?
OB: Oh no.

JC: Never?
OB: No because there isn't any.

JC: That's like a magic button or something.
OB: No I mean, because there isn't any one way fiction is supposed to work. If

there were, everyone would write alike and that would be boring as all get-out. No. What I used to do though, before I began to get any sales, I used to—well I always read a lot—even before I was writing my stories down, but I read even more after I had gotten into my teens and I was writing and sending [my stories] out. I began sending my work out when I was thirteen and getting it back practically by return mail. And I . . . hmm. I just lost my train of thought. What was I talking about?

JC: Well, just before that we were talking about how there was no one particular way fiction worked.
OB: Oh, I was gonna talk about the books I used to, yeah, some of the books I would read were so bad that I would read one and the next day I wouldn't be able to recall what happened in it. And it wasn't like losing my train of thought just now. It was literally, you look at the book and you know you read it and you have to open it and look over a few pages to know what the heck happened. These were really bad, poorly constructed, poorly written books, and they let me know more than anything else. I mean, if people were writing this garbage and getting published I could surely get published.

JC: Were there any other difficulties peculiar to being a Black woman that confronted you?
OB: Yeah, the total lack of examples. It wasn't so much being Black as being ignorant that there were any other Black people out there. Gradually, in my teens I became aware of people but they were like off in the stars somewhere, they seemed so far from me. It was interesting, at the [1994 National Black Arts] Festival hearing some people talk about meeting some of these people. Langston Hughes . . . you think, "My God, it's like meeting . . . Moses or somebody." [laughter]

And, I mean I met nobody. When I was in the twelfth grade, the school I went to, the schools I went to had no creative writing or writing for publications classes. So, I was on my own, the best I could do was journalism. Something I suspect you might be going through. Are you?

JC: Yes.
OB: Anyway, at the end of twelfth grade we were allowed to schedule conferences with people working in our area—the area we hoped to get into. They couldn't find me a fiction writer. They found me a journalist who worked at the local newspaper who kept saying, "Well, I don't know what to tell ya." Then he'd talk a little bit about journalism and then he'd say, "I really don't know what to tell ya." [laughter] I mean, you know, he wasn't being hard or anything, he just literally

didn't know what direction to tell me to go. Just take lots of English classes and that sort of thing and that turned out to be not all that helpful of course. And, I really . . . I had no examples, I had no idea what I was doing wrong in my work. This is true of a lot of people who are beginning to be writers. They don't know what's wrong. They don't know why it keeps getting rejected. I think what a lot of young Black people do, we sit back and say, "Uh huh, it's just racism." And some of us give up thinking it's racism and never knowing it's because we're writing so badly. A friend who is a university professor had some entering students, these are eighteen- and nineteen-year-olds coming into college, send me some papers they wrote about one of my books. And . . . I was amazed. I mean, they were not good. I would hate to think if one of these kids was sending things out and thinking, "They're not publishing me because I'm Black and because I write about Black subjects." I mean, this is probably no doubt my own problem when I was a kid. I had no idea what to do and how to get where I wanted to go, and no idea how bad my stuff was because who could I compare it to? Nobody was writing on the subjects that really interested me and the stuff that I was sending out, I got the idea from reading a lot of science fiction that it was supposed to be about thirty-year-old white men who drank and smoked too much because that's what it all seemed to be about. I didn't realize that all the drinking and smoking was because these authors were being paid by the word. You know, the more words you can stuff in there with him taking a drink or a puff or whatever or lighting up, the more money. I mean, they were getting things like two and three pennies a word for God's sake. So in order to earn a living they had to fatten the story up with a lot of unnecessary stuff. I didn't understand this at the time so I was writing stories about thirty-year-old white men who drank and smoked too much and sending these out and they were really terrible. But the stuff I was writing for myself was also terrible, and I didn't know how to make it better.

JC: So how did you—
OB: . . . but it was the bones of what became my first novels actually. You were going to ask me how did I finally?

JC: Yes.
OB: Well, for one thing I went into PCC, Pasadena City College, and PCC did have a couple of writing courses. They had short story writing, writing for publications, and creative writing. Most of them were taught by a nice elderly couple who wrote children's stories and who didn't have a clue what I was doing and who were perfectly willing to say so even though they tried to be helpful. And I

didn't . . . what I got from them was more along the lines of just plain writing tips. Don't use so many adverbs. Or gee, your transitions here are not so good or non-existent. That kind of thing because often your English teacher just doesn't have that kind of information for you. Also I had to learn that the things I had been learning in English class weren't that useful because it's a different kind of writing. I mean, academic writing is just plain different from fiction. Academic writing is almost required to be tedious. And I had to learn that pretty much on my own. I went to Cal State L.A. and they had one writing class and it was late at night and I couldn't take it because I ride buses. After college I went to a writing class given by the Writers Guild of America, West. That's the people who do screenplays and teleplays. They were having this class for free because they looked around and said to each other, "Why are we all white?" They decided to see if they gave these classes if there were Black and Hispanic kids who would come in and were interested in writing. I was not really interested in writing for the screen, but any professional writer, I thought, could help me. So I went to these classes and the first semester was awful. We had teachers who read the *TV Guide* to us. The problem is, of course, they weren't really teachers, they were writers. They really didn't know what to do. Some of us were so bad that they kind of gave up on the spot. Eventually, though, with the next semester, the second semester of the program's existence, the writer Harlan Ellison came into the program as one of the teachers and also another writer, Sid Steeple. I got into their classes. Sid was teaching novelizations, you know, how to take a movie and turn it into a novel and Harlan was just teaching screenwriting except that I knew, because I had a lot of his books, that he wrote a lot of science fiction—print science fiction. Or at least it was called science fiction at the time—he's not real thrilled with that term. I knew that he could probably help me if I could get him to and he was perfectly willing to so it turned out great. You know, whatever you wrote he would go over it and talk to you about it and you might go home feeling like you didn't much like him but it was the kind of criticism I needed because if you're in school. . . . For instance, I was in classes sometimes where I was the only Black person and you tend to either get ignored or get petted on the head a lot. Neither is in the slightest useful so I was eager to get away from that and Harlan was not interested in doing either. I mean, he was giving up his own time to be there, not getting paid or anything, so he might as well do the job he'd come there to do and that's pretty much what he did. Also, he got me interested in going to Clarion Science Fiction Writer's Workshop. That was the other good writing experience that I had, writing education.

JC: Okay. I had a question that is kind of related to something you touched on. Are you open to adapting your work for the screen or writing screenplays?
OB: I'm not real interested in doing that. I'm a very slow writer and screenplay writing, they really want it fast and any changes, they want that fast too. It's not something that I'm real interested in. I'm liable to do some of it, I did take those classes, but it's not anything I would want to get into and stick with.

JC: So writing is more of a meticulous process for you than a stream-of-consciousness?
OB: Well, why do you think those two things are different?

JC: [laughter] Actually, I'd like for you to show how the two could interact.
OB: Writing is also re-writing. So, sure, maybe you'll go ahead and pour it onto the page, but you'd better go back and fix it or nobody is gonna want it.

JC: Okay, I see. I understand. Have you ever been pressured, especially when you first started out, first got published, were you pressured to de-politicize your work?
OB: My work isn't all that political really. Actually, I was pressured in the opposite direction. I was pressured to politicize it more like, "Why are you writing science fiction? Why are you writing something so unreal? Why don't you write something that would be meaningful?" In the sixties meaningful was the big word and I was supposed to be writing more about Black history or about the struggle or, the thing is, if you let somebody else tell you what you ought to be writing, you're probably gonna write crap. You need to write about the things that interest you. You can always learn to write about the things that interest you. But, if you're writing what somebody else thinks you should be writing, it's like a school assignment and you're probably bored.

JC: That's interesting—
OB: Something that really stirs you up emotionally. Your passion is driving you along and when you are alone with that computer or typewriter or whatever, you need all the pushing you can get.

JC: So what would you say stirs you up?
OB: Well, a lot of things, actually. One of the great things about science fiction is the freedom it allows me to get into anything I want to get into. When I wrote *Parable of the Sower*, the things that stirred me up the most were the things going on right now. The daily news. There are so many terrible things that are going on that no one is paying attention to because they aren't quite that bad yet. I talked

about some of them at the Festival. There are some that I didn't talk about that are in the book. Have you read *Parable of the Sower*?

JC: Yes, I read it not too long ago.
OB: Okay, then you know that in *Parable of the Sower* I talk about the return of slavery, which is real. I mean, that's not something that I pulled out of history; that's something that I pulled out of the newspapers. You know, we already have situations where, here in Southern California, in the Central Valley, or in the South in some of he more rural areas where they'll either bring in illegal aliens and work them and not pay them and forbid them to leave and generally mistreat them and . . . or they'll do it with Black people who are not well enough educated or connected to get out of there, or they'll do it with homeless people who, you know, don't have anywhere to go and are abused. Also, throwaway labor. I mentioned that in the book. There's a lot of that right now. A lot of it, is, right now in the Maquiladora Plants in Mexico, just the other side of the border where people are worked under horrible conditions and they live in horrible conditions in shacks made out of whatever they can make them out of. And when they're around thirty, thirty-five, they're pretty much used up if they haven't been injured or damaged in some way by the kind of work they're required to do and the chemicals, machinery, whatever, they can be tossed aside for younger workers.

JC: I think one of the things that struck me full, in the face, with *Parable* was the issue of privatization. That was what I meant when I said "political." I mean, in terms of dealing with such sweeping social issues.
OB: Yesterday, on National Public Radio, which I recommend to you. Do you listen to it ever?

JC: No, it's been recommended to me before. I'm gonna start.
OB: It's worthwhile. Either *Morning Edition* or *All Things Considered*. And also any Pacifica station you can get hold of is a good source. Especially Pacifica. But, on NPR yesterday there was a piece about an organization. It's a private company that is, at present, running about nine of Baltimore's public schools. And in Hartford, Connecticut, they wanted to take over the school systems. This isn't a matter of bringing in, you know, some big company to help out with your educational system. This is turning your educational system over to a private company. And, you know, what they say may be good and it may not be, but their main effort is to make a profit. All of a sudden, instead of the main focus of education being to educate the children, it becomes to make a profit for this company. And, I mean, that's one little thing. I noticed when I was working on *Parable* that there was a

big fad for privatization. I mean, it was like anything that couldn't be done by private companies wasn't worth doing. That was a big eighties movement. It's apparently not over. I didn't really expect it to be because when you can go in and take over something and fire the people who've earned their seniority and are getting decent salaries and hire some new people in and they're not doing too well, and they don't have any power and they're not unionized, hey, you can probably make quite a bit of money, at least at first.

JC: I'm sure. There are murmurs about that in the District of Columbia as well as in Newark, New Jersey.
OB: I'm curious as all get-out about this company because I can't help wondering what kind of job they are doing. I mean, on the piece yesterday, of course, they were saying they're doing a wonderful job. The teacher's union said they're not, but you would expect that. But I can't help wondering what's really going on there.

JC: That's something I should look into myself. You have a description of yourself which I don't . . .
OB: Oh, that's something I've been sending out for years and years. You want to hear it?

JC: Yes.
OB: Let's see, I should have a copy of it around here somewhere. . . . As a matter of fact I usually have several old copies lying around waiting to be thrown out because they're outdated as far as the books are concerned. Okay, there's a little of this on the cover of *Parable of the Sower*. The title of it is a "Brief Conversation with Octavia E. Butler" and the first question is "Who is Octavia E. Butler? Where is she headed? Where has she been?" The answer is, "Who am I? I am a forty-seven-year-old writer who can remember being a ten-year-old writer and who expects someday to be an eighty-year-old writer. I am also comfortably asocial, a hermit in the middle of Los Angeles." Actually, I don't live there anymore but I'm reading you an old one. "A pessimist if I'm not careful, a feminist, a Black, a former Baptist, an oil and water combination of ambition, laziness, insecurity, certainty, and drive." Are you recording?

JC: Yes.
OB: Oh, good. I can't think how you would get this otherwise.

JC: No, I'm recording. How do all those qualities interplay in your work or does all that come out do you think?

OB: I can look at—what I do as a writer is mine my own life, mine history, mine the news, mine whatever there is, I mean, it's like the whole universe is ore and I have to mine the gold in it. And, of course I can see bits of my own life in what I write. As for those qualities, they hamper me and they push me and there's a lot more to me than that of course. For instance, I'm on the verge of buying a bigger house and asking my mother to come live with me because she's eighty now and she's getting to the point where she might need to move in. I think about this with a certain amount of fear because the way I work, I have a feeling she's gonna believe most of the time that I'm not working at all. I mean, for instance, the ambition and the laziness and the drive, there are times when I will just seem to be wasting an awful lot of time reading books or sitting and staring or listening to book tapes or music or something and then all of a sudden, I'm writing furiously and I have a feeling that the period of what looks like goofing off and loafing is gonna be a problem for us [laughter] because she just won't be able to believe that that's also working.

JC: I'm really glad that you affirmed that because I do a lot of that myself.
OB: But you get the work done right?

JC: Yes. I always say that I'm simmering. It's not done yet.
OB: It's real important not only that you do that but that you get the work done because I have deadlines written into my contracts and they're my deadlines. I decide when I can get the book out and have them write that date into the contract or I write it in. And, it's important to meet those deadlines, of course. If you can't do that, what can you do as a writer? So, in spite of all my flaws and eccentricities and whatever, it's still a matter of getting the work out.

JC: Do your feminist views influence your female characters?
OB: Sure. You see any female characters in my work who just, well, there are a few who seem not to do very much, but they're certainly not top characters.

JC: The thing that really struck me was the redemptive qualities that I saw both in *Parable* and *Wild Seed*. Both of them. That's what led me to ask that question.
OB: What do you mean exactly?

JC: Anyanwu—
OB: Oh, you don't mean *Parable*, you mean *Wild Seed*.

JC: In *Wild Seed* and in *Parable* too because I think that Lauren seems like she's really much more suited to working with the group that coalesces than any of the other people—

OB: Well, that's because she's the one causing it to coalesce. I mean, she does have this dream of bringing these people together and forming Earthseed. As a matter of fact, I'm working on *Parable of the Talents* right now and it's one thing for a teenager to have dreams that other people think are crazy and they kind of put up with them, and it's another thing for a grown woman with a kid or two to have these ideas and people think, "My God, isn't she ever going to grow up?" and "What's wrong with her?" So my character in *Parable of the Talents* has a much harder time with people who don't see her dream as anything but childish nonsense. And the first person among those is her husband.

JC: So when do you expect *Parable of the Talents* to be completed?
OB: It's due in June of next year.

JC: Okay I have something to look forward to.
OB: I mean, it's due for me. Probably a year later it will be published.

JC: There was another question that I had about *Parable*. The recurring fire theme in there, was it at all related to the Los Angeles Rebellion in 1992?
OB: No. It wasn't. It was related to something else entirely. People ask me that a lot. I actually got kind of defensive about it for awhile there. But no, actually I was working on the novel as the riots broke out and I worried about whether I should go back and change the novel because I didn't want to seem as if I was either feeding off or promoting some of the things that went on in the riots. I mean, they burned down my favorite Black bookstore for heaven's sake. They just seemed to burn down whatever was handy. I really, okay, I'll tell you where part of the burning thing comes from. One of my earliest memories is being carried out of a burning house in the middle of—I guess you could say it was the burning desert, only it was night. My grandmother had a chicken ranch out between Victorville and Barsdale here in California and this was very primitive. I mean, we had a well and an outhouse, you know? And we were so far out and we had nothing like a telephone. We had no electricity at this point. So, there was no way to call the fire department. We used candles and kerosene lanterns, and to this day I don't know who did it, but somebody had an accident with either a candle or a kerosene lantern and you know how it is in families—it was my grandmother's—people blame each other. And so I was only about four years old, so I don't know how it happened. I know I was awakened out of a sound sleep by somebody snatching me up and running out of the house with me. This was a house that my uncles had built with their own hands, so it was especially . . . it had everything in it that

my grandmother owned as far as mementos, and records of her children's birth. She had all her children at home so there weren't any other kinds of records. My grandfather was an herbalist, and he helped out as best he could but it was a situation where all sorts of things were lost. But my biggest memory was being snatched up that way and awakened in that particular way and standing outside watching the house burn down.

JC: And that influenced the theme?

OB: A memory that imprints that early you can't help keeping. And as for the walls around the communities, that's another . . . well, the idea of people walling themselves in to keep from getting torched and then finally getting torched anyway, that's something that I see happening a lot now in the L.A. area. People—even poor people—are wanting to build walls or traffic barriers around their neighborhood either to keep the poor people out or to keep the druggies out. Because, I mean, the idea is that if you have an area that has traffic barriers or walls, that the drug dealers will perhaps go somewhere else because they don't like the idea of having only one way in and out. So, there's a lot of that right now. That was the reason by the way that I was willing to extend it to people who are middle class. They should be doing very well because they're professional but they're obviously not doing very well because of the way things have gone.

JC: I've never been to L.A., to California, but I read an interesting book about that called *City of Quartz*. It was really an interesting critique of that in terms of architecture.

OB: Wasn't that about cops or something?

JC: It had a chapter in it about "Operation Hammer." It had a few different things it explored but one of the sections was titled "Fortress L.A." and it just really talked about—he's an architectural critic—and he's talking about how they're building high-rise prisons that look like office buildings so they don't mess up the skyline.

OB: Oh, boy. Well, most prisons are not built around L.A. but there's a city right now—it ought to be a great city for tourism but unfortunately for them it's a city of lower middle-class working people, all white, I guess they're all white, I didn't see any Black ones in the story, they have decided that since they're poor and they really don't seem to be very good at bringing the tourists—it's up near one of our really scenic mountain areas—they have decided that they want a prison. The state is always looking for a place to put prisons. Nobody really wants them nearby and now all of a sudden they're becoming the going industry. It seems like around the country prisons and nuclear and toxic waste dumps are the coming thing. What does that say about our culture?

JC: There is a grotesque story right now, I don't know if you've been following it or not, the Mescalero Apaches are angling for a nuclear waste dump on their reservation. It's called a temporary nuclear waste dump.
OB: Uh, huh. Right. I guess it's only radioactive for a few thousand years.

JC: Well, no, it's temporary because they're supposed to move this stuff after about twenty years.
OB: Yeah, right.

JC: It's especially interesting because the person who is angling for it is a descendant of Cochese. And the person who is most strongly against it is a descendant of Geronimo. And the descendant of Cochese says, "Don't worry, we're gonna have jobs and it's gonna bring money into the community," and the descendant of Geronimo says, "Are you kidding?" And the descendant of Cochese says, "Well, you know, they're gonna move this stuff after about twenty years." And the descendant of Geronimo says, "Are you kidding?" [laughter] We have the guy who is willing to sell out tomorrow to have something good today and we have the guy who's looking toward tomorrow and saying, "We can't do this." The good thing is, and this is usually terrible, but the state itself has decided that they don't really want a nuclear waste dump on the Mescalero Reservation and they're fighting it. Now usually when you hear that the state is fighting some way that the Native Americans have chosen to make money, you know, you're rooting for the Native Americans. In this case I think I'm rooting for the state.
OB: That's understandable.

JC: Some one commented to me about *Parable* that they thought it was a scary book.
OB: Good.

JC: Why do you say that's good?
OB: Well, I mean, it was intended to be a cautionary tale. "Look what we're coming to if we're not careful." And if people see it as scary, it's possible that they'll have their eyes a little wider open. I mean, for instance before NAFTA passed, I used to go around, in my talks I would talk about the Maquiladoras and I would talk about the kind of . . . I would sort of, you know, patch them into our fu-

ture because after all, if companies can go off to Mexico or someplace and employ workers for almost no money and forget about environmental considerations and on-the-job safety then what the heck, why wouldn't they do that? And if they can't leave right now, if it would be inconvenient, all they have to do is threaten to leave and they can lower wages here and get rid of environmental considerations here. Here in Southern California where our smog is just ghastly, we have people saying "Our smog regulations are just too tough. It's bad for business." Of course, we also have businesses leaving the area saying the smog is just awful and they had to get out of there. It's an interesting situation. We seem to be setting things up so that the poor will get a lot poorer and the middle-class will get a lot poorer too, and I don't think a lot of members of the middle-class have figured that out yet. I had somebody review that book, *Parable*, and say, "Well interesting book but she should have been more clear about how we could possibly get from where we are to where they are in *Parable* because I just don't see it." I thought, "You poor baby."

JC: Because we're already there?

OB: We're not there, but we're getting there. The difference in *Parable* is things don't work anymore. For instance, these days if you call the fire department, they'll probably come and put out the fire. In *Parable* they might or they might not and if they do, they'll charge you your head. In *Parable* the institutions still exist, they just no longer work at all. With the possible exception of the tax [laughter] assessors and all.

JC: So is humanity destined to live out that sort of—

OB: Well, I certainly hope not. It's like I said, it's a cautionary tale. And I'm not the only one cautioning. I mean there are a lot of problems that we don't have to walk head-on into. Unfortunately, none of them—very few of them are easy. For instance, there's the conference that's going to be held in Egypt talking about the population problem. How many more people can the Earth support with any degree of comfort and civility? It can support a lot more people if we all wanna have much nastier lives. But if you start talking about something like that it's gonna start scaring people. "Oh, what are you gonna do?" For instance, with Black people, are we gonna find out that we're the ones that they need fewer of? I think the Muslims are wondering the same thing—"Is this a trick so that the non-Muslim world will be more numerous than us? What's going on?" There are always these worries, these concerns. Maybe there is a problem, maybe there isn't, but we don't trust the people who are telling us that there is a problem.

JC: That's interesting because I was researching not tot long ago for an article on what's going on in Baltimore with Norplant. One of the things I came across was the strong sentiment that it was specifically designed for Blacks and Latinos. I think that would have a lot to do with that—

OB: There's always the suspicion that people who never really liked you are finding new ways to make fewer of you or to arrange that fewer of you are made. But the problem is we really do on this planet have a population problem, just as we have a problem building slowly, or not so slowly these days, with global warming. It's not going to be easy to fix any of our major problems. The global warming thing, practically every company that earns its living with fossil fuels, the use of fossil fuels, the production of fossil fuels, I mean anything like that, they're not gonna be in favor of decreasing the use of fossil fuels. I have a feeling that if we had really put our minds to it, we would really be a lot more into solar power or other alternative energies because they're so available. You know, we're told over and over it's too expensive. That's only because so few people are doing it. The more people do it, the more people learn about it, the less expensive it becomes, the more efficient it becomes because the better we learn to do it. It's not something that we're going to do willingly because this society, the human culture, if you can call it that, isn't going to do it willingly. It's not going to make that change until it's forced to make that choice. I think people would rather go nuclear than go solar just because nuclear energy is coming from a centralized source and solar energy, you could wind up, there are a few people who have done this, built self-supporting houses with plenty of electricity—they even sell some of the electricity back to the power company because they have solar energy, maybe a couple of wind turbines or wind mills and essentially, they're pretty much doing what they need to do. They have a, what do you call it, a composting toilet so they can use the contents of their toilet in their garden without giving themselves diseases. It's not very popular because it's more work and it means change. People really, are pretty much comfortable with the way things are until the way things are becomes impossible.

JC: I only have a few more questions. In Atlanta you said something about people seeking power probably shouldn't have it.

OB: Oh, I was talking about my own feelings. I wasn't talking literally about what should or shouldn't be, but that I had somehow developed the idea, or the personal myth you could call it, that seeking power was somehow immoral. And that made it very difficult for me to write this book because I had to first overcome that myth and it was a lot stronger than I had supposed. I had to, I talked about it in terms of my friend's personal mythology and the two personal myths that I use when I talk about that are ones that are almost dead; that the rich are unhappy, that they are specifically unhappy because they are rich, and I still know at least two people who believe that, although I think the eighties knocked that out of most people. And the idea that wisdom is power. I go on to talk about that and say the personal myth is kind of self-protective. I mean, if you're poor, it's very convenient for you to believe that the rich are unhappy. If you are powerless, it's very convenient for you to believe that those who've sought and acquired power are immoral. I mean, maybe they are and maybe they aren't, but it's convenient to believe that. And if you are well-educated, if you've gone through the trouble to get yourself an education, then it's convenient for you to believe that you are among the upper echelons of society, that you've really done it. Maybe you're gonna sit there after that and not do much and want for the power to flow to you and become bitter because it hasn't. Wisdom and power and money are all tools. They are tools that can be used in any way you like. You can use them to tear things up. You can use them to build things up. Once I got that notion in my mind, and it took quite a long time, I was three years just getting ready to write this novel. I wrote and wrote and wrote and wrote and it was all garbage. That was one of my major problems. I couldn't—I had two things—one, I couldn't really accept her being a person who sought power. I've written about power before but it was always power that kind of fell on people. Either they were born to it or somebody thrust it on them in the form of major responsibility as in my Xenogenesis books. So I had two problems. The first as I said was writing about a power-seeker who is also a sympathetic character and the second was believing that a Black woman could be convincing as not just a power-seeker but a power-holder over people who were not necessarily Black and not necessarily female.

JC: Have you, or will you write any nonfiction books?
OB: I don't know. I don't know. If I got a nonfiction idea that got hold of me and wouldn't let go, I might write it. Or I might write it as fiction. I tend to do that more because I find that I like to tell stories. You have to be a lot more careful when you're doing nonfiction. I find that if I can humanize a situation in a fictional story, I'm a lot happier with what I'm doing. By the way, I have written articles.

JC: I have some of them which is actually where this last question comes from. In preparing for this interview I came across an article that you had written in *Essence.*

OB: It's got a line strategically left out of it where I praise one of my teachers and it just sort of disappeared and nobody knows what that was about.

JC: I noticed that.
OB: Yeah, I had a teacher in eighth grade who actually typed my first story for me. I told him what I wanted to do and I showed it to him. I would have typed it but we weren't allowed to take typing yet and my typing was, like two fingers with holes erased in the page and strikeovers and he took it and typed it for me and I still remember him with a lot of gratitude actually, because obviously he didn't have to do that. It's not like he didn't have any work to do or anything.

JC: How do you respond when people ask you what does your work have to do with being Black?
OB: Oddly enough, I don't get that question anymore. I haven't heard that question for a very long time. You know, I mentioned that during the sixties and the seventies I got it a lot. I answered it, really, pretty much the way I did in that piece. It's like saying that somehow, we are set apart from the future and are a part of only our own past. I mean, it's silly. We need to look at the wider world, the wider universe, heck, as much as any other group of people need to.

JC: Thank you.

"We Keep Playing the Same Record": A Conversation with Octavia Butler

Stephen W. Potts/1996

From *Science Fiction Studies* 23.3 (1996). © Science Fiction Studies. Reprinted by permission.

For readers of this journal, Octavia E. Butler literally needs no introduction. Her exquisite, insightful works—especially the three Xenogenesis novels (*Dawn, Adulthood Rites, Imago*) and her award-winning story "Bloodchild"—have been discussed and analyzed more than once in these pages.

One usually has to get up early in the morning to reach Ms. Butler. A private person, she prefers writing in the predawn hours and by eight AM is frequently out of the house on the day's business. She has other claims to uniqueness: she is a native of Los Angeles who does not drive; she is a woman of color working in a genre that has almost none, and she is a science-fiction author who has received a prestigious literary award, to wit, a 1995 grant from the MacArthur Foundation.

The following conversation took place by telephone early one morning in February 1996. It has been edited only to eliminate digressions, redundancies, and irrelevancies and to bridge some technical difficulties; Ms. Butler was given the opportunity to review and amend the finished version.

Stephen W. Potts: Your name has been turning up with increasing frequency in journals (such as *Science-Fiction Studies*) devoted to the serious study of science fiction. Do you read reviews or literary criticism of your work?

Octavia E. Butler: I do, but I tend to get angry. Not when I disagree with someone's interpretation, but when people clearly have not read the whole book. I'm not too upset when they are factually wrong about some incident, which can happen to anybody, but I am when they are inaccurate about something sweeping. For example, somebody writing a review of *Parable of the Sower* said, "Oh, the Earthseed religion is just warmed over Christianity," and I thought this person could not have been troubled to read the Earthseed verses and just drew that conclusion from the title.

SWP: I ask because a substantial part of modern literary theory dwells on relationships of power and on the human body as a site of conflict: between men and women, among classes and races, between imperial and colonial peoples. These issues intersect nicely with the subject matter of your fiction. I was wondering if you were at all familiar with cultural theory.

OEB: Ah. No, I avoid all critical theory because I worry about it feeding into my work. I mean, I don't worry about nonfiction in general feeding in—in fact, I hope it will—but I worry about criticism influencing me, because it can create a vicious circle or something worse. It's just an impression of mine, but in some cases critics and authors seem to be massaging each other. It's not very good for storytelling.

SWP: The first work of yours I read was the story "Bloodchild" in its original printing in *Asimov's*. I remember being particularly impressed that you had taken the invading bug-eyed monster of classic science fiction and turned it into a seductively nurturing, maternal figure.

OEB: It is basically a love story. There are many different kinds of love in it: family love, physical love . . . The alien needs the boy for procreation, and she makes it easier on him by showing him affection and earning his in return. After all, she is going to have her children with him.

SWP: In fact, she will impregnate him.

OEB: Right. But so many critics have read this as a story about slavery, probably just because I am black.

SWP: I was going to ask you later about the extent to which your work addresses slavery.

OEB: The only places I am writing about slavery is where I actually say so.

SWP: As in *Kindred*.

OEB: And in *Mind of My Mind* and *Wild Seed*. What I was trying to do in "Bloodchild" was something different with the invasion story. So often you read novels about humans colonizing other planets and you see the story taking one of two courses. Either the aliens resist and we have to conquer them violently, or they submit and become good servants. In the latter case, I am thinking of a specific novel, but I don't want to mention it by name. I don't like either of those alternatives, and I wanted to create a new one. I mean, science fiction is supposed to be about exploring new ideas and possibilities. In the case of "Bloodchild," I was creating an alien that was different from us, though still recognizable—a centipede-like creature. But you're not supposed to regard it as evil.

SWP: Something similar is going on in the Xenogenesis trilogy, isn't it? While teaching the books in my university classes, I have encountered disagreement over which species comes off worse, the humans or the Oankali. Humanity has this hierarchical flaw, particularly in the male, but the Oankali are the ultimate users, adapting not only the entire human genome for its own purposes but ultimately destroying the planet for all other life as well. Are we supposed to see a balance of vices here?

OEB: Both species have their strengths and weaknesses. You have small groups of violent humans, but we don't see all humans rampaging as a result of their Contradiction. For the most part, the Oankali do not force or rush humans into mating but try to bring them in gradually. In fact, in *Adulthood Rites*, the construct Akin convinces the Oankali that they cannot destroy the human beings who refuse to participate. The Oankali decide that humans do deserve an untouched world of their own, even if it's Mars.

SWP: In the case of both humans and Oankali, you offer sociobiological arguments for behavior: humans are bent toward destroying themselves and others; the Oankali are biologically driven to co-opt the genome of other species and to literally rip off their biospheres. Do you largely accept sociobiological principles?

OEB: Some readers see me as totally sociobiological, but that is not true. I do think we need to accept that our behavior *is* controlled to some extent by biological forces. Sometimes a small change in the brain, for instance—just a few cells—can completely alter the way a person or animal behaves.

SWP: Are you thinking of Oliver Sacks's books, such as *The Man Who Mistook His Wife for a Hat*?

OEB: Exactly. Or the fungus that causes tropical ants to climb trees to spread its spores, or the disease that makes a wildebeest spend its last days spinning in circles. But I don't accept what I would call classical sociobiology. Sometimes we can work around our programming if we understand it.

SWP: The exploitation of reproduction and, by extension, of family arises in a number of your works. Doro in the Patternist novels is breeding a master race and uses family ties with heroines like Anyanwu in *Wild Seed* and Mary in *Mind of My Mind* to help keep them under control. Family ties control the problematic bond between Dana and Rufus in *Kindred*. Reproduction and family lie at the crux of the relationship in "Bloodchild" and between the humans and Oankali in Xenogenesis. Do you intentionally focus on reproductive and family issues as a central theme, or did this just happen?

OEB: Perhaps as a woman, I can't help dwelling on the importance of family and reproduction. I don't know how men feel about it. Even though I don't have a husband and children, I have other family, and it seems to me our most important set of relationships. It is so much of what we are. Family does not have to mean purely biological relationships either. I know families that have adopted outside individuals; I don't mean legally adopted children but other adults, friends, people who simply came into the household and stayed. Family bonds can even survive really terrible abuse.

SWP: Of course, you show the power of such bonds operating in either direction; for instance, Anyanwu in *Wild Seed* and Dana in *Kindred* both ultimately take advantage of the fact that their respective "masters" need them.
OEB: They don't recognize these men as their masters.

SWP: I was putting the word in quotation marks. Are you suggesting that people in subordinate positions should recognize and exploit what power they do have?
OEB: You do what you have to do. You make the best use of whatever power you have.

SWP: We even see that humans have more power than they realize over the Oankali. Especially with the construct ooloi in *Imago*: they have no identity without human mates. Aaor devolves into a slug.
OEB: The constructs are an experiment. They do not know what they are going to be, or when it is going to happen. And they do not need humans specifically, even though they prefer them; they can bond with anything. But they have to bond.

SWP: I would like to go back a bit in your literary history. Who were your authorial influences as an apprentice writer?
OEB: I read a lot of science fiction with absolutely no discrimination when I was growing up—I mean, good, bad, or awful [laughs]. It didn't matter. I remember latching onto people and reading everything I could find by them, people like John Brunner, who wrote a lot. I could pick up Ace Doubles at the used book store for a nickel or a dime, so I was always reading John Brunner. And Theodore Sturgeon—by the time I was reading adult science fiction, he had a considerable body of work. Of course, Robert A. Heinlein. I can remember my very first adult science fiction, a story called "Lorelei of the Red Mist." If I am not mistaken, it was Ray Bradbury's first published story. Leigh Brackett began it and he finished it.

SWP: Can you think of anybody outside of science fiction?

OEB: I tended to read whatever was in the house, which meant that I read a lot of odd stuff. Who was that guy that used to write about men's clubs all the time? John O'Hara. It was Mars for me. I like British between-the-wars mysteries for the same reason. They take place on Mars; they're different worlds.

SWP: Might we suggest that since John O'Hara writes about upper-class white culture, his world would be almost as alien to you as the worlds of science fiction?

OEB: Absolutely. There was a book of his stories in the house, as well as books by James Thurber and James Baldwin. I did not read any Langston Hughes until I was an adult, but I remember being carried away by him and Gwendolyn Brooks. When I was growing up, the only blacks you came across in school were slaves— who were always well treated—and later, when we got to individuals, Booker T. Washington and George Washington Carver. Booker T. Washington started a college, and Carver did something with peanuts; we never knew what. We did not read anything by a black writer except [James Weldon] Johnson's *The Creation*, and that was in high school. We managed to get through adolescence without being introduced to any black culture.

SWP: I was in that same generation, and I remember that it wasn't really until the seventies that we started opening up the canon. Actually, the issue is still controversial, judging from the so- called "culture war" over how inclusive the canon should be or whether we should even have one.

OEB: Yes, it's too bad when . . . well, there was one person I had a lot of respect for, but he could not find a single black person to put into the canon, so I lost my respect for him rather badly.

SWP: On its surface, *Parable of the Sower* looks like a change in direction from your earlier work.

OEB: Not really. It is still fundamentally about social power.

SWP: But it is much more a close extrapolation from current trends: the increasing class gap, the fear of crime, the chaos of the cities spreading to the suburbs, the centrifugal forces tearing our society apart.

OEB: Yes. It really distresses me that we see these things happening now in American society when they don't have to. Some people insist that all civilizations have to rise and fall—like the British before us—but we have brought this on ourselves. What you see today has happened before: a few powerful people take over with the approval of a class below them who has nothing to gain and even much to lose as a result. It's like the Civil War: most of the men who fought to preserve slavery were actually being hurt by it. As farmers they could not compete with the plantations, and they could not even hire themselves out as labor in competition with the slaves who could be hired out more cheaply by their owners. But they supported the slave system anyway.

SWP: They probably opposed affirmative action.
OEB: [laughs] Right. I guess many people just need someone to feel superior to to make themselves feel better. You see Americans doing it now, unfortunately, while voting against their own interests. It is that kind of shortsighted behavior that is destroying us.

SWP: Are these problems somehow unique to American society?
OEB: Oh no, of course not.

SWP: I was sure you'd say that.
OEB: We are seeing a particular American form here, but look at the Soviet Union. When capitalism took over, it is amazing how quickly they developed a crime problem. Unfortunately, the most successful capitalists over there now seem to be the criminals.

SWP: Which is ironic because in classic Soviet Marxist theory the capitalist class was associated with the criminal class.
OEB: That may be the problem. We are getting into murky territory here: I heard about an old man in Russia who tried to turn his farm into a successful private enterprise, but his neighbors came over and destroyed his efforts. He was not a criminal, but to them that kind of individualistic profit-making was criminal behavior. I guess to succeed in Russia you have to be someone who (a) doesn't care what the neighbors think and (b) has a bodyguard. And if you're in that position, you probably are a criminal.

SWP: To get back to *Parable of the Sower*, Lauren Olamina is empathic—
OEB: She is not empathic. She feels herself to be. Usually in science fiction "empathic" means that you really are suffering, that you are actively interacting telepathically with another person, and she is not. She has this delusion that she cannot shake. It's kind of biologically programmed into her.

SWP: Interesting. So what is happening, say, when she feels the pain of the wounded dog she ends up killing?
OEB: Oh, even if it is not there, she feels it. In the first chapter of the book, she talks about her brother playing tricks on her—pretending to be hurt, pretending to bleed, and causing her to suffer. I have been really annoyed with people who

claim Lauren is a telepath, who insist that she has this power. What she has is a rather crippling delusion.

SWP: So we should maintain some ironic distance from her?
OEB: No.

SWP: We should still identify with her.
OEB: I hope readers will identify with all my characters, at least while they're reading.

SWP: Through Earthseed, Lauren hopes to bring back a sense of communal purpose and meaning by turning people's eyes back to the stars. It made me think: the space program of the sixties really was part of the general hopefulness of the decade, part of our sense that anything was possible if we strove together as a people.
OEB: And that was the decade of my adolescence. We keep playing the same record. Earlier I was talking about it: we begin something and then we grow it to a certain point and then it destroys itself or else it is destroyed from the outside— whether it is Egypt or Rome or Greece, this country or Great Britain, you name it. I do feel that we are either going to continue to play the same record until it shatters—and I said it in the book, though not in those words—or we are going to do something else. And I think the best way to do something else is to go some-place else where the demands on us will be different. Not because we are going to go someplace else and change ourselves, but because we will go someplace else and be forced to change.

SWP: Do you think we will be better for that change?
OEB: It's possible. We could be better; we could be worse. There's no insurance policy.

SWP: I gather that we can expect another book to pick up where *Parable of the Sower* left off.
OEB: *Parable of the Talents* is the book I am working on now.

SWP: It will be interesting to see where you go with the story.
OEB: Well, in *Parable of the Sower* I focused on the problems—the things we have done wrong, that we appear to be doing wrong, and where those things can lead us. I made a real effort to talk about what could actually happen or is in the process of happening: the walled communities and the illiteracy and the global warming and lots of other things. In *Parable of the Talents* I want to give my characters the chance to work on the solutions, to say, "Here is the solution!"

SWP: *Parable of the Sower* was published by a small press (Four Walls Eight Windows), as was your collection *Bloodchild and Other Stories*. *Kindred* was republished by a small press (Beacon). As a successful science-fiction author, what made you turn to less commercial publishers?

OEB: I had probably reached some kind of plateau in science fiction, and I couldn't seem to get off it. I knew I had three audiences at least, but I couldn't get my science-fiction publisher to pay any attention. I could tell them all day and all night, but they would answer, "Yes, that's right," and then go off and do something else. You know, the best way to defeat an argument is to agree with it and then forget about it. I had wanted to try one of the big publishers not normally associated with science fiction, and then my agent came up with this small publisher. I thought I would take the chance.

SWP: Would you like to break down some of the walls between generic marketing categories?

OEB: Oh, that's not possible. You know how we are; if we kill off some, we will invent others.

SWP: I ask in part because I noticed that Beacon Press published *Kindred* as a book in its "Black Women Writers" series.

OEB: Yes, I mentioned having three audiences: the science-fiction audience, the black audience, and the feminist audience.

SWP: And being marketed through such categories doesn't trouble you.

OEB: Well, they're there, as I was just saying, and there's nothing you can do about it.

SWP: I remember that during the New Wave of the sixties—

OEB: Oh, where is it now?

SWP: —I was among those who believed that science fiction was moving to the forefront of literature.

OEB: Well, parts of it did move into the mainstream. In other cases, people simply did not call what they were doing "science fiction." I mean, Robin Cook did not announce that he was doing medical science fiction, and Dean Koontz does not publish his work as science fiction. And there are a lot of people who write science fiction although the word does not appear anywhere on the cover or inside. It doesn't mean they don't like science fiction; it means they want to make a good living.

SWP: As I pointed out initially, your treatments of power, gender, and race coincide with many of the interests of current literary theory, and your own race and gender inevitably come into literary critiques of your work. Has being an African-American woman influenced your choice of theme and approach?

OEB: I don't think it could do otherwise. All writers are influenced by who they are. If you are white, you could write about being Chinese, but you would bring in a lot of what you are as well.

SWP: I cannot help noting—as you yourself observe in your essay—"Positive Obsession"—that you are unique in the science-fiction community. While there are more women working in the field than there were thirty years ago, there are few African Americans, and I still cannot think of another African-American woman.

OEB: I have heard of some who have published stories. The ones who are actually writing books are not calling themselves science-fiction authors, which is right because they are actually writing horror or fantasy. For instance, the woman who wrote the lesbian vampire stories, the Gilda stories, Jewelle Gomez—she's not science fiction but she is fantasy, and that's in the family. But I don't think she even presented her work as that.

SWP: Do you think many people are still under the impression that science fiction is primarily a white male genre?

OEB: Yes. In fact, sometimes when I speak to general audiences they are surprised there are a lot of women in science fiction. Because people do have a rather fixed notion of what science fiction is; it either comes from television or they pick it up somehow from the air, the ambience.

SWP: Any last words to the science-fiction critical community about how to approach your work?

OEB: Oh, good heavens, no!

SWP: [laughs]

OEB: As far as criticism goes, what a reader brings to the work is as important as what I put into it, so I don't get upset when I am misinterpreted. Except when I say what I really meant was so-and-so, and I am told, "Oh, but subconsciously you must have meant this." I mean—leave me alone! [laughs] I don't mind attempts to interpret my fiction, but I am not willing to have critics interpret my subconscious. I doubt they are qualified.

An Interview with Octavia E. Butler

Charles Rowell/1997

From *Callaloo* 20:1 (1997), 47–66. © Charles H. Rowell. Reprinted with permission of The Johns Hopkins University Press.

Rowell: At the end of your interview with fiction writer Randall Kenan, you said, "I don't feel that I have any particular literary talent at all. It [writing] was what I wanted to do, and I followed what I wanted to do, as opposed to getting a job doing something that would make more money . . . it would make me miserable." As I think of the number of books of fiction you have created and the many awards you have received (including a MacArthur Foundation Fellowship) for your work, I begin to wonder, what did Octavia mean when she made that statement to Randall?

Butler: It's a problem that I have quite often encountered with would-be writers—and I'm sorry to say especially black would-be writers. So many of these would-be writers are afraid they don't have the talent. And I actually wrote about this in an essay in *Bloodchild and Other Stories* (1995). But what I mean, I guess, is that I had to learn my craft. And I mean I had to learn it, bit by bit, by doing things wrong, and by collecting years and years of rejection slips. But I kept writing because I liked doing it. The quote that you read is a bit condensed from the original. I did have lots of jobs. I worked at all sorts of things. Anyone who has read my novel *Kindred* (1979) can find a number of the kinds of jobs that I had, from blue collar to low grade white collar, clerk typist, that kind of thing. And I did these jobs because I had to live, but always while I was doing them and between jobs I wrote, because it was the only thing I actually cared about doing. All the other jobs were just work to keep a roof over my head and food on the table. I felt like an animal, just living in order to live, just surviving. But as long as I wrote, I felt that I was living in order to do something more, something I actually cared about.

Rowell: What is it then that you're talking about if it's not talent you have as a writer?

Butler: I'm talking about learning your craft. And practicing it, and learning as you practice it, even though it often hurts to be told that you're doing some-

74

thing that doesn't work in your writing. Writing is very personal, and it does hurt sometimes to be told that something is wrong with some work you really love and feel is perfect. Your writing is an expression of your inner feelings and thoughts and beliefs and self. One of the reasons it is difficult to learn to write professionally is that that kind of thing is so painful; rejection is so painful. It sounds as though you are personally being rejected, and in a sense you are—no matter how much somebody tells you not to worry, "It's not you; it's just the work." But the work is you; so it hurts. You need to go through that, and you never really stop going through that, even though you've learned to write professionally; you go on learning. If you don't go on learning, then your writing becomes stale, and you do the same thing over and over again.

Now sad to say, doing the same thing over and over can be lucrative for some people. But most often it's just a form of death, literary death. In that essay that I mentioned—it's called "Furor Scribendi" and it's in *Bloodchild and Other Stories*—I talk about the ways in which you gather and train your writing skills. Of course I talk about reading, I talk about writing every day, and I talk about having a schedule, about keeping that writing schedule. Even if you can write only one hour a day, to actually do that writing is very important. To do your reading is also important. You use your reading not only to learn about the mechanics of writing but also to learn how other people have written to gather information that has nothing to do with your writing because everything goes into the well. And when you begin to write, it's surprising what you suddenly find coming out. The things that come out of your writing are often things that you are on friendly terms with, even though you perhaps never intended to write about them. Say a year ago you read a very intricate book about the geology of California. You read it because there was an earthquake and you were curious, and then later you find yourself doing something that relates to the geology of California or geology in general. But you did not read that book so you could write about geology. You read the book for amusement and information, but eventually it does come out. Anything that happens that makes you emotional is almost certain to come out in your writing. I say to students, anything that doesn't dismember or kill you will probably come out in your writing. You go on learning to write for as long as you live and write. If you don't do this, if you're not willing to do this, you might want to *be* a writer, but you don't really want to write.

I think there are many people who want to *be* writers because they think that it is a good thing to be, that it is important or whatever. But they don't actually want to get down and do the work. So they wind up talking about how they're going to write the great American novel someday. There's so much you can do that will contribute to the writing. One thing, for instance, is to keep a journal. I mentioned how important emotionally felt experience is. If you keep a journal and let yourself overflow with the things that affect you, the things that make you joyous, the things that make you furious, the things that make you jealous; if you can be honest with your journal and not write about what you had for breakfast or what load of washing you did (nobody's going to care about that ever), but what you felt and what you care about, you will discover that these are things other people feel and care about. It's difficult sometimes I think, especially for men, because they feel that they are revealing themselves in public, and they might feel uncomfortable about that. But it's one of the exercises that I like to give students when I'm teaching a writers' workshop. I want the students to delve into their emotional experiences. Since emotional experiences tend to be personal, I want my students then to fictionalize an emotional experience with the same emotion. It does not have to deal with the same emotional experience. It just has to deal with the same emotion, which I then ask the student to turn into a story. It's just practice for writing honestly, writing what you feel and what's important to you.

Rowell: I have no doubt that the established writer and the literary critic understand what you mean when you say, "Learn your craft." But I am not certain that the beginning or developing writer and the general reader understand what you mean. Will you say more about what you mean when you talk about learning one's craft?

Butler: First of all, if you're in school you should take writing classes. The great thing about writing classes is not only that the teacher might provide you with information that will help you improve your writing, but that the other students in the class are an audience. So often new authors will argue that they didn't really mean what everybody thinks they meant, that they meant something else altogether. That's when, if they're really going to be writers, they learn to say what they meant and stop arguing about what other people are seeing in their work. That's one of the major difficulties in communication. Sometimes we writers tend to be alone too much, and we write for ourselves. We can't help doing that. But later we discover that we haven't really communicated what we think we communicated. That means that the writing needs to be fixed. Fixing it doesn't mean that you won't be misinterpreted. Inevitably you will be. It just means that people need to work harder to do it. Another kind of exercise that I have students go through is to look at their trouble spots. For instance, if they have difficulty with beginnings—they have wonderful stories to tell but don't know where to begin or how to begin—I have them look at work that they enjoy reading, novels

or short-stories—it doesn't matter. I then ask them to copy half a dozen beginnings; I ask them to copy them directly, word for word. It's difficult to say how
much to copy, anything from the first couple of paragraphs to the first page. It's
just a matter of finding out how each writer gets into the story that the writer
is telling. And in this case it's taking those half dozen or so beginnings (more is
okay, but fewer is not a good idea) and figuring out what each writer has done in
order to begin. They find dialogue beginnings, they find action beginnings, and
they find the kind of beginning that gets you immediately into a mystery. They
also find descriptive beginnings. Learning what other people have done by way
of beginnings helps them to understand what's possible. This is not about imi-
tating someone else's beginnings; that's why I want at least a half a dozen. This is
about learning what is possible. One of the big problems we have as writers is that
we either know too much or not enough. Sometimes we manage to know both at
the same time. We know that there is an ocean of possibilities out there, and we're
overwhelmed. And we don't know how to take from that ocean just what we need.
Sometimes focusing on what other people have done (not just beginnings, but
transitions, descriptions of important characters, for instance, those elements of
fiction writing that give people trouble, in general) may help beginning writers.
I like my students to go through their own favorite works—not something I pick,
but something they actually like—and copy down what the writers have done and
figure out why it works. This is something that I have used on any number of
problems, and in fact it's something that I am usingright now on a problem that
I'm having.

Rowell: Could you share that writing problem?
Butler: [*Laughter.*] Maybe later.

Rowell: Okay. Two elements of your background fascinate me: your family background and your formal, higher education. I would like to begin first by talking
about your family background. Like many African-American writers and scholars
of our generation, you come from a working-class family, one whose roots are in
Louisiana, where you never lived, of course. Your mother was a domestic, in California, where you've lived all of your life. Has that working-class background, as
far as you can tell, contributed in any way to your work as a fiction writer? One
can probably say, on a superficial level, that you used Louisiana—that is to say,
nineteenth-century Louisiana—as a setting in *Wild Seed* (1980).
Butler: Yes, for part of *Wild Seed*. I don't know enough about Louisiana to talk
about it knowledgeably. I did some research to use it as a background for *Wild
Seed*. My mother's life and my grandmother's life and the little bit I know of her

ancestors' lives were very hard and very terrible. These were not lives that I would have wanted to live. I mean the reason my mother did domestic work was not only that she was black, but because she was the oldest daughter. This meant that after only three years of education, she was pulled out of school and put to work. The oldest son, who was a couple of years older than she, got a chance to go to school. But as the daughter she was the one that was kind of sacrificed, I guess you would say, and sent off to work. She never really got back into education.

She was born in 1914, so she was a child quite a long time ago. Her mother chopped sugar cane, and she also did the family laundry, not just her own family but the white family for whom they worked. She washed clothes in the big iron pots with paddles and all that. That was hard, physical labor. It's no wonder she died at fifty-nine, after having a lot of children and working her life away. This is the kind of life that she had no choice but to live. The reason I mention the place is that there was no school in that area—no school for black children, and racial segregation was very rigid in those days. There was no integrated schooling in that part of Louisiana. My grandmother and grandfather moved to a more urban area to get the kids into school. My mother was already about seven or eight years old. Because she was big, and obviously not a kindergartner from appearance, they put her in the third grade, which meant that she was suddenly confronted with concepts she knew nothing about. To the end of her life, she felt that she was stupid and couldn't learn, because she was presented with all these concepts that other kids had been taught early on and that she had never been confronted with at all. She really learned quite a lot, but she felt inferior. She was physically courageous, willing to take on whatever came. But emotionally, intellectually, she felt that she was inferior, and she always kind of, figuratively, ducked her head when it came to anything requiring intellectual competence. I used to try to talk to her about that, but I think it was something so ingrained that it was something she was never able to get away from.

Her big dream for me was that I should get a job as a secretary and be able to sit down when I worked. My big dream was never to be a secretary in my life. I mean, it just seemed such an appallingly servile job, and it turned out to be in a lot of ways. I can remember watching television, which is something, of course, that my mother as a child never had access to, and seeing secretaries on television rushing to do their bosses' bidding and feeling the whole thing to be really kind of humiliating. I was occasionally taken to work with my mother and made to sit in the car all day, because I wasn't really welcome inside, of course. Sometimes, I was able to go inside and hear people talk about or to my mother in ways that were obviously disrespectful. As a child I did not blame them for their disgusting behavior, but I blamed my mother for taking it. I didn't really understand. This is something I carried with me for quite a while, as she entered back doors, and as she went deaf at appropriate times. If she had heard more, she would have had to react to it, you know. The usual. And as I got older I realized that this is what kept me fed, and this is what kept a roof over my head. This is when I started to pay attention to what my mother and even more my grandmother and my poor great-grandmother, who died as a very young woman giving birth to my grandmother, what they all went through.

When I got into college, Pasadena City College, the black nationalist movement, the Black Power Movement, was really underway with the young people, and I heard some remarks from a young man who was the same age I was but who had apparently never made the connection with what his parents did to keep him alive. He was still blaming them for their humility and their acceptance of disgusting behavior on the part of employers and other people. He said, "I'd like to kill all these old people who have been holding us back for so long. But I can't because I'd have to start with my own parents." When he said *us* he meant black people, and when he said *old people* he meant older black people. That was actually the germ of the idea for *Kindred* (1979). I've carried that comment with me for thirty years. He felt so strongly ashamed of what the older generation had to do, without really putting it into the context of being necessary for not only their lives but his as well.

I wanted to take a character, when I did *Kindred*, back in time to some of the things that our ancestors had to go through, and see if that character survived so very well with the knowledge of the present in her head. Actually, I began with a man as main character, but I couldn't go on using the male main character, because I couldn't realistically keep him alive. So many things that he did would have been likely to get him killed. He wouldn't even have time to learn the rules— the rules of submission, I guess you could call them—before he was killed for not knowing them because he would be perceived as dangerous. The female main character, who might be equally dangerous, would not be perceived so. She might be beaten, she might be abused, but she probably wouldn't be killed and that's the way I wrote it. She was beaten and abused, but she was not killed. That sexism, in a sense, worked in her favor. Although if you could take the character and give her life and ask her if she thought she had been favored, it would be likely that she wouldn't think so, because of what she suffered. But, anyway, that's a long-winded answer. And that's how I came to write *Kindred*.

Rowell: You have referred to yourself as growing up as "an out kid." Did you read a lot? What did you read as a child? What do you mean when you said you were "an out kid"?

Butler: I was not an out kid because of my reading or writing, at least not at first. I was an out kid because, as an only child, I never really learned to be part of a group. At first it didn't matter. When you are four years old in preschool, kids tended to play by themselves anyway. I was like most of the kids. You know, the kids talked together, but they didn't exactly play together. Later on, I really knew more about being around adults than I knew about being around other kids. This made me very awkward and strange around kids, and, unfortunately, children have a pecking order and it was very much in effect. If you're pecked and you don't peck back, then you'll go on being pecked. If you're a little chicken, you die of it, but if you're a little kid, you only want to die of it. I spent a lot of time getting hit and kicked and not really knowing what to do about it, because if you're most of the time around adults and they hit you and you hit them back, it's definitely not a good idea, especially black southern adults of that day. So it took me awhile to learn to hit back. It was strange for awhile because I was bigger than most kids my age. That meant, by the way, that I was originally being bothered by kids who were older than I. The ones my own age pretty much left me alone, but the older ones saw me as a marvelous target. Later, when I realized that I could fight back, I discovered that I was a lot stronger than I had thought. I hurt people by accident. I had a lot of empathy, and hurting somebody really bothered me. So I found that I was hesitant to hurt them for those reasons. That was just elementary school. Elementary school is very physical for kids. Later there are fewer fights because, after all, fights are more dangerous as you get older, you could really do damage. So later I had few fights, but a lot more social ostracism.

By the time I was ten I was writing, and I carried a big notebook around so that whenever I had some time I could write in it. That way, I didn't have to be lonely. I usually had very few friends, and I was lonely. But when I wrote I wasn't, which was probably a good reason for my continuing to write as a young kid. I read a lot also, for the same reasons. I discovered the library back in kindergarten, I guess. We didn't have a library at the school, but we were not that far from the main city library in Pasadena. The teachers would have us join hands and walk down to the library together. There we would sit, and someone would tell us—or read us—a story. Someone would also talk to us about how to use the library. When I was six and was finally given books to read in school, I found them incredibly dull; they were Dick and Jane books. I asked my mother for a library card. I remember the surprised look on her face. She looked surprised and happy.

She immediately took me to the library. She had been taking me home, but now she immediately took me to the library and got me a card. From then on the library was my second home. In a way, reading and writing helped me not to be lonely, but in another way they permitted me to go on being an oddball as far as other kids were concerned. So reading and writing both helped and, I suppose in some ways, hindered.

I often wonder what kind of person I would have been if my brothers had lived. I had four older brothers. My mother had difficulty carrying a child to term. And she lost them all, either at birth or before they should have been born. I wonder what kind of person I would have been if they had lived and if I had had more of the society of kids when I was a kid. But, anyway, since I didn't have that, I made my own society in the books and in the stories that I told myself. I began telling myself stories at four. I can recall the specific time when I began doing that. I couldn't go out and play when I was being punished. I saw other kids having a good time. I lived near some of my cousins at that point, and it was less than a year that we were living there. It was sort of fun, for that little period, having them nearby.

You also asked me about TV and film. That's interesting, because I think my first strong influence was radio. Not because I'm so terribly old—although I guess to some people I might seem so—but because at first we didn't have a television. There were still radio dramas on. I was introduced, for instance, to characters like Superman and the Shadow by way of the radio. The Whistler and Johnny Dollar, *My True Story*, and other programs. Radio was fun; it has been called theater of the mind, and it really is. As a young child, you have no idea what the adults mean when they say a lot of different things, and you imagine all sorts of things. For instance, I was a small child during the McCarthy era, when we finally got television. There was a program on television called *I Led Three Lives*. It was supposed to be the story of an American who was a double agent pretending to be a communist, but actually working for the FBI. A wonderful fellow, yes. Anyway, every now and then during this program he would talk about someone having been "liquidated." You can just imagine a little kid sitting there wondering what "liquidated" means and imagining them being dissolved in a mixing bowl or something. Everything was theater for the mind at that point for me because I had no idea what most things meant.

Movies didn't play a big part in my life because my mother felt that movies were sinful. We didn't go. Then we did go when I was about seven, because my stepfather would take us to the movies. My father died when I was a toddler, almost a baby, and I really don't have any strong memory of him. When I was about seven, my mother thought she might marry again. My potential stepfather would take us to the movies. My mother would go because it was someplace she could take me along, too, and she didn't have to pay for a baby-sitter. I got to see, for instance, *Invasion from Mars*. This ridiculous movie—and I think they've done a remake of it—is about a little boy who sees a flying saucer land, and the flying saucer people are turning everybody into them, by doing something to the backs of their heads. They finally grab his parents and do it to them, and then the whole thing turns out to be a dream. That gave me nightmares. I, by the way, enjoyed my nightmares. I had wonderful fun with my nightmares. Some of them really scared me to death, but they were all so much fun. They were like movies that scared me to death on television. When movies came on television, they, in the eyes of my mother, were somehow not evil—or at least she did not say they were. I was smart enough never to question this, but it did occur to me. It also occurred to me to shut up. So I did watch movies on television. I could watch over and over again. I think they were the ones that caught my attention and held it. There was something called Channel 9 Movie Theater back when there were RKO stations. Channel 9 was an RKO station. You could watch the same movie every night for a week and twice on Sundays or something like that. It's been a long time, so I don't really recall. Some were science fiction movies, and some were Fred Astaire dancing along. I think those movies that I had the chance to watch over and over were the ones more likely to have the greatest effect on me—not so much those that I only saw once. The television, once we got one, was a great friend to me; I spent a lot of time with it.

Rowell: Will you say more about what you were viewing and reading—how, for example, radio, television, and books might have helped to shape you as a writer? You mentioned seeing science fiction movies—for example, *Invasion from Mars*.
Butler: It almost had to be defined as science fiction, if Mars was somewhere in it. Actually, it wasn't *Invasion from Mars* that mattered. It was just a movie that I described. The movie that got me writing science fiction was *Devil Girl from Mars*. That was just one of the old sub-genre of science fiction movies that talked about how the people of some other world have used up all men. So this beautiful, gorgeous, Martian woman has come to Earth to get some more men. The men, of course, don't want to go to Mars, a planet full of man-hungry women; the men, they want desperately to stay here. It was a silly movie, although it wasn't as bad as I make it sound. I watched it as a kid, and it seemed a silly movie to me, so I turned it off and I began writing. My idea was, gee, I can write a better story than that. And since the story that I had seen was supposed to be science fiction,

I began writing science fiction as I thought of it then, even though I didn't know much in the way of science. What I had already discovered was that I liked science documentaries, whether they were television movies or the kind of films that teachers showed at school. I was probably one of the few who really liked those films. They tended to be rather preachy and dull. But, quite often, they gave me something to think about, taught me something that I didn't know about before. I got my first notions of astronomy and geology from those little films. I guess I was interested enough in astronomy to learn more because the second book I ever bought new was a book about the stars; I bought it to learn more. I knew that what I was writing was completely imaginary because I didn't know anything about Mars or anyplace else out there in space. I wanted to know more, so that's when I went and bought the book about the stars.

Rowell: When was that?

Butler: I was twelve then. Before that, I had bought a book about horses because, when I was ten, I was crazy over horses, even though I had no contact at all with them. I bought a book about the different breeds of horses, and I was writing a kind of—I guess in a way you could call it—either part of a novel or a long soap opera about a marvelous, magical wild horse. And it couldn't end because then what would I do? So I just wrote on and on and on about this marvelous, magical wild horse in number two pencil in a notebook. After a while you couldn't read most of the pages, because they were so smudged. Anyway, that was some of my early writing.

I went on writing science fiction because I enjoyed it. I enjoyed reading and hearing about science. I enjoyed finding out what was real, or at least what everybody assumed was real then and what wasn't. I enjoyed trying to understand how the universe worked. I think if you're going to write something like science fiction, you do need that basic interest in science and not just a desire to write about spectacular things that you know nothing about. I can remember a young man who sat next to me on a bus. I like to talk to people on buses, since I write them all the time. Sometimes people are interesting. But this young man didn't make conversation, and he said, "Oh, science fiction. I've always wanted to write science fiction, about creatures from other galaxies." I said, "Why do they have to be from another galaxy?" And we talked a bit, and I realized he didn't know what a galaxy was. It was just something he had heard. And this was a young man in college. To him a galaxy and the solar system were pretty much the same thing. And I realized that there probably are people who want to write science fiction and who might be good at it, but who have the wrong idea of it. They've gotten their idea from television or movies. And they think science fiction is anything weird that they choose to write. That is not what science fiction is. If you are interested in science fiction, I hope you are also interested in science. Or you just might want to call what you're writing fantasy. Fantasy has totally different rules from those in science fiction.

Rowell: What are some of the elements or characteristics that distinguish science fiction from fantasy and other related forms of prose fiction? Then there is also speculative writing. There are also horror stories.

Butler: Science fiction uses science, extrapolates from science as we know it to science as it might be to technology as it might be. A science fiction story must have internal consistency and science. Fantasy can make do with internal consistency. Speculative fiction means anything odd at all. Sounds nice though. Labels tend to be marketing devices. All too often, they mean anything, and thus nothing.

You can make an easy division—science fiction and fantasy. Obviously they both have a tendency to be fantastical, but science fiction basically uses science, and uses it accurately up to a point. It extrapolates from sciences. Fantasy goes where it likes. All that is required of fantasy is that it remains internally consistent. You can be comic the way *The Hitchhiker's Guide to the Galaxy* is comic. But you have to be careful about the kind of science fiction that gets to be called science fiction on television and sometimes in movies. That kind of stuff would not be considered science fiction if you were trying to publish it in a magazine or as a book with a publisher.

Rowell: You and many other writers usually recommend to other writers that they should read if they want to become writers. You've already done so in this interview. I find myself telling developing writers the same. What do you really intend to convey to them when you tell them to read? How does the practice of reading, as you view it, contribute to a writer's development? Now, I, of course, assume you're recommending that they read the best writing.

Butler: Not at all.

Rowell: I am appalled sometimes when I meet some young poets, for example, and they tell me that they've been reading certain poets who are very bad writers. Some of these young writers have never heard of the work of people like Rita Dove, Jay Wright, or Robert Hayden, for example.

Butler: I hope they'll read a little of everything. I am alarmed by adults who say to little children, "Oh, my God, I don't want my children reading comic books,"

"I don't want my children reading the Goosebumps series," or "I want them only to read enlightened literature," which bores the crap out of kids. Understandably, it wasn't written for them. I recommend anything that gets them into reading. When they're older, when they're in high school, when they're in college, even then a little junk food for the mind won't hurt, as long as that's not all they read. I can remember a science fiction writing teacher telling me most young would-be science fiction writers read too much science fiction. I didn't really understand what he meant at the time. I thought if you were going to write science fiction, you should read it, which is, of course, true. But if it's all you read, then you just wind up reproducing what someone else has done.

I have to be careful what I say to younger people, because every now and then someone will come up to me and say—"Oh, this touches on reading, but is not just reading." "What should I major in at college to become a writer?" I have to stop myself from saying that it's not so much what you major in at college or even that you go to college. It's that you read. I'm more likely to say, "What you should major in is something like history. Maybe you should take a good look at psychology and anthropology and sociology. Learn about people. Learn about different people. When I say history, I don't mean to tell you just to study the kings and queens and generals and wars. Learn how people live and learn the kinds of things that motivate people. Learn the kinds of things that we unfortunate human beings do over and over again. We don't really learn from history, because from one generation to the next we do tend to reproduce our errors. There are cycles in history. Even look into things like evolutionary biology; that goes back further, for instance, than history, further back than cultural anthropology would go. Learn all you can about the way we work, the way we tick.

Read all kinds of fiction. In school you're going to be assigned to read classics, and that's good, that's useful. A lot of it is good writing and will help you with your writing. But a lot of it is archaic good writing that won't necessarily help you with what you are doing now. So read the current best sellers; read something that is maybe going to spark a new interest in you.

I used to, and I still do this every now and then when I am between projects. I'll go to the library and do what I call "grazing," which means that I'll wander through some department in some place that I can't ever recall having been before and just browse the titles until something catches my attention. Then I'll build into something that I know nothing about. Sometimes it's something that interests me a lot. Sometimes it's something that after a few pages bores me. I was just at the library about a week ago, and I had this big load of books and tapes, audio tapes. And I said to the library clerk who checked out my books, "I'm starting a new project, and I really don't know what I'm doing, so naturally I have to get a lot of books." If you know what you're after, a few books will do it. But if you have no idea, you've got get this big mountain of books.

I love audio tapes. I'm a bit dyslexic and I read very slowly. I've taken speed reading classes, but they don't really help. I have to read slowly enough to hear what I'm reading with my mind's ear. I find it delightful. I learn much, much more and better if I hear tapes. I can recall when I was a very little girl being read to by my mother. Even though she was doing the domestic work that I talked about, she would, during my very early years, read to me at night. And I loved it. It was, again, theater for the mind. As a matter of fact, I think anybody who has children couldn't go wrong by reading to those children at night just as the kids are falling asleep. I love the tapes now, possibly going back to that memory but also because I happen to learn things better by hearing them than I do by reading. I had book tapes and I had books, and I brought them home and started "grazing."

Rowell: What are the books that are still important to you today that you've been reading? I mean, Octavia Butler, the writer. And what are some books that you return to, probably return to ever so often, not just merely for enjoyment, but for form or language or character development? Are there such books that you go back to from time to time?

Butler: There is a book that was recommended to me when I was a student; it's called *The Art of Dramatic Writing* by Lajos Egri. This is a book that I go back to when I get into writing trouble, and it helps sometimes. It's old. If you haven't read Ibsen, it might mystify you a bit. The way Egri teaches in this book has been very effective for me. I often recommend it to students. He's very clear in what he's saying. Sometimes writers writing books about writing aren't. They assume that you know perhaps more than you do, but Egri doesn't. He just tells you without being condescending; it's very basic, but it's also complex and very clear somehow. He's done a very good job in that book. As for novels that I like, they're not classics for the most part. They're novels that took me someplace that I'd never been. For instance, one of my favorite books—and I emphasize the word book here because I'm not talking about the movie—is *The Godfather*, because that book took me to another world—not necessarily a real world, but it did make good guys of some rather unpleasant people. It did take me to another world. Oh, yes, a book like *Shogun. Dune* is one of my favorite science fiction novels. There are just any number of favorite science fiction novels. Those are a few. I don't know what kind of list you are looking for here, but those are a few.

I love specialized dictionaries and encyclopedias—these are usually one or two volume encyclopedias. For instance *The Oxford Companion to Medicine* is sitting here right next to my knee. It's something that I have to be careful with, because it has British spellings and some things that surprise me still. I have dozens and dozens of specialized dictionaries covering everything from geography to anthropology to psychiatry to religion. I've got a two-volume set about religion in America and about ancient Egypt. You name it, and I've probably got a specialized dictionary that touches on it. I use them for more than just looking up things. If that's all they were for, I would suppose that a regular encyclopedia would do it. To whet my appetite when I am shopping for ideas, to just find things—that's another reason I use them; it's another form of grazing. I find things that I perhaps wouldn't have thought of before and maybe wouldn't want to read a long article on. Just going through and finding something in, for instance, the American Medical Association's *Encyclopedia of Medicine* would be useful, or discovering some animal or something in my dictionary of land animals really has managed to surprise me. Or finding something in my encyclopedia on invertebrates. That one is really good for science fiction, because some of the invertebrates seem so other-worldly. It has all sorts of things. As I said, you name the subject, and I'll probably go to a specialized dictionary or encyclopedia that touches on it.

Rowell: What do you mean when you say "shopping for ideas"? I like that.
Butler: When I'm "shopping for ideas," I'm just looking for something that catches my attention and that evokes or provokes an emotional response from me. For example, I have a book about animals without backbones. I also have a particular aversion to some invertebrates, really a phobia. I ran across one, a picture of one that made me drop the book. The thing is something like maybe an inch long and utterly harmless and doesn't even exist in my part of the country, I'm happy to say. It is a revolting little creature, and I'm really glad it's not bigger. I wound up using part of its appearance to create the alien characters in my Xenogenesis books, *Adulthood Rite* (1988) and *Imago* (1989). Every now and then there's something that's made a big impression. Some things make small impressions. I was wandering through a book about guns awhile back and hadn't thought about using the information I was finding at all until I wrote a book called *Clay's Ark* (1984). Then I realized I had to go back and find that book and use some of that information about guns. Again, I had to use it in *Parable of the Sower* (1993). Reading fills the well. Reading fills the well of your imagination. You can return to the well and draw the water that you've put in there. You can also think of it as a bank. You can go back and take out that intellectual money that

you've put away. If you don't read and your bank account goes down to nothing, you can't really go to it to take anything out. So your writing is going to be pretty impoverished. It's going to be totally confined to things that you somehow have learned without reading, which means that you might be a one-book writer, if you're a writer at all.

Rowell: Your formal education is for me a study in itself. That is, you graduated from Pasadena City College, a two-year college, and you attended but did not graduate from California State. But you later took creative writing classes at UCLA at different periods.

Butler: I took writing courses wherever I could find them. If somebody said "writing course" and "free" in the same sentence, I was probably there. Later when I was earning a little bit more money at the horrible little jobs I mentioned, I was able to go and take classes at UCLA. As a matter of fact, I sold my first novel while I was taking the class from Theodore Sturgeon at UCLA. It was the novel I had sent away before I got into the class, of course, but I got the very, very conditional acceptance while I was taking his course. I remember it, because I took the acceptance letter to Sturgeon. Sturgeon, by the way, is a very well-known science fiction writer. He's dead now, but he was a very well-known writer. I liked his work because he was such a good craftsman. Sometimes science fiction writers were more pulp writers than they had to be because they didn't bother to learn. I'm talking about the old-time science fiction writers now, the ones who were more concerned with the wonderful machine than with the people who were supposed to be having something to do with the machine. They didn't characterize very well. Their women characters in particular were stick people, puppets, and Sturgeon, even though he was easily old enough to be my father, didn't write that way, and a few others didn't write that way. I especially paid attention to their writings. And when I had this chance to take a class from Sturgeon, I grabbed it.

This was an interesting sort of class. It taught me something about writers. By the way, I don't believe that Sturgeon ever graduated from high school. He made a comment when he was teaching the class, an extension course: he said probably America is the only country where a man who never graduated from high school can teach at college. He might have had a point. I don't think that writing is something you have to go to a university to learn, although education of any kind helps. *Writing is something that you're going to teach yourself, no matter how many classes you go to.* The classes, as I said, are audiences, and they help you to correct the obvious problems.

One of my problems, when I took my first college writing class, was that I punctuated by instinct. I had no strong idea of punctuation, and my spelling was horrible. I don't think I had ever heard the word dyslexic. I had done something about my vocabulary—this goes back to when I was twelve. I may have been younger than twelve, but back when Kennedy was running against Nixon. My family was all for Kennedy, and nobody liked Nixon. We were Californians, and we'd seen a bit too much of him. I wanted to find out more about Kennedy, because everybody seemed to like him so much. And I would tune in on television and get the news and hear Kennedy talking. I couldn't understand half of what he was saying. At twelve years old, you know, and it never occurred to me that some of this might have been deliberate. I didn't know about politicians in those days, but not understanding him devastated me really. I felt so depressed, because I realized that I was even more ignorant than I thought. I wanted to learn more words; I wanted to understand better what people were saying, especially people that I thought of as being important, you know, people who went on television and said things. That pushed me to read things that were perhaps a little bit more difficult than what I had been reading. It also pushed me into nonfiction. It made me pay more attention to English teachers who recommended things that I might not otherwise have paid any attention to. I had learned early on that often I couldn't finish a book if it was assigned for me to read. I read too slowly, so I learned to scan, but scan is the wrong word. I learned to kind of read in summary. You know, the beginning, the end, and a little bit of the middle, and I could usually fake it pretty well. My grades weren't that bad, but I started paying closer attention. I started to try to write in what I thought of as more sophisticated English, which meant my writing became stilted and strange and just exactly what you would expect from a kid who was trying to pretend to be older than she was. I don't know whether I mentioned it, but I started sending things out, submitting things for publication when I was thirteen. So this meant that some editors were getting the most awful garbage from me, but the writing helped me to go on learning more about the way English is used.

I was working while I was going to Pasadena City College, so I took three years to get through two years of college. And the last year and the last semester was in 1968, which was very strange, because we had assassinations for midterm and finals. Very, very bad. Martin Luther King and Robert F. Kennedy. PCC had its first black lit class in 1968—its very first—and it was a night class, which was a good thing, because I was working full time then. A professor, a marvelous black woman, came over from California State at Los Angeles. I'm sorry to say that I can't remember her name at this moment; it's been awhile now since that course. But I really liked her, because she challenged us. I couldn't get through all the books, although I think I did a pretty decent job faking it. I always loved essay tests, because they allowed me to show off, and she gave all essay tests. You know, you can show off pretty well if you've read part of the book. She introduced me to writers I'd never heard of and to a literature I knew almost nothing about and to words I'd never heard before. She would deliberately use them. If we looked mystified, she would define them in context, and I could see her doing it, but I wasn't offended by it. She was that good. And I'd never had a teacher like her before. If I am ever going to say that a teacher was inspiring, she definitely was. I had a few others who were, but she was one of the last. That's why I remember her. I wish I could think of her name. That's odd because I can recall the names of all of my elementary school teachers, most of my junior high teachers, but after that they kind of blur.

Rowell: Let's imagine that today you were commissioned to write a book on what one calls "the writing life." What would be the first thing you'd say about it? You know, a lot of people have called it solitary.

Butler: Well, I've already talked a lot of the reading and the writing on an everyday schedule. I've also talked about keeping a journal and taking classes. One of the most important things you must do to be a writer is that you have to find your own way. I mentioned earlier using models from published writing—that is, copying down half a dozen beginnings or transitions or endings or character descriptions or whatever. You might also look at the lives of a half dozen writers to see what they do. That doesn't mean that you'll do what any of them do, but what you'll learn from what they do is that they have felt their ways. They have found out what works for them. For instance, I get up between three or four o'clock in the morning, because that's my best writing time. I found this out by accident, because back when I used to work for other people I didn't have time to write during the day. I did physical work, mostly hard physical work, so I was too tired when I came in at night. I was also too full of other people. I found that I couldn't work very well after spending a lot of time with other people. I had to have some sleep between the time that I spent with other people and the time that I did the writing, so I would get up early in the morning. I generally would get up around two o'clock in the morning, which was really very much too early. But I was ambitious, and I would write until I had to get ready to go to work. Then I would go off to work, and I'd be sleepy and grumpy all day. It's a good thing that my mother was a nice Baptist lady who taught me not to cuss. I learned to cuss later, but I also learned that I could put a sock in it when I had to, because I generally felt so bad while I was working that I would have been happy to cuss most people out when they said anything to me. Fortunately, I had enough control not to do that. I learned that I really liked the early morning hours before it got to be light, when I'd had some sleep and it was still dark out. That's one of the reasons I like the long nights of winter best. I think the other reason I like winter best is I live in southern California, where winter means occasional rains. I love writing while it's raining.

Rowell: Will you allow me to enter the privacy of your writing space and stand over your shoulder while you're working and observe the process while you work? Let's say now you're creating "Bloodchild" or "The Evening and the Morning and the Night," short narratives.

Butler: Well, it's sort of hard to do that. It's hard because I'm not watching myself write. I realize that most of the time people would think that I wasn't working at all, because maybe I'm just sitting here. Maybe I've got some music on the radio—not so much the radio, but a tape or a CD in the stereo. For instance, when I was working on *Parable of the Sower*, I had a lot of ecological audio tapes. I can't watch television while I'm actually doing the original work. I can watch television if I have to rewrite something, but I can't watch television while doing original work, because I do tend to watch it. But I can have anything on the tape recorder or whatever, and I had tapes of Nova and other programs that I had taped—books as well—about ecological problems, because those play a big part in *Parable of the Sower*. The ecology, especially global warming, is almost a character in *Parable of the Sower*. So I had a lot of those tapes on, and you can imagine my having them on over and over again. I don't think anyone else could stand it. I've heard other writers say this, too. I don't have a family living here with me, so I'm not annoying other people. But I've heard other writers say they had to write with headphones, because they played the same piece of music or the same whatever over and over again.

This goes back to what kind of habits writers should establish. Whatever works for you, as long as it isn't physically detrimental. I mean, I don't really recommend that you go and have a drink. I don't think your writing is going to be improved by it. And, for the sake of your health, don't sit there with a cigarette; it's probably not going to help you either. Do anything that helps you. For instance, some people, like me, need to be in a certain location, at a certain time of day. Maybe they have clothes that they like to write in. I have a friend who writes in the nude. He just shuts the door and goes to it. Whatever works for you. I remember a kind of paraphrase, a quote from Maya Angelou; I don't recall the exact words, but paraphrased it kind of goes like this: if you have to hang by your feet and smear honey on your legs to get yourself writing, then do it. You know whatever works.

That goes back to how do you get into the writing life. Well, you get into the writing life by finding out what works for you and then doing it. The best way to find out is by seeing what other people do and usually rejecting it. By the way, one of ways I get ideas is to look through books of quotations. I'm bound to find in the book of quotations—the longer the better—something with which I violently disagree. Once I've done that, then I have to think about what I really think, what I really believe, and why and how to support it. It's no good to just say, "Oh, that guy's an idiot." I mean it's a matter of having actually to think about things. One of the nice things writing does for you is to make you think about things, think of other people's lives, think about what other people might believe, for instance, other people's religions, which fascinate me. Anything that isn't what you're familiar with.

One of the problems I had at school was that I was already into looking at things from a lot of points of view. This is junior high school, especially when people are incredibly rigid, because they've gone to the trouble of learning something and it's got to be the one and only true way. You remember how that goes in junior high. Even in high school you could get laughed at by possessing a different opinion or doing something that the group didn't know about and therefore didn't approve of. For me though it was always fascinating to find out what else there was—what's out there that I don't know about, what's out there that I've never even thought of. If something out there grabbed my attention to read more about, I'd go to the library and find out something else.

Rowell: In your interview with Randall Kenan, you said that "the wall next to my desk is covered with signs and maps." Why are they there? I hope that question is not too personal.

Butler: That's not particularly personal. At the moment they're not there because I'm beginning something. But by the time I'm half way through this project, the wall will be covered again. I like maps. When I was writing *Parable of the Sower*, I had maps of the areas that my characters were traveling through. I went to the map store and spent a lot of money buying detailed copies of maps of different parts of California, going up to and over the Oregon border because I wasn't quite sure where my characters were going to stop. But once I realized they were going to stop in Humbolt County, which is one county south of Oregon, I got a nice big detailed map of Humbolt County, and hung it on the wall so that I would understand where they were and what kind of terrain they were in. Aside from the map, I also had vocabulary lists filled with words that I habitually mis-spell or words that are specific to this story that I've never used otherwise. They were reminders of what story this particular book is telling, what story this par-ticular chapter is telling. I also had character lists. I guess you could call them cast lists. In *Parable of the Sower* I had a number of families, a fairly sizable com-munity in the first part of the book, and in order to keep people straight I had to make lists of the families—for instance, who was in what family. Actually I never even used most of those people. They got mentioned occasionally—some of them did—but most of them never showed up on-stage except as part of a crowd. But it was necessary that I knew who they were and where they lived and how they re-lated to my character—what she thought of the family. This family was crazy and this family was really super-dependable. You know the kind everybody went to if they had a problem. This family was a little odd because the old lady snooped. This family was weird because there was this guy who was really kind of a snitch. If he could find something bad about you and spread it around, he'd love to do that; and when my character's parents had problems with the police, he was the one who went to them and threw suspicion in their direction, in secret of course. There were all these people who were doing all these things, and I had to know about them even if they never personally stepped on-stage. So that was up there as part of the wallpaper, you might say, and almost anything that was giving me trouble was up there. The reminder. I was not only writing in the first person but in journal form, which made it very difficult to foreshadow anything. If my character couldn't know what was coming, then I had to arrange for her not to know—but still to be the intelligent woman I was writing her as. Had she been a fool, it would have been easier. But she was not a fool. So I had to let people see what was coming without necessarily having her see it as clearly as the readers did. And she did see, to some degree, what was coming; but, when it came, it was worse then she could have foreseen. So I had notes with regard to foreshadowing future trouble, and I also had notes about religion, because she sort of forms her own religion. I had to do research; I looked into a number of different religions. I put what I discovered up there on the wall, if it at all related to the book. Some-times it got so awful that I had to take things down because there were notes on top of notes and notes hanging from notes. It looked like a hodgepodge; it was. My office usually looks like a tornado blew through. No other room in the house looks like that, but my office seems inevitably to be a total wreck.

Rowell: What were you trying to do in the Patternmaster saga?
Butler: I was trying to tell a good story about a strange community of people. I

find myself doing that over and over again. That's not all I was trying to do. In each book, I was trying to do something a little different. But overall to gather these people and start this community that didn't work very well, if you noticed. There are people who think that they've won, so everything's fine. But they were really not very nice, the Patternists. When you get to *Patternmaster*, you'll see that. Really they were pretty awful. You wouldn't want to live in that society. And why were they so awful? Well, they were so awful because they had, shall we say, a bad teacher. And it didn't really occur to me until I had been working on the series for awhile that I might have been making some comment on Black America. Once the thought came to me, I realized that I probably was commenting on Black America. Then I had to ask myself how I felt about that—that I was perhaps making a comment on learning the wrong thing from one's teachers. I realized that maybe it was something that I needed to think about and maybe it was something that I needed to say, so I certainly wasn't going to stop saying it or deny having said it.

Rowell: You, Samuel Delany, Steve Barnes, and Charles Sanders (he lives in Canada) are our only science fiction writers. That makes you different from other African-American writers.

Butler: Well, there seem to be more coming around now. But they're mainly fantasy and horror writers. There is Jewelle Gomez who wrote *The Gilda Stories*, a story about a black lesbian vampire. Winston A. Howlett and Juanita Nesbitt—both black—have also written novels: *Allegiance* and *The Long Hunt*. They write together. Howlett has also written with a white writer named Jean Lorrah. Tananarive Due has two novels, *The Between* and *My Soul to Keep*. HarperCollins is her publisher. Her second book is not out yet, but will be soon. There are other black science fiction writers out there. Unfortunately, they have not achieved prominence, but they're out there writing.

Rowell: Will you talk about what it was like for you in the early days, as opposed to present times—you a black woman writing science fiction?

Butler: When I first started with my writing, I guess people didn't think I looked like a writer. I don't look like what people think a writer is. I have difficulty just conveying the idea that I write for a living—conveying it in person I mean. Somebody would ask, "What do you do?" And I would answer, "I'm a writer." I learned to say I write for a living, although even that didn't penetrate sometimes, and usually their comment would be, "Oh how nice. Maybe someday you'll sell something." That was bad enough, but there were also those people who, when I said I'm a writer, went on to talk about other things. Later they said, "Well, what do you do for a living?" In one case, at a party, I actually said to a woman, 'Well, what did you think I meant when I said I was a writer?" She said, "I thought you were talking about your hobby." I can understand what she meant, because here in Los Angeles everybody is a writer. Everybody is going to write that wonderful book someday, or they've got that wonderful book in their bottom drawer, but the publishers are so small-minded and can't see how wonderful it is. Someday they're going to self-publish it. Actually one of the Los Angeles TV stations several years ago did a person-on-the-street interview, in which a journalist would walk up to people walking on the street, and ask, "How's your screenplay?" Nine out of ten people talked about the screenplay they either had written or were writing. In this area there are so many people who call themselves writers, and either don't write at all or who write to the bottom drawer or who are crazy. There are so many odd things going on that it is not easy to get through to people that you are a writer. After so many times of telling people that I write for a living and after hearing them tell me, maybe someday you'll sell something, I started to say, "Wait a moment. I just told you I write for a living. I did not tell you that I'm independently wealthy. I told you I write for a living." At that point, from the tone of my voice, they figured that they better change the subject.

As far as being a black science fiction writer here, my early isolation helped me. On one level, I was aware that there was only one other black science fiction writer that I knew of—and that was [Samuel] "Chip" Delany. I was aware of him because he was one of my teachers at Clarion. Before that I'd seen his work, but I didn't know he was black. Harlan Ellison was one of my teachers with the Screen Writers Guild of America, West's free classes. As I said earlier, when anyone said free and writing classes in the same sentence, I was there. So that's how I ended up in these classes learning screen writing which I don't like at all. Harlan mentioned the Clarion science fiction writers workshop and asked me if I was interested. I think the first question I asked him after what Clarion was, was this: Are there going to be any other black people there? You see, it was going to be held in a little tiny town in the hills of Pennsylvania. He said, Chip will be there. That was the first time I knew Samuel R. Delany was black. He was the only black science fiction writer I knew about.

I remember my first science fiction convention. I went to that while I was at Clarion. A group of us was going to go down to Pittsburgh to a science fiction convention that was run annually there. It was called Phlange. I didn't know what it was about, but other students gave me the idea that it was fun, so I went along. One girl had a van, and we all piled in, fourteen or fifteen people in one van. That was in 1970. We went down to Phlange, and I was totally out of my element. I didn't have a clue as to what was going on. I wandered about and saw one black guy in the whole place. I walked up to him, and said, "Are you a writer?" He said, "No. Are you a writer?" I had no confidence, so I said, "No." I wasn't a published writer. We wandered off in different directions to find more important people to talk to. It wasn't a matter of anyone coming and saying you can't come in here, it's all white. It was just a matter of my not really knowing socially how to get in. I would just show up at these things, and, since nobody would throw me out, eventually I learned my way around a little bit. I never was very social; that's sort of a carryover from my childhood. Some science fiction writers are extremely social. Harlan certainly is. And then there are some of us that are practically reclusive. We barely get out of the house, and that's me more than it should be, I suppose.

Being found by other black writers was interesting, too. I was not known as a black writer, not because I was being ignored but because I have never liked the picture that was taken of me. I suppose I really look like that, and there's nothing I can do about that. I guess always I hope I'll look better or something. I've never allowed a picture on the back of any of my books. Black writers did not know I was black, but a couple of experiences helped that. I was asked by the *Washington Post* to review two books: one was Claudia Tate's *Black Women Writers at Work*, a book of interviews, and the other one was *Confirmation*, a huge anthology of black women writers edited by Amina and Amiri Baraka. After I went through the two books, I wondered why I was not in them. Then I thought, "I'm not in here because nobody knows about me." I had been in *Essence*, but apparently it hadn't reached anybody. One of the editors at Doubleday—her name is Veronica Mixon—did an article on me for *Essence* Magazine, but it didn't attract any particular attention. At any rate, I reviewed those two books. Then I went to a gathering of black writers here. I also attended a gathering of black women of the Diaspora writers at Michigan State University. I think that's when people began to realize, "Oh, she's black." There I was surrounded by other people who had maybe read my stuff, because I write with black characters. Suddenly these people discovered that I am black. So I guess that's when I began to be known. The little bit I did *Essence* Magazine helped. Another writer, Shelley Anne Williams, did an article about me in *Ms.* Magazine—back when *Ms.* was more commercial. I guess the more exposure I got, the more people realized, "Oh, yeah, she's black." I began hearing from people who were interested in me because I am a black writer as well as people who were interested in me because I write science fiction or because I am female.

I always try to convince my publishers that I have these three specific audiences for all my work—and occasionally another audience. For instance, I tried to push the idea that a New Age audience would be interested in *Parable of the Sower*, but I was never able to get it over with the publishers. They tend to think that you're going to appeal to one audience, and for most of my career it's been the science fiction audience. I was kind of confined there. I got another letter from another writer who asked whether she should worry about being put into this kind of category, the horror category or the science fiction category or whatever. I said, as long as your publisher doesn't put you there, it's fine. If your publisher won't advertise you to anybody but to one very small community, then you're in trouble. I know because I've been in that kind of trouble. I was in it for a long time. Some of them wouldn't advertise me at all. And none of them would send me out on tour until I got to this very small publishing company that was originally called Four Walls, Eight Windows. My editor, Dan Simon, did see that it might be possible to send me out on tour, and he did do that. No one else had. Dan's new publishing company is Seven Stories Press. Before that I had only gone out speaking when I was invited. Someone else paid for the travel because I wasn't making much money.

Rowell: What was the response of your white readers who did not know that you are black?

Butler: By the time I went out on the tour that Dan sent me on, I was pretty much known, because my face had shown up quite a few places. There was a book called *Faces of Science Fiction*, and I was in that. I was also in some of the science fiction reference books—like encyclopedias or guides. I had attended conventions. So I don't think I shocked anybody in particular, except for some British people who came over here and asked if I would come and be interviewed for their television program. The man told me afterward that he hadn't heard that I was black, but he didn't seem to have a problem with it. He just didn't know. By the time I went out on tour, I was pretty much known.

"Radio Imagination": Octavia Butler on the Poetics of Narrative Embodiment

Marilyn Mehaffy and AnaLouise Keating/1997

"'Radio Imagination': Octavia Butler on the Poetics of Narrative Embodiment" was first published in *MELUS: The Journal of the Society for the Study of the Multi-Ethnic Literature of the United States* 26.1 (Spring 2001) and is reprinted here with the permission of *MELUS*.

African American science-fiction author Octavia Butler's work is thematically preoccupied with the potentiality of genetically altered bodies—hybrid multi-species and multi-ethnic subjectivities—for revising contemporary nationalist, racist, sexist, and homophobic attitudes. Yet a curiously polarized dualism has dominated the critical response to this thematics: while Donna Haraway and Amanda Boulter praise Butler's novels for the way that they consistently "interrogate reproductive, linguistic, and nuclear politics in a mythic field structured by late twentieth-century race and gender," Charles Johnson dismissively cites Butler's fiction's tendency to "plunge so deeply into fantasy that revelation of everyday life . . . disappears" (Haraway 179, emphasis added; Johnson 115–16). Is Butler's science fiction radically revisionary, as Haraway and Boulter propose, interacting with the anatomical idioms of, specifically, everyday contemporary representation? Or, as Johnson proposes, do its frequent otherworldly themes and characters, and subsequent classification as fantasy, render Butler's work socially disjunctive or, as even a more positive critique like Eric White's depicts it, race-blind science fiction?

Our interview with Octavia Butler centers on several sets of questions having to do with the narrative embodiments inhabiting Butler's fiction: with the efficacy of science fiction as an ideology-bending genre; and with the possible connections between Butler's texts' unorthodox embodiments and her relative marginalization from the canons of United States literature, both African American and "mainstream." Butler's relative marginalization within canonical contexts resonates as well in her work's peculiar position within the genre of science fiction. Recently, she has been the multiple winner of science fiction's highest awards, the Hugo and the Nebula; in 1995 she was awarded the MacArthur Foundation Award, popularly called the "young genius" award. However, Butler's work has never, as she related in our interview, "fit in" with conventional expectations for either canonical or science fiction literature. For many years, science fiction was written by, primarily, "white" men for "white" male adolescents. With very few exceptions, women of any color did not write science fiction, female characters were generally portrayed as sex objects, and men of color rarely wrote or appeared in science fiction novels or stories. Thus, Butler's entry into this genre represents an unusual and significant breakthrough. Her novels introduce strong female protagonists, usually African American, and characters of many colors.

In this way her work complicates traditional science fiction themes—global and local power struggles, for example—by inflecting such struggles with the implications of gender, ethnic, and class difference. As Butler explains in another interview: "It is a writer's duty to write about human differences, all human differences, and help make them acceptable. I think science fiction writers can do this if they want to. In my opinion, they are a lot more likely to have a social conscience than many other kinds of writers" (Harrison 33).

Further, in a 1995 autobiographical essay, Butler addresses the challenges directed to science fiction's efficacy, as a genre, for representing struggles specific to African American history. She responds to the question, most often asked by African American readers, "What good is science fiction to Black people?" by answering:

> What good is any form of literature to Black people? What good is science fiction's thinking about the present, the future, and the past? What good is its tendency to warn or to consider alternative ways of thinking and doing? What good is its examination of the possible effects of science and technology, or social organization and political direction? At its best, science fiction stimulates imagination and creativity. It gets reader and writer off the beaten track, off the narrow, narrow footpath of what "everyone" is saying, doing, thinking—whoever "everyone" happens to be this year. And what good is all this to Black people? ("Positive Obsession" 134–35)

Like the opening critical commentary we cited from Donna Haraway, Charles Johnson, and Amanda Boulter, our questions in this interview engage the unorthodox, always embodied, thematics of Butler's work, and its potential for social intervention. But we are also interested in the formal promise of Butler's science fiction to revise, as well, what Robert Stepto identifies as "American acts of reading." For instance, if, thematically, Butler's work frequently envisions the "horror and beauty" of an alternately embodied global populace, how might these refigured, hybrid categories of subjectivity structurally undermine readerly recognition, and therefore readerly mastery, of stereotypic, discretely raced, gendered, and sexualized subjectivities? That is, in its unorthodox formal aesthetics, how much political power and efficacy might Butler's science fiction, or any radical author's fiction, promise as a revisionary social project?

Toni Morrison, for instance, cites the authorial uses of hierarchized black and white bodies, the "demonizing and reifying [of] the range of [skin] color on a palette," as the founding metaphor and formal convention defining canonical United States literary narrative, (white) nationalist identity, and colonialist habits of reading (7). With respect to subjective categories of gender, Luce Irigaray similarly questions the formal uses of female bodies for structuring modern representation: "without the exploitation of the body-matter of women, what would become of the symbolic process," including literary narrative, "that governs society?" (85). Furthermore, most postmodern critical thought, in many ways exemplified in Morrison's and Irigaray's work, calculates "the body" as a metaphor and formal narrative convention. Within this context, what is the ideological impact of Butler's apparent return, thematically, to the nineteenth-century genetics of flesh—sociobiology, eugenics—which prompts contemporary biological "truths" of discrete, identifiable categories of race, gender, nationality, and sexuality?

Our interview with Octavia Butler centers on these questions and others having to do with the poetics and politics of narrative embodiment: Butler's formal links between hierarchies of subjective corporeality and global environmental destruction; the efficacy of textually restructuring popular representations as a mode for achieving more equitable personal and collective social relations; the crucial influence of a writer's body on the shape of her work; science fiction's longtime preoccupation with alternate corporealities, and the genre's marginalization as a credible component of United States literature; and, finally, Butler's perception of her critical location within the canon of African American women's writing and within modern United States literature as a whole.

We chose "Radio Imagination," Octavia Butler's self-described term for her artistic aesthetics, as the introductory phrase for our title because, for us, the term recapitulates Butler's unorthodox formal aesthetics. A "radio imagination" invokes and, for readers, invites a corporeal visualization of characters, yet short-circuits the foundational optical mastery of those characters that Toni Morrison and Robert Stepto associate with modern habits of reading. As in radio narration, the socially built body of the speaker, or, in Butler's fiction, of the character's body, is initially displaced and delayed, rendered off-screen or off-stage, invisible, at least with respect to ethnicity and sexuality, if not always to gender or nationality. The "punch" of such an aesthetics, according to Butler's comments in the interview, allows readers to "see" and to "hear" characters' situational relations and "problems" before classifying those relations within familiar idioms of race, gender, or sexuality.

Yet, paradoxically, "radio narration" thereby subsequently intensifies, for readers, the irreducible significance of corporeal identity to those "problems" and relations, but without the initial optical instruction, and therefore without the accompanying stereotypic associations, of legibly inscribed bodies. Despite formally demoting corporeal appearance as a defining legible idiom, however, Butler explains that the body is "all we really know that we have"—"all we really know that we have is the flesh." Complementarily, the narrative embodiments of her fiction advocate a therapeutic reclamation of that flesh as a primary site and signifier of knowledge and communication, both personal and collective, both material and narrated. Acknowledging the exploitative narrative uses of what she calls "body knowledge," Butler claims here, does not necessarily entail renouncing the flesh, but, rather, re-imagining and reassembling it within an ethics of survival.

MM: As you know, the critical focus of our interview project is the use of bodies as a formal narrative convention in American literary texts, that is, how bodies— usually human [laughter]—are inscribed and constructed to serve narrative purposes. For instance, how do or do literary bodies mirror stereotypes and biases from other popular culture texts like advertising, or television and film, or political discourse? We're interested in how particular texts race bodies in certain ways; and how specific sets of value and aesthetics become attached to particular categories of ethnicity as a result. And, as well, how do literary constructions, in turn, interact with or impact popular perceptions? We're studying writers who devise different approaches to familiar categories of subjective identity—gender and ethnic identity and sexual identity; and how those re-imagined bodies might affect readers and, therefore, popular perceptions about subjective categories like race and gender and sexuality. Here's where you come in because your books, it seems to us, are all about recreating bodies in different ways.
OB: Well, this sounds interesting. But what you seem most interested in is appearance. I began writing back when I was twelve, and I'd already been reading science fiction. Later, when I realized that people actually publish this stuff, I realized that I had been writing about people for years and I'd never seen any of them. I have the kind of imagination that hears. I think of it as radio

imagination. I like radio a lot better than I do television; and, really, I have to go back and try to imagine what characters might look like because when I began writing at age twelve, I couldn't. What I had to do was go back and sort of paint the characters in. What would I like them to look like? I had a character in *Patternmaster*, a very early character. This is somebody that I ran across when I was twelve even though he had a different name. He had lived in my head for over a year when I finally thought, "I gotta know what he looks like." But everything I imagined, or tried to sketch in, was a disappointment because somehow without this kind of—not bodilessness, because, actually, it was very sexy—he was not what I imagined.

MM: And your books are very sexy, by the way! I always think that—that they're a real turn-on—but I never hear anybody talking about their sexiness.
OB: I hope so because one of the signs—I put signs on my walls as a reminder while I'm writing—is "sexiness," not only sexiness in the sense of people having sex, but sexiness in the sense of wanting to reach readers where they live and wanting to invite them to enjoy themselves.

MM: Maybe this is a good time to ask you my vision question since it's related to your talking about how you don't see characters first. A physical function of the Oankali and the Oankali-human constructs that intrigues me is their ability to see without eyes, by means of sensory tentacles or patches rather than human optics. Are you commenting on the prevalence in modern times of optical vision as the privileged mode of seeing and knowing others and their bodies?
OB: You're probably putting more into it than I actually did, but this is something that is left over from my days of being down in the basement in the corner with J. B. Rhine and company. There were books about strange people, books about people who had unusual abilities or deficiencies. Every now and then there would be something about someone who had photosensitive tissue in some strange place. If they couldn't actually read with it, they could at least detect light and dark, or vague images, that kind of thing. I thought, "This would be good," because I wanted these characters to look alien. I go from not paying any attention to how my characters should look to recognizing that it's very important how they look, especially if they're not supposed to be human. I need to help my reader visualize them even though what my reader sees won't be what I had in mind. My characters have their photosensitive tissue elsewhere, and they have a type of vision that's at least as efficient as the human eye. It's just not where you would expect it to be.

ALK: Since we're talking about characters' bodies and how you see them, I think this question goes to that issue. One of the things I'm fascinated to find in your work is the way that you mark bodies by their colors rather than by characters' ethnicity. And you only mention color when it's contextually important to the story. For instance, in *Kindred* readers don't realize that Dana is "black" until page 24, and that Kevin is "white" until page 54. This is something that completely astonishes my students.

OB: That's writing. If you have the character look in the mirror, and you say, "Notice her soft brown skin and her doe-brown eyes," that's too obvious.

ALK: I think you're underselling yourself. "Race" is one of the areas I study, and, over and over, I see other writers mark ethnicity in extremely obvious ways. Generally, they state characters' ethnicity in the opening pages, and you don't do that. Was the delayed description of color in *Kindred* deliberate?

OB: Yes, that delay was deliberate because of the kind of book I was writing. If I had given the characters' race away earlier, that aspect would have had less impact and possibly the reader wouldn't react, but, instead, maybe discard that information and then start wondering what the problems were later on. But what if I hit the reader with it in a very dramatic way? In that case, ethnicity, based in history, based in antebellum slavery, as a component of Kevin's and Dana's relationship, would have a lot more power and a lot more saying power.

ALK: Even in *Survivor*, it's not until Alana thinks back to her parents and provides readers with a visual description that we learn her mother was black and her father Asian. It just kind of comes through as a description, and not until page 27. You do the same thing in *Dawn* and the same thing in *Parable of the Sower*—when ethnicity fits the context, we learn about it within that particular context. You don't appear to use ethnicity to influence or predetermine readers' perceptions of a character.

OB: Which is also something in my life. I had a friend when I was in junior high and high school who was of mixed background, and I never knew that until somebody else mentioned it. It turns out her parents lived next door to one of my relatives, and one day I learned that her mother is Japanese and her father is black. Afterward I thought about it, and I thought, "Well, gee, I've been thinking all this time that she was Latina." It didn't change anything about the way I thought about her except that I was intensely curious about her life. How is her life different because she's from this unusual situation?—unusual at the time. But in my life a lot of times there have been situations where either I didn't know or I found out late or something like that, and it's been a lot more interesting. I don't know what it would have been like if I had known immediately. Probably I would have just put it away and forgotten about it, but, again, the punch.

ALK: When you were talking earlier about the "bodiless" character in *Pattern-master*, were you referring to Teray? I don't think you ever really do identify him physically.
OB: Well, He was my first boyfriend [laughter]; and he had this wonderful bodiless body, where he could be marvelously sexy and good looking without my actually ever defining what that meant. So I guess I carried that forward into the fiction. It had not occurred to me that I hadn't described him, but you're right. I was in such a habit of not describing him and when I tried, it didn't work at all.

ALK: His personality comes through perfectly.
OB: He's very young and he's still learning to be a man.

MM: Perhaps of all the writers we hope to interview, with the possible exception of Gloria Anzaldúa, your work most obviously imagines human bodies in ways which belie familiar ideals and expectations, not only in terms of race and ethnicity, but also with respect to gender, sexuality, and species. For instance, in the Xenogenesis Trilogy sex becomes an activity involving three genders, not two or one. For reproduction, the ooloi—the Oankali third gender—puts together or, as you call it in the Trilogy, "assembles" the offspring out of the genetic material from the two species, human and Oankali. Pleasure isn't necessarily associated with reproduction. And parenting in families changes, too: It involves five parents of two different species; and, again, the parents are of three genders and two species. Do these revised gendered and sexed bodies inhabit primarily a fantastic realm, or are you suggesting that popular narratives in categories of "family," "male-female," are actually inadequate to express sexuality and gender?
OB: Oh, I'm sure they are.

MM: Or inadequate to produce and rear offspring?
OB: Well, one person can rear offspring, and now that cloning is on the horizon, one person can also produce offspring. Most people would just love to reproduce themselves and then, of course, be immensely disappointed if they do it, because it won't be them.

MM: So, then, are these different configurations of family, sexuality, and gender simply fantastic, imaginative, and fun, or are you doing something political where you're saying that popular narratives or traditional expectations are just really not adequate to express sexuality?

OB: I was trying to stretch minds. You remember in these three books [the Xenogenesis Trilogy] there is the idea that human beings have two characteristics that don't work well together.

MM: Yes, the "human contradiction."

OB: Hierarchical behavior and intelligence. Unfortunately, the hierarchical behavior is the older behavior, which is true; you can find it in algae, for goodness sakes. So sometimes the one in charge shouldn't be. That's why I begin the story with the idea that we've one-upped ourselves to death in a nuclear war. What I intended to do when I began the novels, what I really wanted to do, was change males enough so that the hierarchical behavior would no longer be a big problem. So, yes, I did have a perception-altering idea in mind. Not that women aren't hierarchical, but we don't tend toward mass murder.

MM: It's not usually the women who start wars.

OB: Yes. We're much more likely to figuratively stab one another in the back, sadly.

MM: Which saves bodies, in a way [laughter].

OB: But I'm not sure I really managed what I set out to do. I wound up with a somewhat different hierarchical system, chemically controlled as with DNA, but, instead, pheromonal. I wanted to work with ways of having my characters function without having them function in traditional ways. But there's also the fun element. When I was a kid, I used to read science fiction stories that talked about, for example, an alien race with twenty-seven different sexes, every single one of which is absolutely essential to reproduction. But then the stories would never tell readers how sex worked, what the characters did for pleasure, exactly. So I wanted to have the interesting task of figuring out exactly how a different form of sex might work biologically.

ALK: On the "human contradiction"—which you describe as the genetic combination of intelligence and hierarchical behavior that compels humans to use their intelligence to evaluate, rank, dominate, and control others—it's a central theme in Xenogenesis. The Oankali believe this contradiction will ultimately doom humans to extinction. Is that your perspective as well?

OB: It's a real possibility now that the Cold War is over; look at how we are hunting for someone else to hate.

ALK: So, like the Oankali, you see hierarchical behavior in humans as a genetic characteristic?

OB: Yes, I do, when you consider that our hierarchical tendencies go back to algae. Anything living, if it feels threatened, will try to push the other thing out of the way. I saw this on a PBS show once, and I have looked for it again ever since. There's a particular kind of marine algae that grows on rocks on beaches. When two clones of algae grow around the same rock and eventually meet, instead of going the other way or going down into the sand or to another rock or something, one poisons the other. They actually both try to poison one another, but one is successful. So the simple hierarchical behavior goes all the way back, I suspect, to the beginning of life. And intelligence has not made us better. For instance, when I was in Peru doing research for the Xenogenesis books, we went to a number of the equivalent of national parks in Peru. Actually we wound up not being able to go to one because someone had come in during the night and cut down a lot of the trees, nice big virgin growth. Anyway, of the ones we went to, one of them had two flocks of macaws that used to fly in to be pampered by the tourists. These were very tame birds; they were wild, and lived on their own, but they would fly in every day. They would happily sit on your shoulder and take whatever food you gave them, and bite you on the ear if you didn't give them any. When there were no tourists out there feeding them, there was a roost that had been set up—a pyramid with long slats, then shorter and shorter going toward the top—and I don't know if the birds knew what they were doing, but those birds spent all their time fighting to see who would sit at the top.

MM: The birds did? That's discouraging, isn't it?

OB: No, it's entirely normal. That's what I mean. And, by the way, no bird ever got to sit there for more than three seconds.

MM: It was constantly in question, then—there wasn't really one bird that stayed up there?

OB: It meant that the fighting was continuous.

MM: So there was always that challenge of claiming the authoritative spot?

OB: Yes.

ALK: I know that intelligence can be used to devise even more hierarchical and new strategies to get to the top but, also, don't we have to hope that it can be used to figure out different ways of reacting?

OB: Sure, but the dangerous thing is that the more hierarchical we become, the less likely we are to listen to our own intelligence or anyone else's. During the

Gulf War, I remember, there was an Italian student who had come to the U.S. to go to college in California for a while. The other students were wearing American flag patches on their sleeves to show support for the war. He felt that he shouldn't do that because he wasn't an American and he was going to be going home to Italy, and finally the U.S. students harassed him to such a point that he just left. Sometimes we lose all awareness of what we should be doing, what makes sense, what's intelligent, and just let that hierarchical stuff go to our heads, which, I guess, is where it is anyway. The other thing is that my mother developed a dislike of cats because she stopped two male cats from fighting one time, and they split her lip right down the middle. Even stepping between two men is a very dangerous thing. They might stop, but they probably won't because real fighting is much nastier than what we see on television. So I can't help wondering if our intelligence has much of a chance. Look at what we're doing to the environment. We know we're damaging it, but we can't stop. The people who are making the money out of this keep telling us, "Don't worry. It's OK." We who are comfortable may not believe them, but we don't push very hard.

ALK: So, in the Italian student's situation with U.S. students, you're connecting hierarchical behavior with a fear of difference?—The U.S. students' fear of a different perspective?
OB: Sure. I may be wrong, but it all seems to be part of the same thing.

ALK: You might be right; but as an educator I want to think there is more hope for human nature.
OB: Of course there is. For instance, on the news this morning I heard that there are now women executives climbing to the top of Fortune 500 companies. They're sitting at the top saying, "Oh, there's no more problem. There's no more glass ceiling, so we no longer need affirmative action. Don't worry; all you have to do is work really hard and you'll be fine." I thought, "That's the worst problem: The women who make it to the top have to pretend to be men." Of course I don't mean taking on physical male characteristics or acting like men, but in that way, they do seem to take on the characteristics of the people that they most try to imitate.

MM: So all of this hierarchical behavior, too, goes back to genetics?—which many of us don't want to believe because it seems so closed, so deterministic. The idea that subjectivity is reflected primarily in genes harks back to the age of eugenics, for instance, doesn't it?
OB: But we still need to look at some of those possibilities. For instance, several years ago one of my friends became really annoyed with my interest in

sociobiology. I said, "Wait a minute. If you, for instance, are suffering from PMS and you know that you have PMS, there are going to be certain things that you don't do because you know that you will do them badly and hurt yourself or hurt someone else. But if you don't know that this is a biological thing that's going on with you, maybe you'll try to just bull your way through. You'll say, 'Oh, I'm just being self indulgent,' and try to push through with it and may really hurt yourself." Another friend should not use sharp objects during that time because she will hurt herself, and she has stitches to prove it. Before she realized this, she often did hurt herself because those were the times when she wanted to do something with the sharp object, cut up salad or meat or whatever, or even go out and whack limbs off a tree.

ALK: So you're saying that knowledge of the body can be used to empower and not necessarily to determine?
OB: Yes. Sure!

ALK: Well, the determinism is what scares me about sociobiology.
OB: Don't worry about it.

ALK: How can you not worry about that?
OB: Don't worry about the real biological determinism. Worry about what people make of it. Worry about the social Darwinism. After all, if sociobiology, or anything like it (people don't really use that term much any more for obvious reasons), is true, then denying it is certainly not going to help. What we have to do is learn to work with it and to work against people who see it as a good reason to let the poor be poor, that kind of thing—the social Darwinism: "They must be poor because of their genes," that kind of foolishness.

MM: When you gave the example of your friend with PMS, you were talking about women looking after themselves and knowing certain things about their own bodies, and then conducting themselves as a result in certain ways. But there are still people who make jokes about how women can't ever be president because they'll have access to that red button during their period and we'll all be blown up.
OB: And men have access to it no matter how crazy they are.

MM: Exactly.
OB: This is what I mean: What's made of genetics—body knowledge—is what's important. What's made of biology is that the people who are in power are go-

ing to figure out why this is a good reason for them to stay in power. Look at the tests that show that women have better linguistic abilities: Yet, how many of our ambassadors are women? How many of the politicians are women? This is not looked at; instead, the argument goes that women don't have the mathematical abilities . . . every now and then. So we're much more likely now to be penalized for whatever we're assumed not to have. We're much more likely to find that whatever little genetic thing that's discovered is going to be used against us. Recently I was sitting on a panel with a man who had just gotten his Ph.D in genetics, and he was going to be working with the Human Genome Project. He was gung-ho, very much, for it. I said to him, "But doesn't it bother you that this is going to be used for a considerable amount of crime against people? It's going to be used by insurance companies who will refuse to insure people who have certain tendencies even if they never develop the disease. It's going to be used by employers who will find it an excellent reason not to employ certain people who need a job. Ways will be found to use this against people." And he said, "Those people can always get a lawyer and sue." But the people who this is going to be used against are the people who are going to be the least able to get a lawyer and sue! When I suggested this, he replied, "Maybe that's true, but the work still needs to be done," and the truth is that the work will be done. So I think that really what we need to do is fight those reactions. They're bad reactions. They're the kind of reactions that serve as political bullying.

ALK: The rhetoric is so powerful, though, because science is the "truth," so if science says these things about bodies, they must be truth.
OB: But it isn't science that makes the sociological connections. We manage to do that without the benefit of science. Again, consider the fact that women are better with verbal skills: why isn't the popular perception, then, that they would make better diplomats?

MM: Because they're the bodies of the culture and they bear the children.
OB: So!?

MM: They have periods, and so they're dangerous. I'm just saying what I think is still a fairly popular consensus.
OB: But that doesn't make any sense when you notice how men behave toward one another.

MM: Oh . . . we agree.
OB: It's not women with their periods who were out there starting shooting wars.

MM: You're saying that body-knowledge could, possibly, dehierarchize, or maybe re-hierarchize, social and political relations, then? In your work, body-knowledge carries a great deal of authority, unlike most postmodern thinking and writing which calculates the human body as primarily a discursive entity— perhaps in defensive response to the ways genetics studies have often allocated political power and influence according to hierarchies of raced and gendered bodies— again, movements like eugenics, for instance. For these postmodern thinkers and writers, race, gender, sexuality, are all metaphors. One's body can only be known through language or some other medium of representation. The body, for them, is a thing, in other words, which only language and narrative can bring to life and make known to ourselves or to others. In contrast, in a great deal of your work, the body is the central communicator. Spoken or written language is frequently inadequate for communication. Among the Oankali [Xenogenesis Trilogy], for instance, the flesh knows. Akin calls it an Oankali "certainty of the flesh." In this way your work grants a great deal of authority to the body and its metabolic processes and powers beyond discourse.

OB: Because the body is all we really know that we have. We can say that there're always other things that are wonderful. And some are. But all we really know that we have is the flesh. As a matter of fact in my next book, *Parable of the Talents*, there's a verse about that which begins "self is . . . ," and the verse goes on to talk about this concept.

MM: And what does the verse say a "self" is?
OB: Pretty much, body.

ALK: But people know their bodies so poorly; human beings don't usually know their bodies well at all.
OB: This goes to what we were saying earlier. Some things we are afraid to know; there's danger in knowing. We know a little bit about our bodies, and then along comes somebody writing a book invoking genetics, saying, "Well, what we know proves that some groups of people should be given vocational training, because they're not really intelligent enough to absorb an education like us, who are, somehow, apparently, better folk."

MM: So identifying some as, for instance, candidates for vocational training alienates those groups—as objects of inquiry— from their bodies because they're perceived and objectified in those ways?
OB: I mean that that's what's done with body knowledge.

MM: Hierarchy . . . again.
OB: Um hm.

ALK: My favorite character out of all your writing is the protagonist in *Wild Seed*, Anyanwu. She knows her body. She knows bodies at every level, it seems to me.
OB: Actually, when I wrote her, I felt very insecure about what I was having her do. I tried to make it seem logical, but I felt very uncomfortable about it and then when I got to the Xenogenesis books, I understood more of what I was trying to get at. So the nice thing about writing is that you do keep discovering not only things about the world but things about yourself.

ALK: In December of this year we're presenting a paper at the MLA conference in Toronto on your work. One of the things that we're arguing is that you invent what we're calling "new orders of difference," communities with different categories of kinship relations and racialized gender. Would you say that you're trying to create new types of community in your writings?
OB: I'd say more that I don't try to create communities; I always automatically create community. This has to do with the way I've lived. I just bought a new house, where there really isn't much in the way of community. People don't know their neighbors, but I went to the houses on each side of my own and introduced myself. The neighbors said, in effect, "That's nice," and that was the end of it. I'm used to living in areas where there's real community. My little court that I've talked about where I lived for about six or seven years has six little houses right-angling off the street, and it was a community in the real sense of the word. We all knew each other and if one of us was going away for a few days, we'd tell the others. We didn't all like each other, but we all knew each other and, since we were going to be living there, we made an effort to get along. When I was growing up, I lived in my grandmother's house. She owned it—a huge old house— and the neighborhood had changed. It had gone light-industrial and the houses were selling cheap, so she bought this enormous thing and had it cut up into apartments for her children to move into with their families, and this was a community. It was a good thing, too, because it was a really bad neighborhood, and it was also good because my father wasn't there. He died when I was a toddler, a little bit earlier, really, and since he wasn't there, it was good that I had uncles living in the other apartments because that meant that the street people knew that I had these big uncles: "Don't bother her; she's so-and-so's niece." So I've always lived in clusters of people who found ways of getting along together even if they didn't much like each other, which was often the case. My character Anyanwu at one point

actually says that she makes communities around herself. All of my characters either are in a community like Lauren in *Parable of the Sower,* or they create one; she does that, too. My own feeling is that human beings need to live that way and we too often don't.

MM: *Adulthood Rites* is my favorite of your books. In it, there's a line at the beginning that, for me, imbeds the too-uncommon kind of community you're talking about in altered bodies, the result of gene trading in the book: Nikanj tells Lilith that "trade means change. Bodies change, ways of living must change. Did you think your children would only look different?"
OB: Exactly!

MM: So are you saying, then, that in order for society to change, the body must change genetically?
OB: I'm saying it will change, for whatever reason, if we leave the earth, for instance. Or, it is changing already, actually. People who reach my age and can't see very well to read without glasses, now can still do productive work, without servants to help us. That's a change, and other changes: now we can travel a lot more widely and this is good, but it also means we can bring each other our diseases. So we're changing in those ways. All of a sudden we're able to contend with diseases we never even heard of. Change is inevitable, and it won't just change one thing.

MM: When I read that passage from *Adulthood Rites,* I think of contemporary social relations. It seems like the conventional political wisdom is that we can talk out our problems, contemporary global problems or local social problems, and thereby change perceptions and advance to a more just and egalitarian system. But in so many of your books, especially the Xenogenesis Trilogy, talk as a way of changing perceptions is not enough. In your books, bodies have to be genetically, as well as visibly, altered, in order to alter the human contradiction.
OB: The Xenogenesis books looked at one possible way—but I don't think for one moment that aliens will actually come down and fix it for us. When the Oankali do fix it for humans in the Xenogenesis books, the humans don't like it and they wouldn't.

MM: Even Lilith.
OB: She wasn't that thrilled. In *Parable of the Sower,* I deal with another possible way: I talk about us as we are, and I give us—I don't give it; nature seems to have given it (I never heard of a culture that didn't have a religion)—a religion. Lauren uses religion as a tool. So I use that tool as something that she can use to help

people who follow her and those who are influenced by them, to save themselves. Now her idea (and this is an old science fiction idea) is that the one insurance humanity can take out is to scatter among the stars. This is one way, probably, that some of us will survive somewhere, because of the way we've been going. We go in these strange destructive cycles, and we do it over and over again. I was reading the Will and Ariel Durant history and, especially in the first book, over and over again the marauders come in and they take over and kill and torture and maim and steal. It's horrible. The marauder king finally settles down and says, "I'm going to try to make a really good society here for my people," and he starts to do things that are actually useful, not always, obviously. But in several cases this happens: he starts to initiate actions that are useful: arrange for better care for the sick, and see to it that children get what they need. The more he does this, the more he steps on the toes of people who had a really good thing going before, exploiting whoever he's trying to help now, whether it's children or old people or whomever—women. Then those people who had earlier been at the top of the hierarchy begin to stir up the populace: "Don't you realize that this guy is your enemy?" This is what they're basically saying although they never put it quite that boldly. They find things to say about him that either make the people laugh at him or that make them suspect him of doing something behind their backs. In some way they diminish him in the eyes of the very people he's helping. Then after a while the populace can be encouraged to help bring him down. It seems to work every time; it never works as clearly as I've just said it, but it's the same pattern over and over again. I don't really have much hope for us as a species, especially if we become more technologically aware and if we all stay here on earth. Just talking through problems isn't an adequate solution.

MM: Related to my question about bodies changing in the Xenogenesis Trilogy, and therefore, as Nikanj says, "ways of living" changing, I'm fascinated by the third gender in the Xenogenesis Trilogy and how it alters the mechanics of heterosexual couplings.

OB: Well, the men don't like it because they feel they're being made into women. And that's not really what's happening. That's the way they see it because the men aren't at the top of the hierarchy any more, biologically or sexually. But the ooloi are not necessarily taking away any male functions. Genetically, the men are still male. But in the Oankali system, "male" doesn't carry the connotations of power and authority that it does in human systems. I don't know whether you've noticed—there're two differences in hierarchy that a lot of readers and reviewers tend not to notice in the Xenogenesis books. One is that the Oankali have no traditional government. Instead, they come together by way of the nerve systems of their various chips and appendages, and they get a consensus; that's how they make decisions. And the other is that the ooloi, who seem to have so very much power, make no personal genetic contribution to the offspring. It really hurts them in that sense, not hurts them, but they're cut off in that sense from their own young. So those two differences bend the usual hierarchy. The Oankali are hierarchical, but not in the same ways as humans; they have some natural brinks on their tendencies.

MM: What might be the effect on readers of a text like yours revising these, and other, hierarchies in this way, for instance the threesome of gender and of sexual activity, rather than the usual twosomes?
OB: To bend their minds a bit? That's what I'd hope for, but the problem there is the same problem with Lauren's hyperempathy: people don't read carefully. Reviewers typically account for Lauren's hyperempathic powers as something supernatural—as a type of extrasensory telepathy—when I didn't write it that way. I guess that, with fiction, readers don't feel they need to read carefully; so many assume over and over again that the ooloi are just a combination of male and female. Even though in the Trilogy I say clearly over and over again that the ooloi are something different—not simply a combination of two, but a third gender altogether—and that they don't act like either men or women, readers usually see what they want to or what they expect to.

MM: So, if readers, as you say, "don't read carefully," then what's the purpose of writing such reconfigurations, . . . or of having readers know about them? If people don't read carefully, then can there be any relation between writing fiction and political commentary and struggle?
OB: Do you mean, do I think I influence political commentary?

MM: Do you believe there is a relation between the two? For instance, my impression is that even many academics in our field believe that reading and studying literature is more an escape from . . .
ALK: That it's just entertaining.

MM: That it just entertains people rather than having a political function or having some influence to change the hierarchies of bodies and social relations we've been talking about, for instance.
OB: Let's look at some fiction that seems to have had quite an influence recently and long term. What about that book which a lot of the survivalists are so hot

on?—*The Turner Diaries* by Andrew Macdonald. It looks forward to a time when there's a terrible race war, and his side wins. It's become an underground cult classic—said to have influenced Tim McVeigh and the whole separationist movement. Every now and then it's in the news because some new, pardon me, nut group decides to bring about, or tries to bring about, their agenda. Then there's that antisemitic one, *The Protocols of the Elders of Zion*; I'm not sure people think of that now as fiction, but I'm sure back when it was written, the author knew it was fiction, whoever the author was far back into antiquity—it was brought back by the Czarists to demonize Russian Jews and, later, by the Nazis in Germany. I came across it in my research on how a country goes Fascist, the major theme of my new novel [*Parable of the Talents*]. A lot of readings that shouldn't have effect might just have it because they're taken so seriously, even something like the Biblical book of Ruth. The question about the book of Ruth is whether it's fiction or not because it's so unusual. It's pressing for a kind of tolerance that the books which follow it certainly are not. That kind of tolerance is not there. Instead, the later ones suggest, "Get rid of these foreign wives," which seems to me grotesque: "Here, take your family and shove them out the gates." But that one and the book of Job—both of these are fascinating fiction, but they have found their ways into our everyday religious discourse and had a heck of a lot of influence. If nothing else, they're at least fascinating to talk about and a lot of people do believe them literally.

MM: Do you see your texts as political?

OB: I have a character (I keep doing this to you)—I have a character in *Parable of the Talents* who says, "We have to stay out of politics. We don't want to get noticed. Things are too hot right now." There is a real Fascist running for president and my character is afraid the Fascist will win. My character and his friends are in the process of building up their business. At first, it's really basic barter and trade. Then, gradually, as they acquire a truck, it becomes wholesaling. They're doing more, and other people are afraid because one of the things that the Fascist is saying is, "It's these non-Christians, these cultists who've gotten us into all this trouble." And my character and his business partners are saying, "We've gotta cool it; we don't want to be noticed. We don't want to get into politics." But the female protagonist remarks, instead, that "To be human is to be political." That's pretty much the way I feel.

MM: So your texts are political. You do see your texts as political?

OB: Everything is political in one way or another.

MM: We see your texts as very innovative, and we believe that they . . .
OB: I'm not entirely sure that they are, but thank you.

MM: That they also represent a political struggle. We're wondering—with the way the world is (and we've talked about the Gulf War and all of the other conflicts having to do with various hierarchies even though there is no longer a Cold War)—if there's a relation between fiction and political struggle, as you've said you believe there is, how politically effective is textual innovation and struggle? Can the type of remodeled hierarchies, including remodeled bodily hierarchies in terms of gender and ethnicity, or sexuality, for instance can they make a difference in popular attitudes?
OB: When I buy a book, I say that if I get one idea from this book it's paid for itself. When I write a book, if I influence one person who goes on to influence others, then probably I've done something worthwhile if the influence is good. Nobody can see how long their books will last or how much influence they'll have, so I just assume that at least I can make a few people think. I don't know what will come of that, possibly nothing, but you never know what that one kid, for instance, sitting in the back of the room is going to wind up doing. You're both teachers, so I'm sure you're very much aware of this. That one kid is liable to someday be able to say "yes" or "no" to something very important: "Yes, we'll kill off the rest of this nasty Amazon forest," or, "No, we won't." I don't really believe one person alone will make that decision, but that's something that's important.

MM: So you do believe that textual innovation and struggle are or can be, politically, positively effective.
OB: Can be, but there's no guarantee.

ALK: Relatedly, how would you like your writings to influence and affect readers? You've already said that you want to make them think, but I wonder if you could be more specific, for instance if you had a lot of power and knew you could influence readers in certain ways. Would you want to influence them, and, if so, how?
OB: That's a genie in a bottle sort of question. If I knew that I could and did it, I hope that I would have the good sense not to do it most of the time. And if I did do it, I'm hoping that it would have something to do with the environment. I can make any number of people think about what we're doing to the environment without affecting what we're doing to the environment. But maybe

they'll remember when they get older. It's obvious, for instance, that global warming is already taking place. All signs say "yes"; none of them say "no," but there are still scientists who'll look at one sign and say, "This one sign is questionable and maybe, therefore, it's not really happening." I write a book like *Parable of the Sower* in which global warming is practically one of the characters, and maybe it becomes more real to young readers who don't yet have any power but who might someday. Maybe they're more able to admit, "Yes, of course it's happening, and if we can't stop it, we have to at least start paying attention to it and preparing for it and not making it worse."

ALK: Since 1980 or so there's been a proliferation of works by African American women—Alice Walker, Toni Morrison, Paule Marshall, Terri McMillan, among many, many others. Have you read and been influenced by them?—As a writer, how would you situate yourself among them?

OB: Not really. For one thing, we all seem to have come around at the same time. I came into writing first by way of my fantasies, magic horses and all that, and then by way of science fiction. So I had the flaw that so many young science fiction writers have. I read too much science fiction. It was practically all I read when I began as a writer. So these women writers you've mentioned are people that I discovered much later and, I think, late enough so that I don't think they had that much of an effect on my writing. However, Toni Morrison did make me aware that there are ways to use words, ways that I hadn't been using. I came in by way of pulp science fiction which had begun to annoy me even before I began to think about what else I might do. So writers like Toni Morrison who use the language so well made me aware of other possibilities.

MM: How would you situate your work within the context of U.S. literature as a whole?—that is, not only how it fits into the science fiction genre, but how it fits with more canonical literary traditions.

OB: I've never been good at fitting in. You can fit it in for me.

MM: I ask that question because we both teach from the *Heath Anthology of American Literature*. We both teach the Survey of U.S. Lit courses, and we're surprised that your writings aren't included in the 1865–Present volume.

OB: Well, is that because the anthology was published a while back?

MM: No the most recent edition is only two or three years old, and the new one is coming out in November. If you're not in the upcoming new edition, would you like to be?

OB: Sure. Why not? At least I'm now in the *Norton Anthology of Afro American Science Fiction.* You can look me up in the *Oxford Companion to American Litatature,* that kind of thing.

MM: That's good, but I want to see your work in the *Heath Anthology of American Literature* too, not only as a science fiction writer, that is, but also as a part of U.S. lit as a whole. That would also be a way, perhaps, for our field not to marginalize science fiction as a genre so much.

OB: It's interesting what gets called science fiction. Robin Cook came in writing bad science fiction, and he says that, before reading his work, most people didn't know anything about science fiction. It was brand new to most readers, and they were impressed with how innovative he was!

MM: So to what do you attribute his success, then—a more mainstream success than most science fiction writers enjoy?

OB: To a couple of things: he was very smart in the way he did not sell to a small science fiction publisher. He found a mainstream publisher, and he's an MD; he wrote about medical subjects, and he got in. And now he can write about aliens coming to earth, and it's still a big deal because he's Robin Cook.

ALK: The classifying is so interesting because Margaret Atwood's *The Handmaid's Tale* isn't, surprisingly, labeled science fiction. And it deals more with the future than, for example, your *Parable of the Sower,* which of course is labelled as science fiction.

OB: Yes, they're equally un-science fiction-y books—Atwood's even more so because she has this future that is totally non-technological; it gets harder and harder to see how we would get to a non-technological future without a terrible war or something, simply because people find technology so convenient. So it isn't likely that they would just give it up. It was an interesting book

ALK: How would you say your own body has influenced and perhaps shaped your writing?

OB: Not so much my body, but other people's reaction to it. I grew up as out-kid. I think I was first called ugly in first grade, and I went on being called ugly all the way through junior high school. If you're called ugly that long, you start to believe it. You also start to expect it so that, after a while, when people become too polite to do that you assume that they're thinking it, and you start to miss it in a horrible sort of way. So I was out-kid, and I assume that I was out-kid because I was ugly. Actually, I was the most socially awkward person you can imagine, still am to some degree. And I was an only child and never really learned to work with other people very well. Because of this, because I was so ostracized and because I was so shy, the writing was a real refuge for me. So, in that sense, I guess you could say my body helped to make me a writer.

MM: In the writing process itself?.
OB: In other people's reactions to me. I was six feet tall when I was fourteen or fifteen, so that also helped. Boys figured I did it on purpose.

MM: What about specific texts? You said that other people's reaction to your body influenced your writing. Can you think of any specific ways of writing or specific characters or specific texts that were influenced?
OB: I tried being a small person—I tried to experience being a small person in *Mind of My Mind* and in *Wild Seed.* That was interesting because then I had to think of some of the problems that a small person might have to deal with, and to think as a small person. My first attempt at being as big as I am was in *Survivor.* Here I have a character who is not necessarily fat, but she's very tall and androgynous-looking. I used to be mistaken for a man a lot, and, occasionally, somebody would try to chase me out of the ladies room, which used to upset the hell out of me.

MM: What would you say?
OB: I was deeply offended.

MM: What did they do when you corrected them? Did they apologize?
OB: No, people tend not to apologize for mistaking me for a man. On the phone for instance, because I have a deep voice, people will often call me "sir," and my standard response now is just to say, "I'm a woman." Some of them don't hear me; some of them say, "What?" And some don't say anything; they just go on as if I haven't spoken. And some say, "Oh, I'm sorry," and they change their pronouns and their manner of address, so it's been an interesting life. The size thing has been the biggest influence. I had a friend when I was in junior high school who belonged to the same religious denomination as my mother. We both had the same prohibitions: no dancing, no makeup, no short dresses, although we did roll them up a bit; in other words, if it felt good, you couldn't do it, and let's not even talk about boys! And so, as a big person, bigger than most boys, my reaction was to dive into the writing. My friend's reaction, when she began to get to a rebellious age, was to go out and get pregnant. That was an act of rebellion. I saw this happen to other people, and I thought, "What's the future in that?" She missed a year of school; eventually she dropped out altogether and she couldn't get a decent job, so she found herself a husband. For one thing, she was about half a foot

shorter than I was. So I figured I couldn't really take her track as far as men were concerned because, at that point, men were still looking at me and saying things I didn't really want to hear. I looked at other friends I had. In one neighborhood the girls living on both sides had decided that they wanted to prove they were women, so they got pregnant, and one of them more than once. I looked at them both, and I saw no future. Where are they going? One of them eventually wound up cleaning houses, which didn't appeal to me at all, and the other one just had a lot more children and eventually got married. None of this was in the vaguest bit appealing to me. Part of what I'm saying is that my body really got in the way of any social life that I was likely to have had. But, on the other hand, it did push me more into the writing because I was in the habit of thinking about things. Writing does encourage you to think about things. I would look at something before I leaped into it, and that's not really an adolescent characteristic: Typically, adolescents just tend to leap all too often.

MM: Now there are students waiting to talk with you. Thank you for being so forthcoming. We totally enjoyed our interview with you. This has been a thrilling two days, and we're grateful that you came to us in the high plains in the midst of a tornado warning.
OB: Well, I think if I'd heard about the tornado . . . I might not have come!

MM: Thank goodness you didn't, then!
OB: I've enjoyed this very much, too.

Works Cited

Boulter, Amanda. "Polymorphous Futures: Octavia E. Butler's Xenogenesis Trilogy." *American Bodies: Cultural Histories of the Physique.* Ed. Tim Armstrong. New York: New York UP, 1996. 170–85.
Butler, Octavia E. *Dawn.* New York: Warner, 1987.
———. "Positive Obsession." *Bloodchild And Other Stories.* New York: Seven Stories P, 1996. 123–35.
Haraway, Donna J. "A Cyborg Manifesto: Science, Technology, and Socialist-Feminism in the Late Twentieth Century." *Simians, Cyborgs, and Women: The Reinvention of Nature.* New York: Routledge, 1991. 149–82.
Harrison, Rosalie G. "Sci Fi Visions: An Interview with Octavia Butler." *Equal Opportunity Forum* 8 (1980): 30–34.
Irigaray, Luce. "The Power of Discourse and the Subordination of the Feminine." *This Sex Which Is Not One.* Trans. Catherine Porter. Ithaca: Cornell UP, 1985. 68–85.
Johnson, Charles. *Being and Race: Black Writing Since 1970.* London: Serpent's Tail, 1988.

Morrison, Toni. *Playing in the Dark: Whiteness and the Literary Imagination.* Cambridge: Harvard UP, 1992.

Raven, P. H., and G. B. Johnson, *Biology.* 4th ed. Dubuque, IA: Wm. C. Brown, 1996.

Stepto, Robert. "Distrust of the Reader in Afro-American Narratives." *Reconstructing American Literary History.* Ed. Sacvan Bercovitch. Cambridge: Harvard UP, 1986. 300–22.

White, Eric. "The Erotics of Becoming: Xenogenesis and The Thing." *Science Fiction Studies* 20.3 (1993): 394–408.

Addendum

In two phone interviews subsequent to the original in-person conversation at Eastern New Mexico University in May 1997, Octavia Butler talked about the two *Parable* novels as, at once, interconnected and different from one another. Both novels, she claims, represent "warnings": about the dangers of a fundamentalist religion-driven national politics, as exemplified in Pat Robertson's 1992 run for the U.S. presidency, and about the climate changes, emblematized by global warming, occurring in the two fictional landscapes and in contemporary real time. Yet, further, Butler reiterated Olamina's self-conscious use, herself, of religion as a "tool" for transforming the relation among diverse populations and between humans and the Earth: "I had in mind how certain historical populations have used religion to focus a group toward long-term goals—such as building cathedrals or the pyramids. I wanted Lauren to envision, but then also to focus the Earthseed group toward, the goal of changing human attitudes about and treatment of the Earth and of each other. And a big part of that vision was to formulate not a national government but, instead, multiple communities, self-governing and—supporting, but also interactive with each other. In Lauren's religion, the Earthseed group's going back to the Earth, as at the end of Sower, means being alive again, literally and spiritually. Unlike a fundamentalist sensibility where immortality means death and transcendence, Lauren wants to give her group immortality by returning to the earth. And it was important to me that Lauren had some success. . . . By the end of *Talents*, Lauren's too old to go to the stars and she has no descendants going—Larkin won't go—but others are going. So the ending is ambiguous: There's some success for Lauren, some failure, and a lot of hope. The other ambiguity here is that if we humans are, as Lauren believes, and as I believe, a part of Earth in significant ways, then perhaps we can't, or shouldn't, leave and go to another world. The system of Earth is self-regulating, but not for any particular species, in the same way that the human body has its own metabolic logic. Perhaps the Acorn community represents the most logical way to halt the damage we're doing to the Earth and to ourselves as humans."

With respect to narrative form, Butler talked about the differences between *Sower* and *Talents*: "In some ways, having several narrators in the second novel serves, subtly, to, I hope, undermine the single-minded guiding voice of *Sower*—Olamina's. This is as it should be: *Talents* isn't the coming-of-age story that *Sower* is. Olamina doesn't have the only truth. I wanted Lauren's daughter Larkin to be heard as well, as one spokesperson for a later era; but her story, and her life, is very different from Lauren's—Larkin never had the intellectual leisure, for instance, that Lauren did for formulating a religion like Earthseed and a plan. Unlike Lauren, by the time Larkin gets an education, she's already an adult." Butler related as well how the early drafts of *Talents* changed after her mother's 1996 stroke and death: "In January 1997, when I got back into writing the novel, it had become a mother-daughter story." Additionally, we queried Butler about the narrative pattern in her previous books where, as we commented in the original interview, there's typically a delay in readers' learning a character's ethnic origins until, and unless, that information becomes central to the narrative; unlike these, *Talents* marks characters' racial or ethnic identity much sooner and more directly than does any of her earlier novels, including *Sower*. She commonsensibly replied that "By the time many readers get to *Talent*, they already know most of the characters from *Sower*. So they're accustomed to multi-ethnic and multi-cultural communities and blended bodies and identities. Besides, there's more at stake—life and death stakes—at this stage of the Earthseed community's development than there was early in the Parable story."

Finally, Butler related that after writing *Talents* she had envisioned four more novels in the *Parable* series: the third, *Parable of the Trickster*; the fourth, *Parable of the Teacher*; the fifth, *The Parable of Chaos*; and sixth, *The Parable of Clay*. She imagined that none of the four after the first two would have characters in common, though the stories would be interlocking. However, after re-writing the introduction to the third novel in the Parable series "at least 150 times," Butler says that she has permanently "killed" the series: "It was too hard to write the first sequel; and now I'm focusing on and having fun with a completely different text and a new narrator." The name of the new text is *Mortal Words*, which takes an epistolary form, daily letters written by a woman in her ninety-ninth year, the last written on her hundredth birthday. After a lifetime in Southern California, Octavia Butler has recently moved to Seattle, Washington.

Congratulations! You've Just Won $295,000: An Interview with Octavia Butler

Joan Fry/1997

From *Poets & Writers Magazine* (March/April 1997). Reprinted by permission of the publisher, Poets & Writers, Inc., 72 Spring Street, New York, NY 10012. www.pw.org.

Octavia E. Butler may be the only African-American woman currently writing science fiction for a living. In person, with her close-cropped hair, six-foot height, and strong features, Butler cuts an imposing figure. As the author of ten critically acclaimed novels and several prizewinning stories (collected in her most recent book, *Bloodchild and Other Stories*), she has set an equally imposing track record.

Some critics call Butler a futurist; others claim she writes speculative fiction. Butler, who is adamant in her dislike of labels, does not consider some of the stories in *Bloodchild* science fiction at all: "I'm a storyteller," she insists. However critics categorize her, they're unanimous in praise of her vivid imagination, which makes her work both compelling and believable.

Butler, who was born in Pasadena, California, wrote her first three novels—*Pattermaster*, *Mind of My Mind*, and *Survivor*— about a race of telepathic people selectively bred by a "transmigrating soul" named Doro, who changes bodies the way normal humans change clothes. All told, there are five novels in Butler's Patternist series, but *Mind of My Mind* is easily the eeriest because it's set in present-day Forsyth—a fictional southern California town that bears an uncanny resemblance to Pasadena.

Butler's main philosophical concerns in her novels are the abuse of power, the destruction of earth's resources, and the different ways of being "human." But she is never openly didactic. Her popularity rests on her gift for characterization—like their creator, many of Butler's protagonists are smart, strong-willed black women who can, in the face of grim circumstances, be very funny—her "spare, vivid prose" (*Kirkus Reviews*), the scary plausibility of her plots, and the authenticity of her settings, which range from slave-era Africa in *Wild Seed* to an alien planet in *Survivor*.

Butler, who once described herself as "a pessimist if I'm not careful," wrote her second series of novels, the Xenogenesis trilogy, out of her suspicion that humans have an inborn genetic conflict between their hierarchical behavior (which she defines as "simple one-upmanship in any form") and their intelligence, which often causes them to act in a self-destructive manner. In Butler's view, humans are incapable of living in peace with one another—or even with the creatures in their environment.

Just around the time of her forty-eighth birthday (she was born in 1947), Butler's telephone rang. The person on the other end informed her she had received a $295,000 MacArthur Fellowship. To date, the only major change that Butler made in her life is to buy a house and move from Pasadena to neighboring Altadena. She didn't buy a fancy new car because she doesn't drive—she's dyslexic and prefers taking buses. And even though she finally bought a computer, she is finishing her latest novel on an old-fashioned manual typewriter.

JF: What were you doing when you received word that you'd won a MacArthur Fellowship?
OB: I was sitting at my desk either writing or reading, which is what I'm usually doing in the middle of the day if I'm at home.

JF: Did you believe it?
OB: Not at first. In the past, people who called and told me I'd won something were lying. They were telephone solicitors who wanted me to buy something. So I thought it might be some kind of scam, and I had better listen very carefully.

JF: Did you get the money all at once?
OB: No, it's paid over a period of five years. I think that's a good thing for people in the arts, because one of our problems is that it's either fat times or starvation times. I had gotten into the habit of putting whatever money that came in from writing or speaking into the bank and paying myself a salary, but there have been times when there was so little in my account that it became a problem.

JF: What was the first thing you went out and did, once the reality sank in?
OB: Well, the reality sank in a long time before the money arrived. So I didn't do anything unusual.

JF: How long have you been writing science fiction?
OB: Since 1959, when I was twelve, but people only began paying me for it well enough to support me since 1979.

JF: I've heard you talk about the blue-collar jobs you held before you had established yourself as a writer. You said that one of the few good things about them was that nobody required you to be pleasant.

OB: Or to smile. That isn't my nature, so it was very nice to be just as grumpy as I felt, because I was getting up early in the morning and writing and then going to work, and the last few hours of the day I was pretty much on automatic. I remember working in a mailing house; I don't even know if those places still exist. They had both machines and people putting together pieces of mail for advertising. It was like an assembly line at a factory, only a little more complicated. You might be doing something with each piece of mail, not just putting them together. You did this over and over and over all day until your shoulders wanted to desert to another body. The only thing I could do to keep myself somewhere near conscious was to sing, very softly, to myself. I don't have the most wonderful singing voice, and the supervisor kept walking by giving me funny looks. Finally she came up and asked, "What are you doing? *Talking* to yourself?"

JF: She must have thought you were losing it.

OB: People did lose it. That's why I wrote "Crossover" [one of the stories in *Bloodchild*]. I was watching a woman who was clearly going crazy, and there was nothing anybody could do. She had to work at this horrible, boring job, and when she went home, she had to take care of her ailing mother. That was her life. I'm not sure very many people could have held on.

JF: "Crossover" is about a woman who works in a factory and is greeted one night by an ex-boyfriend just out of jail—except he's not really there. What makes the story science fiction?

OB: It's not.

JF: Then what is your definition of science fiction?

OB: Well, it's nice if you use a little science.

JF: So science fiction doesn't necessarily mean space aliens and alternate universes.

OB: It doesn't necessarily mean anything at all except that if you use science, you should use it correctly, and if you use your imagination to extend it beyond what we already know, you should do that intelligently. The reason I've stayed with science fiction to the degree that I have is because you can do almost anything in it. But you have to know about a subject before you can play with it, so I do my research first.

JF: I've noticed that. You're very knowledgeable about a variety of subjects: medicine, biology, zoology. . . .

OB: I'm not, really, but I know how to use the library. And I'm curious about those things anyway, so I'll read idea-producing magazines like *Scientific American* or *Discover* or *Natural History* or *Smithsonian* that tell me things I didn't know before and perhaps direct me to books I wasn't aware of.

JF: Why did you start writing science fiction?

OB: Because of a movie I saw when I was twelve called *Devil Girl from Mars.* I thought, "I can do a better story than that." Of course what I wrote was awful, but I didn't know it. I was having a good time. By the time I was thirteen I was bothering editors with my stuff. One thing that contributed to my fascination with the universe in general was the time I spent on my grandmother's chicken ranch between Victorville and Barstow [in California's sparsely settled high desert], and being able to look up and see the stars and realizing there are parts of the world that human beings don't dominate.

JF: The book of yours most people seem to read first is *Kindred.* Why is that?

OB: It's accessible to people who normally don't read science fiction. *Parable of the Sower* is another one. *Kindred* is the story of a black woman who unwillingly travels back in time to the antebellum South and has to fight like hell to survive slavery. She's a struggling writer, and before her trips begin, she and her husband are both holding jobs that I had actually held—food processing, clerical, warehouse, factory, cleaning, you name it.

JF: How long did that period of your life last?

OB: Ten years, from 1968 through 1978. After *Patternmaster* came out in 1976, I started working more sporadically, at temporary jobs. I didn't get an awful lot of money for that novel; I've gotten more money for the best of my short stories— but also, things cost a lot less then. The last job I held was in a hospital laundry. In August. Bad. And this was after I had written and sold three novels. When I got the money from the third, I was able to quit and go off to Maryland to research *Kindred.*

JF: Who influenced you as a writer?

OB: My all-time favorite writer is Frank Herbert, who wrote *Dune.* He wrote a lot of other books, too, and then he wrote a mainstream novel that let me know what to expect if I ever tried it. The jacket copy proclaimed, "His first serious novel." Theodore Sturgeon influenced me—he was a real craftsman. I probably liked *The*

Synthetic Man, which was originally called *The Dreaming Jewels* [in subsequent reprints the book has reverted to its original title], and *More Than Human*, the best. The writers who influenced me most tended to be those who were the most prolific. John Brunner was *very* prolific—my favorites are *Polymath*, *The Whole Man*, and *The Long Result*. Harlan Ellison was a major influence, particularly his short story collection *Dangerous Visions*. As a kid, I also read a lot of Felix Sultan. I wasn't allowed to go to the movies, so whenever I heard about one that sounded interesting I would go to the library and check the book out. Sultan tended to write about animals as though they were human—more accurately, as though they were knowingly, although not always willingly, *subject* to humans. In *Bambi*, for instance, man is always referred to as "He," with a capital letter, as in "God."

JF: After *Kindred* you wrote *Wild Seed*. That's a book a year for five consecutive years. How did you manage to be so prolific?
OB: I was like a lot of writers. I had all these ideas stored up I had been trying to write for years. Once I was able to actually finish a novel, the flood gates opened and I was able to finish the others, too.

JF: You wrote the Patternist novels first, but you wrote them out of sequence— some are prequels to others, and so on. If someone wanted to read them chrono- logically, what's the order?
OB: I wrote them completely out of order, yes. Chronologically, *Wild Seed* would be the first, then *Mind of My Mind*, *Clay's Ark*, *Survivor*, and *Patternmaster*.

JF: What I enjoyed about the Patternist books, *Mind of My Mind* in particular, is what I also enjoyed about *Parable of the Sower* and your story "Speech Sounds": you show a disintegrating urban society—substance abuse, random violence, murder—that really isn't much different from what we see right now.
OB: You're right, it's not that far from some of the problems we have. I tell in the afterword to "Speech Sounds" that we all have some kind of communica- tion deficit that shuts us off from one another. So we wind up not understanding one another, and sometimes envying people who seem to understand each other better.

JF: I was wondering if "Speech Sounds" had anything to do with your dyslexia.
OB: Not at all, because dyslexia hasn't really prevented me from doing anything I've wanted to do, except drive. I can read, for example, but I can't read fast. I never had a problem reading because I was lucky enough to be taught before I got into school by my mother and grandmother.

JF: I've noticed that you give talks and then usually have a question-and-answer period. You don't give readings.

OB: No, I don't, because I tend to read things that aren't there. I once volunteered as a reader at the Braille Institute. I felt that I'd been pretty lucky, and I wanted to give something back. So I thought, "At least I can do that." I didn't realize how badly I read aloud until I began reading to these unfortunate blind people who had to listen to me. One of them finally said, "What's the matter? You can *see* it, why are you doing that?"

JF: Some critics claim you write speculative fiction and others claim you write science fiction. What's the difference?

OB: I would say that speculative fiction is *any* kind of nonconventional fiction, from Borges to Isaac Asimov. But I don't make any distinction. Labels are something that people just absolutely require, and there's nothing I can do about it. As I've said before, I write about people who do extraordinary things. It just turned out that it was called science fiction.

JF: Are there any other black women writing science fiction? Or do you prefer to be called African-American?

OB: Oh, Lord—labels again! Either one is fine. No, I don't know of any. When Kris Neville was alive, his wife Lil Neville sometimes had a part in his writing— she's black and he was white—but they wrote only under his name.

JF: What was the origin of your Xenogenesis trilogy?

OB: Well, I got the idea back in the early 1980s . . . from Ronald Reagan.

JF: This I want to hear.

OB: Early on in his administration he used to talk about "winnable nuclear wars" and "limited nuclear wars," and he had this lackey who ran around talking about how if we had a nuclear war you could save yourself if you dug a hole. After you dug the hole you put a door over it and threw dirt on the door and then got down in the hole. After the bombs were finished, you could come out again and start up life. I thought, "The American people put these idiots in positions of power—and they're going to *kill* us! If people actually fall for this crap, there must be something wrong with the people!"

So I set out to figure out what might be wrong with us. I put the problem into the mouths of my alien characters, the Oankali. To them, humans have two characteristics that do not work well together. People are intelligent—no problem, the Oankali were happy to see that—but also we are hierarchical. And since our hierarchical tendencies are older, they tend to focus and drive our intelligence.

So I began the books after the end of a horrible nuclear war in which we've one-upped ourselves to death.

JF: In *Dawn*, the first book of the trilogy, your female protagonist awakes to find herself the captive of the Oankali, a group of nonviolent genetic engineers. The woman, who's black, is named Lilith and she's instrumental in starting a new race of human-Oankali beings. I did note the significance of her name, but it made me wonder what other clues I'd missed.

OB: When I write, there are always lots of levels. The first level is, here's an entertaining story; enjoy yourselves. And then there's whatever I put underneath. For instance, there's the young black man Lilith is introduced to by the Oankali. Lilith was an adult when the Oankali got her, but he grew up with the Oankali. Even though he's physically grown, he's never had a chance to learn to be the responsible man he might have become under other circumstances. His situation is, in a way, reminiscent of the survival characteristics that black people developed as a result of slavery, characteristics that were useful in slavery but detrimental later. It's hard to suppress ideas people have in their heads just because they're no longer appropriate, especially when it's a matter of mothers teaching their children. So some of the things that are really hard to talk about in the black community I talked about in *Dawn* and in *Mind of My Mind*. I have no idea who picks up on them and who doesn't. I think some of the academics do, because they expect you to do things like that.

JF: *Mind of My Mind* is a very violent book—beatings, incest, murder. What exactly are you referring to?

OB: The fact that you have Doro, who has kidnapped a bunch of people and bred them and used them, and after a while, when they're strong enough, they do nasty things to him. But they also do nasty things to everybody else, because they've learned that's how you behave if you want to survive.

JF: Do you think that's another legacy from slavery?

OB: I don't think that black people have made peace with ourselves, and I don't think white America has made any kind of peace with us. I don't think we really know *how* to make peace at this point.

JF: That's one of the recurring themes in your books. All the humans, with very few exceptions, are capable of betraying one another. Put these individuals into groups and they're even worse.

OB: That's why there's such a problem. And to tell the truth, even if we did know how to get along there would be problems. Even when people are the most absolutely homogeneous group you could think of, we create divisions and fight each other.

JF: In your Xenogenesis books you don't hold out much hope for human civilization as we know it.
OB: We do keep dragging each other back to various and sundry dark ages; we appear to be in the process of doing it again now. And when we're not doing that, we're exploiting our resources to such an extreme degree that they're going to disappear. On National Public Radio there was a woman who spent a number of years studying wolves that had migrated down from Canada into Glacier National Park. At one point she said something like, "If I were a wolf I'd stay in one place until I had used up the resources and then I would move on, but the wolves don't do that." And I thought, "Aha! The wolves have figured something out, at least on a biological level, that we *still* haven't!" In family bands, when humans lived that way, we didn't stay in one place until there was nothing left. We moved on. Right now it seems that people are being encouraged to see the environment as their enemy. Go out and kill it. If they're really unlucky, they will succeed.

JF: According to the jacket copy on one of your books, your chosen themes are feminism and race.
OB: No. Those are my audiences. My audiences are feminists, blacks, and science fiction readers, with some New Age people as well. There are mainstream readers, too, who don't fit into any of those categories, who read me just because they enjoy my work.

JF: Another motif I've noticed is metamorphosis. In your Patternist books you call it "transition," but some of your Xenogenesis characters undergo similar changes.
OB: We all go through them. I guess the most obvious metamorphosis is adolescence, and after that comes middle age. Adolescence can be an unpleasant metamorphosis. It's the only time I seriously considered suicide.

JF: Another motif you return to is the ability to share another's pain.
OB: In the Patternist books, it's actually being a telepath. People who come through transition are no longer feeling anything they don't want to feel, unless somebody stronger is inflicting it on them. The ones who are stuck in transition—maybe they're stuck in a kind of adolescence—are the ones who don't live long because they're wide open, and they're suffering.

JF: One last question about motifs—this one I noticed particularly in the Patternist books—is incest. Where did that come from?

OB: I explain in the afterword to my story "Near of Kin" that when I was a kid, I was a very strict Baptist. I was raised to read the Bible, really read it, every day. And I noticed that a lot of these Old Testament types were marrying near relatives— Lot's daughters got him drunk and had sex and produced two whole new ethnic groups. I thought, "Wow—instead of getting struck by lightning, they get a reward. They get to be the mothers of whole new people!" I found it very intriguing. In fact I titled a section of *Wild Seed* "Lot's Daughters."

JF: In *Survivor* you're very hard on traditional Christianity.

OB: I wrote the first version of *Survivor* when I was nineteen as a result of the rebellion I was feeling, breaking away from my upbringing and all that. The other day I was talking to some high school students, and a young woman with a very severe look on her face said, "Why do you call yourself a *former* Baptist?" And I thought, "Oh, my. Let's not corrupt the children." So I said, "Well, I belonged to a very strict Baptist sect. Dancing was a sin, going to the movies was a sin, wearing makeup was a sin, wearing your dresses too short was a sin—and 'too short' was definitely a matter of opinion with the ladies of the church. Just about everything that an adolescent would see as fun, especially the social behavior, was a sin. And I'm not talking about sleeping around. I finally reached a point where I really didn't believe I was going to get God mad at me if I danced."

JF: Where do the philosophical ideas in *Parable of the Sower* come from?

OB: From me, really. One nice thing about writing is that it forces you to look at your own beliefs. My character got her *Books of the Living* by my going through a lot of religious books and philosophical writings and stopping whenever I found myself in agreement or violent disagreement. Figuring out what I believed helped me figure out what *she* believed. And the answers began coming to me in verse. I needed the verses because I was having such trouble with the novel—trouble in the sense that I had problems with my main character being a power seeker, and trouble in the sense that I was slipping into rewriting my old stuff, which is what writers do after a certain point. Either you're a young writer and you're rewriting other people's work, or you're an old writer rewriting your own.

JF: Which of your books has sold the best?

OB: *Kindred* has been in constant circulation the longest. It was out of print for a while, but it went back into print before any of my others, and it's used in classes more than my other books.

JF: Why do you think mystery novels are increasingly being treated as serious literary fiction while science fiction is still relegated to genre status?

OB: I had a friend at Cal State L.A.—I went there for a long time and collected a lot of units in different majors, but I didn't graduate—who would not read science fiction because it was trash. I tried to explain to her that science fiction wasn't all trash—it *contained* trash like anything else—and I mentioned a book that she liked, George Orwell's *1984*. I said, "That is classified as science fiction." She said, "It can't be science fiction. It was good!" Do you know Sturgeon's Law?

Theodore Sturgeon was a well-known science fiction writer. He's dead now, but supposedly he was on a panel at a science fiction convention once when somebody complained to him, "Ted, 90 percent of science fiction is shit." Sturgeon said, "Ninety percent of *everything* is shit." And, unfortunately, a lot of people have been trained to believe that science fiction is juvenile, and by the time they're fourteen they should be beyond such stuff. Science fiction suffers from its *reputation* for trashiness and immaturity, which makes it easy for people to judge it by its worst elements.

JF: You're clearly concerned with specific social and environmental issues in your work. Is most science fiction escapist, or are there other writers doing what you do?
OB: Oh, goodness, lots of them. Sure. Some write about the problems that I write about, and others write about other problems. Some look for technological solutions and others disparage technological solutions. Some think the world will go to hell and others think it will turn into ice cream. You have the same wide variety in science fiction that you have any place.

JF: What are you working on now?
OB: A novel called *Parable of the Talents*, which is a continuation of *Parable of the Sower*. I examined a lot of the problems in *Parable of the Sower*, and now I'd like to consider some of the solutions. Not *propose* solutions, you understand—what I want to do is look at some of the solutions that human beings come up with when they're feeling uncertain and frightened, as they are right now. When people don't know what they're frightened of, they tend to find things. Ridiculous things. United Nations helicopters are going to drop down and put them in concentration camps. It's so silly you don't think anybody would believe it, but there are people out there who do.

JF: Has winning the MacArthur Fellowship changed anything about your life or your writing?
OB: No. The nicest thing it's done is allowed me to buy a better house than I could have afforded before. And I like the security of knowing how much I'll be earning—especially now that I'm writing this novel. It was due last year, but I had

to tell Four Walls Eight Windows "What I have here is not publishable. I've got to redo it. I'll return the advance, if you like." They said, "No, no, go ahead and rewrite." I had never done anything like that before, but I couldn't send them what I had.

JF: Do you wish the award had come earlier in your career, for instance when you were working at some of those blue-collar jobs?

OB: If you had asked me then, I would have said, "Oh, absolutely!" But now I have the luxury of being able to say I'm glad it came when it did, because not having money forced me to establish habits of working, habits of depending on myself and not on others to do something for me.

JF: The practice of giving large cash awards to individual poets and writers has come under fire recently, the argument being that the money could launch the careers of dozens of young aspiring writers, or put them through college, or feed the hungry, et cetera.

OB: But that's the excuse used to get rid of anything you happen not to like! Let's abolish the space program because we're not feeding the hungry. We can do both, if that's what we choose. I don't think the two are incompatible. And I wouldn't have thought so before I got my award, either, just for the record. As a matter of fact that's one of the arguments in *Parable of the Talents*. My character has an opponent who says, "What's wrong with you? There's just too much here to do on earth to even be thinking about the stars." And she says, "You're perfectly free to do whatever you like to help people here on earth. I'm certainly not neglecting them, but we have our own destiny."

Octavia Butler

Mike McGonigal/1998

From *Index Magazine* (March 1998). Reprinted with permission of Index.

For more than two decades, Octavia Butler has crafted intense, transcendent fables, stories which have as much to do with the future as with present and past. One of her best-known books, *Kindred* tells the story of an African-American woman who is unexpectedly transported back in time from Southern California in 1976 to a plantation in the antebellum South.

Entranced with sci-fi books from an early age, Octavia Butler decided at thirteen that she was going to make a living as a writer of science fiction—despite her aunts telling her that "Negroes can't be writers." But through years of menial jobs and rejections from publishers, Butler kept writing and prevailed. And with ten books to her name, she is highly regarded as one of the few African-American women writing science fiction today. She has won all of sci-fi's top prizes—the Hugo, Nebula, and James Tiptree awards, and in 1995 received the prestigious MacArthur "Genius" award.

Genius, however, is a word she's unlikely to offer on her own behalf. For a 1996 book jacket, she described herself as "a forty-eight-year-old writer who can remember being a ten-year-old writer and who expects someday to be an eighty-year-old writer. I'm . . . a pessimist if I'm not careful, a Black, a former Baptist, an oil and water combination of ambition, laziness, insecurity, certainty, and drive."

Octavia Butler's work like all the important writing done in the genre of science fiction, is also concerned with what might be called *science fact*. It is imaginative writing but it is firmly grounded in the world in which we live, where we come from, and in the bodies and minds we inhabit, not only physically, but morally and spiritually.

Mike: I recently read *Kindred* for the first time, and one of the things that made the story so frightening is that there's no real explanation for why the main character, Dana, is being thrust back in time.

Octavia: I was much more interested in taking a black woman of now and sending her back to then, and having her cope. I wanted to do a novel about feelings as much as about history. Because I recognize that a lot of young people did not really understand on the level of feelings—they could quote facts for you—but they didn't really understand what it might have been like to live then. And frankly, *Kindred* doesn't tell them what it would have been like. *Kindred* is a clean version of slavery. In the same way that some of the Holocaust novels and TV shows have been rather clean. You don't really want to know the intimate details of what people had to go through, because they're so ugly and awful. And frankly, in a weird way, boring.

Mike: How you did research the book?
Octavia: Oh, my! First off, I went to my own bookshelves, and realized that I only had ten books that could possibly relate, and most of them were very superficial. A problem with overall histories is that they tend to be so superficial they're really useless if you want to write about individuals living in that time. And then I went to the library.

Mike: What year were you writing that book?
Octavia: Let's see, I finished it in '78, and it was published in '79. I was looking into black history at a perfect time—a lot of the results of the sixties and seventies were there on the shelf. A lot of slave narratives that were no longer in print were there. My problem then was that I had to localize things. I found that although I could get a lot of information on slavery in general, slavery in Maryland was not that easy to get information on.

Of course, there were stories of Harriet Tubman and Frederick Douglass, because they were both Marylanders. But I felt that if I could do it, I needed to go to Maryland. I sold a novel called *Survivor* before I should have and went off on a Greyhound bus, because I didn't really have very much money.

Mike: You "rode the dog" for a couple of days?
Octavia: Three and a half.

Mike: Oh, goodness!
Octavia: I've been cross-country several times on the Greyhound, so I knew how it was going to be. And I got there, Baltimore, strange city, and I went over to the Travelers' Aid, and said, "Can you direct me to an inexpensive hotel that isn't actually dangerous?" And the place where I stayed, I really was a bit worried. But I'm very fortunate to be six feet tall and rather formidable-looking. I was able to base myself in that crummy little room and go to the Eastern shore on the bus—to the library and to the Historical Society. I collected a lot of information and walked my feet off. My feet never hurt so much. I also went down to Washington DC, to

Mount Vernon. I bought everything I could on Mount Vernon, the plan of the place, and took pictures of the various dependencies. They had not restored or rebuilt any slave cabins. And they never said the word "slave." They said "servant." So there was obviously a game going on. But I could still get the idea. And I came home and in fact put a plan of Mount Vernon on my wall, and used that.

Mike: It seems you put a lot of research into your work.
Octavia: I don't do the kind of work that involves doing research and not writing. I do the research and the writing at the same time, and one stimulates the other. When I need to know something specific, I go hunting for it. As I hunt for it, I find other things. And that sometimes causes the novel to turn in directions that I had not really expected.

Mike: Is that usually what the process is like for you?
Octavia: The novel always changes as it's being written. It doesn't always change for the same reasons, but it always changes. It has to be able to. If you absolutely are rigid and you only have the original idea and nothing else, at some point you're liable to wind up using your characters as puppets.

Mike: You're fascinated with biology and medicine, but anyone could have figured that from your novel *Clay's Ark.*
Octavia: I suspect so, yeah.

Mike: How does this fascination manifest itself with you, though?
Octavia: I worry about these things.

Mike: Do you read technical and scientific journals?
Octavia: Not so much journals, unless you want to call *Scientific American* and *Discover* journals. I was just looking at Richard Rhodes's book *Deadly Feast,* which is a scary enough book, really fascinating. I was fascinated by preons back when I first read about them in *Scientific American* a couple of years ago . . .

Mike: You were fascinated by what?
Octavia: The protein that causes Mad Cow Disease and several other dementias. The book is basically about the kind of behavior that's led to what was eventually called Mad Cow Disease—the kind of warnings we had ahead of time, that we paid no attention to. And the kind of thing we're liable to wind up doing to ourselves if we don't pay more attention to what we're doing now.

Before that, I was very much fascinated by Laurie Garrett's book, *A Coming Plague,* which deals with a lot of the public health problems we've already had, and the ones we're storing up for ourselves in the future. And I can remember picking up *Medical Detectives* by Burton Roche. But I didn't pick these books up because I thought, "Gee, I better keep up." They already were talking about subjects that fascinated me. I like to just go in the library and graze.

Mike: In writing your books, you don't just have a story to tell, characters to develop, and an environment to describe. Ideas seem very important, as well, to be developed.

Octavia: That's the nice thing about science fiction, really. Back when I was a kid and began reading it, it was called the literature of ideas. And I think it still qualifies as that, as long as you recognize that anything can be bad, just as anything can be good. You can have video game science fiction on the screen, in movies, and you can also have science fiction that makes you think. I prefer the second kind.

Mike: Your ideas tend to be big, and I imagine that's why you've written books in series.

Octavia: Also, there is the weakness that some of us have as writers, which I don't think many of us talk about: once you've gone through the trouble of creating a universe, you want to play in it for a while. And it's actually fun. I've had people say, "Oh, you just wrote that trilogy for money." I'm not sure I'm the kind of writer who could just write a novel for money. An article, maybe, but not a novel. For me, a novel is too big and too personal.

Mike: As a writer, even when you start to sell your work, it always seems to be feast or famine—and usually much more famine.

Octavia: What I learned to do when I began to do novels, was to pay myself a salary. When you get a nice advance—well, there's nice and Nice—you put that away and you pay yourself a salary. Because otherwise it's going to disappear and you're going to look around and say, "What do I do now?"

Mike: And I can't take these things back that I don't really need.

Octavia: Well, back before I got anything like a novel advance, I wound up pawning several of my possessions and never being able to claim them. So you learn from things like that once you do start to get some money.

I was lucky, I had an extra typewriter. And any time I got really low on food, I would go and pawn that. It didn't really work, but I could fix it so that it worked for a test, and I could get some money on it. And I never stuck anybody with it. It was the one thing I would get back. It was finally stolen, but it was just a period of my life that I had to go through.

Mike: I've been through times where I've had to sell pretty much everything.

Octavia: Um-hm. I had a nice accordion that had to go. My mother got it for me when I was a kid. I mean, you'd think the words "nice" and "accordion" wouldn't really fit together, but it was a nice accordion. So that was back then, and once you've been through that, you really want to take every precaution not to have that kind of thing happen to you again.

Mike: In the introduction to the story "Bloodchild," I loved reading how you'd always intended to write "a pregnant man story."
Octavia: Sometimes the best work comes from the collision of two completely unrelated ideas. There was the pregnant man idea, and then there was the insect phobia. And the way that I had to write out my fear, to lessen it.

Mike: Now, for people who aren't aware of that story, you're talking about the fear of . . .
Octavia: The fear of certain slimy invertebrates.

Mike: And what is it that they do?
Octavia: Well, in this particular case, it was the botfly. It lays its eggs under the skin and you carry around a little pet for a while, a little maggot that's lunching on you, and growing.

Mike: The idea, of course, is that it's much worse to do what would seem to make perfect sense—get rid of it immediately?
Octavia: Where I was, in the Amazon rain forest, you couldn't. Because you would inevitably get an infection that would be much worse than just having a little maggot under your skin. We were told that if we got them, we should leave them there and either go to the doctor and have them removed when we got home or just let them grow up and fly away.

Mike: That's a horrible idea.
Octavia: I didn't get one, but I understand that toward the end they can be rather painful in their eating.

Mike: One would certainly think so. But you're still able to make that such a sympathetic story.
Octavia: A love story sort of has to be because it is a love story. And for me, making it a love story, as opposed to turning it into *Alien*, was one way of lessening the impact of what I found so horrifying—the idea of being a kind of mother to these little maggots. I was glad to be able to do the afterword to that story because I wanted to point out that A) it wasn't a story about slavery, and B) that it was a story about paying the rent. Too many writers have written about going to other planets and star systems in exactly the same way they would write about going from England to America, or from England to Africa.

Mike: Or be even slightly like travel as we've known it until now.

Octavia: Yes, it's going to be a whole other order of immigration, if we ever get to that point. There won't be the Navy sailing across the sea to protect you, or the cavalry coming over the hill, or any such nonsense. I doubt very much that it will be anything like what I've written, of course. We're going to have to make some kind of accommodation, and it will probably be something that we've never done before. That's one of the reasons I began writing *The Parable of the Sower*, because I began with the Gaia hypothesis. I don't even know if you want to hear this . . .

Mike: Oh, of course I do.

Octavia: I got very interested in the Gaia hypothesis and what it would mean to us if we became immigrants to other worlds in other solar systems. I wondered what it would mean if we really were part of an earth organism in some literal way. You know, what sort of problems we would have—rejection problems, call them.

I wanted to deal with that, and to have my characters have a good reason to go into interstellar space. Because it's unrewarding, it's uncertain. It's definitely unprofitable and extraordinarily costly, if we ever do it. I chose religion because religion can make us do all sorts of things that are otherwise unprofitable and extraordinary.

Mike: And that was their reason to leave?

Octavia: Yes, my characters would go because of their religion and would experience this kind of possible rejection. They would land on another world, and the other world would have a kind of an antibiotic reaction against them. I wanted to work with the kinds of accommodations people would have to make, not necessarily with other people, but with the planet itself, if it's a living planet. If it wasn't a living planet, they wouldn't have a chance of surviving there, not without support. I'm interested in the accommodations they would have to make that would not involve shooting anybody, or getting shot. I guess I'm reacting to the video game aspect of space opera that's so popular right now.

Mike: And you connect that kind of work to colonialist attitudes.

Octavia: It's fascinating to think about, and I don't think we've thought enough about it. It startled me, when I began going to science fiction conventions, that a lot of people hadn't really thought about it. They really did tend to think of going to other worlds or meeting aliens as though they were meeting other humans. I don't think we will meet other intelligences, frankly. But if we did, the differences would be so extreme. We don't have a clue.

Mike: In your Xenogenesis series the reproduction process is so strange.

Octavia: When I was a kid, I used to read science fiction in which authors would casually remark, "This species has twenty-seven different sexes and every single one of them is absolutely essential for reproduction." And then they would go on and talk about something else. I always wanted to know what in the heck they did!

Mike: Sex can seem like such an alien thing—even between two humans.

Octavia: Well, if you get into a little natural history and biology, it can seem even more alien. And fascinating. The idea, for instance, that some sea creatures have such an extreme sexual dimorphism—size difference—that the male is an appendage on the female. They make the attachment when they're very young, and the female keeps growing and the male doesn't. Or the way viruses reproduce. I mean, there are all sorts of fascinating possibilities that already exist and that we know about.

Mike: Do you see disease as a potentially positive agent?

Octavia: I understand why we've gone about things as we have, in fighting disease, because disease appears to be fighting us. You don't stop and think how beautiful that tiger is if it's got you by the arm. But there are so many things we could be doing with micro-organisms, because it isn't absolutely essential that they be disease organisms. We've already proved it to some degree with the use of viruses to alter genetics. It hasn't worked very well, but we're learning. Things like monoclonal antibodies.

I think we'll learn, if we survive, to partner them more than to fight them. That's really going to be our only chance, because in fighting them, all we've really done is cull them and make them stronger. And preons are even more fascinating. Here you have something with no genetic material, and it's a protein. And how does it hurt? It does harm by way of its shape. It communicates that shape to other proteins of its kind in the body. So you wind up with something that is communicable and something that, in a way, can be transmissible through the generations.

Mike: And also, like the alien organism in *Clay's Ark*, aren't preons transmissible inter-species?

Octavia: Yes, and good point. Preons are very good at jumping from species to species. Of course, we've helped them a lot, and we still are. It's very important when something like preons or AIDS comes up, to recognize not just the science of the situation, but the politics, and the economics. Sometimes in science fiction we don't pay enough attention to the economics and the politics and the religion because we are fascinated by the science.

Mike: In your work there seems to be a general interest in what it might be like to be post-human. Do you think much about what the next change will be, after being human?

Octavia: History gives us the only other worlds we know of that are definitely populated, and by creatures almost like us. And I have a feeling that we're not all that like the people who came before us. We're like them, but we're not like them. So in a way, if you want to know what we're likely to become, probably the best thing to do is look back and see what we've been. It doesn't mean that we're going to travel a straight line. I mean, some of the changes are definitely social. But for instance, if we spend a lot of time making it possible for some particular kind of disability to be transmissable and not to be lethal, then later on that disability could spread through the community and become something more than either. I don't know if that's making sense, but . . . it can become something necessary.

Mike: Or it could be something . . .
Octavia: That can also wipe us out, but you never know.

Mike: If you don't mind, as one last question. You've described yourself as being comfortably asocial. How so?
Octavia: I like spending most of my time alone. I enjoy people best if I can be alone much of the time. I used to worry about it because my family worried about it. And I finally realized: This is the way I am. That's that. We all have some weirdness, and this is mine.

Octavia Butler and Samuel R. Delany

MIT Cultural Studies Project/1998

From MIT Cultural Studies Project Website, http://web.mit.edu/m-i-t/science_ fiction/transcripts/butler/_delany index.html (site accessed in 2006) © MIT Cultural Studies Project. Reprinted with permission of MIT Cultural Studies Project.

The Value of Literacy

Henry Jenkins: This is a question partially directed toward Octavia because it picks up on some of the stuff you were just talking about. I was just re-reading *Kindred* over the weekend, and I was really moved again by the issue of literacy—the slaves' hunger for education, for the ability to read and write and the risk that's involved in that context of teaching literacy. And it reminded me of two other moments in your writing—one of which you referenced, the "Speech Sounds," the loss of literacy, the loss of language altogether, and the dystopian world that's created there.

And the other is a moment in *Dawn* when Lilith demands writing implements, demands books, and is told, "Well we can fix your mind so that you don't need any of that stuff. You can simply remember things and we can modify you." And she seemed to think that something fundamental to her humanity would be lost at the moment in which her mind is modified so that she no longer needs the ability to read and write. And I thought that those three moments juxtaposed together posed some powerful questions about how important the issue of literacy is in your writing and the way in which you think about the world. And I wondered if you might want to build on that a little bit more.

Octavia Butler: Hmmm. It's obviously very important to me, and because I come from the kind of family I come from, I don't think it could be otherwise. My mother was taken out of school after about three years of education and put to work. She didn't get to go to school until she was about eight years old and, unfortunately, they put her in the third grade. So you can imagine what kind of education she had; she was very fortunate to be able to read and write at all. She focused so strongly on the need to be able to read and write and to get along in the world in ways that she wasn't really able to do.

I think literacy was probably a lot more popular when it was the forbidden fruit. That's a terrible thing to say, but I'm afraid it may be true. Any forbidden fruit is desirable. When I was a kid, there were so many older people pushing me that I wouldn't have dared to drop out of school; at least, not before I got out of high-school. I remember talking to a younger guy—he was about ten years younger than I was—and I said something like, "How could we possibly have done anything but go on to school and try to make something of ourselves with all those people pushing us." And he said, "What people?"

I don't know. I don't know how well this answers your question but what I'm seeing, especially in the black community, is that there isn't that hard push as much as there used to be, and that's frightening. That scares me.

Samuel Delany: I don't know whether there's anything more important, really, when all is said and done. My grandfather was born a slave; he was a slave in Georgia. And our emancipation came when he was seven years old. Quite illegally, he had been taught to read and write before emancipation, so that when he was seven years old, he already knew how to read. And after emancipation, there wasn't time to learn how to read; he couldn't have learned afterwards because when his family was on its own, there simply wasn't the time to get that sort of education.

He ended up as the vice-chancellor of a black college, and the whole purpose of this college was to teach other blacks to read and write, and also teach them many, many other things as well. It was a very practical, hands-on education. It was a college, but there were cooking classes; there were lots of classes in how to lead your life. And so my family has always been involved with that from the very, very beginning. But, dare one say, if his owners had not decided that they were going to let this kid learn how to read beforehand, my family and my family history would have been very, very different.

The reason he was the vice-chancellor is because the chancellor had to be white for legal reasons because there were papers that had to be signed and what have you, and black signatures were not valid on these papers. But in the same way that he would not have been the vice-chancellor of a black college, I wouldn't be a college professor today, I don't think.

There isn't any problem that I can think of in the United States that doesn't finally go back to education because education is how you learn how to solve the problems, even if we haven't solved them now. And I think black, white, gray, or grisly, I think education is really our most important problem right now.

The Future of Literacy

Butler: I've wondered, and this may be the audience to put this question to, what the likelihood is of a future in which reading is no longer necessary for the majority of the people. I don't much like the look of that future, but I wonder if when computers, for instance, can be addressed verbally, can be spoken to, whether it will still be necessary for people to be able to read and write. Do you have any thoughts on that?

Burstein: Well one of the things that I was recently reading was an essay by Spider Robinson which points out that reading is actually difficult. He was walking along the street in his hometown, and I think it was in Vancouver, where he saw that somebody had written on a piece of sidewalk and immortalized in stone a nice big heart with the names "Tood and Janey forever." He couldn't believe that anybody in this society would go to the lengths of naming their son "Tood." So his only conclusion was that young Todd didn't know how to spell his own name, and what he found to be worse was that this is somebody who is old enough to have the hots for Janey and possibly produce progeny and yet he cannot spell his own name.

And in this essay, Robinson points out that television and radio in some ways is the most natural way for us to receive information because there's less decoding that has to go on. Perhaps, Samuel Delany can talk more about that. There's less decoding of the symbols. The information is presented there right for you, whereas when you're reading, you actually have to learn to decode the symbols before you get a full-flavored understanding of the story. And although it can spark our imaginations more, once it becomes as simple as it is now to have the information presented visually and orally, he wonders what's going to happen to reading. You thought the World-Wide Web was slow because it was just a problem of computers; it's our way to make sure people keep reading the stuff rather than just looking at the pictures.

Michael McAfee: To sort of answer your question, the first thought that comes to my mind is: Reading and writing itself will be necessary because all our languages developed somehow from the need to put down a permanent symbol for someone who might come along later and have to look at it. Whether it's standardized English or not is another question, depending on our desire to communicate with people outside a certain area. If all of a sudden, I decided that "Oh, I only need to talk to about fifty people, and we all come up with our own little slang terms, or even our own little ways of jotting them down, there's really no need for me to have to do standardized English." So that might be a way of a communications breakdown in the future, rather than the erasing writing and reading altogether.

Craig McDonough: I'd like to directly address Octavia's question. As a perceived need for literacy drops, what we may see is a growing despotism of those who can read, who can control the information flow. And getting back to the fragmentation, the balkanization of language through slang may become a way that some people would possibly use to control segments of the society—the same way that in the past, people think and react to their neighbors differently on the basis of religion, color, or small shifts in language. You see it in very insular areas. There are places where you can still go today and you can live there for forty years and you're still one of their flatlanders rather than being somebody who has lived there.

Butler: It sounds like history swinging around to an educated priesthood again. It's odd. We tend to think whatever we have is going to be lasting forever. Whatever we knew when we were able to learn what our society was made up of will last forever, and then it doesn't. And we wind up with something very strange.

Alan Wexelblat: I'm a graduate student at the Media Lab here. To answer Octavia's original question, I think it's important, first of all, that we remember that literacy is a relatively new invention. It's only been around a couple of thousand years, and at its arrival it was decried as leading to the downfall of the training of men's, of course, men's minds.

And the second thing is that I think it's important that we not confuse literacy with education. I agree with the point that you made about the importance of education, and I do see a future coming in which literacy will not be the ultimate prerequisite for education as it is in our society today. I think new technologies will allow that shift in the expected and necessary skills for participating in our culture. I suggest to you a book by Neil Stevenson called, *The Diamond Age*, which is essentially a book about how to educate children.

One of the things he posits is that there are several parallel languages. There's a sort of written textual language, but there's also a sort of commonly used pictorial language which, for example, enables people who can't read words to actually operate appliances. That is, they look at the pictorial symbols and they figure out how to operate the food processor or whatever it is, based on the pictorial symbols.

In particular, a lot of the work within the Media Lab has been oriented towards trying to figure out how to teach children to learn through a philosophy called, "constructionism," that Seymour Papert, one of the professors there, pioneered. In it he basically argues that learning happens through building, not by reading about things or listening to things, or even watching things, but rather by being involved in the construction and building of artifacts. I would like to see a world happen very soon in which that philosophy was more widely accepted, in which there were not just microscopes for every student but also full lab science kits, and kids could actually build little science projects and try out experiments and do things and build things. I think that learning would happen a lot better in those environments and that literacy, or lack of literacy, would be a lot less of a problem, if that were to happen.

Delany: The point is, of course, that literacy has not been around, as you say, that long. We could lose it in another seventy-five years, and the world would continue. We survived the first three and a half million years without being able to do it; if we're going to be around for a million or so more, maybe we'll survive that without it, too.

Nevertheless, I think literacy does do certain things. It has certain good things that should be encouraged. I'm not a believer in the replaceability of one medium by another. I think the media are irreplaceable, and it's very easy to fall into the argument that, "Ah, literacy is dying before television and movies and what have you." And while that, indeed, may be the case, I still think television and movies are really good things, and really interesting things, and that fascinating things go on there. But I also think fascinating things go on in texts, and I think we'd lose something if we lost our textual facility.

Butler: I agree with you, we would go on, but this is rather like a discussion that I can recall having on a science-fiction panel. Someone was saying about global-warming, "Well, the temperatures have been different before, and things have changed before." And I said, "Well, you're absolutely right, of course, but there weren't nearly so many of us, and we hadn't organized our society around certain things being so, that we grow this crop in this area and that we feed this many million people with it." That kind of thing.

I think that losing literacy would change us drastically, change the kind of society that we have, and I think we would develop a kind of literate priesthood, whether they were a priesthood of God or of something else. They would be the people who knew the secrets, and I don't really see that as a very nice world to live in.

Delany: But we could also develop an illiterate priesthood, you know.

Phil: I'm in the computer entertainment industry. In the computer entertainment industry, literacy has vanished. Whereas in 1984 about one third of the best-selling game programs were text-based games, by 1986, there were none—zero—on the market. And, in fact, I've just read a couple of interviews with John Romero and Ken Williams where they're asking, "How can we get the rest of the text out of the games. How can we get rid of these text-bubbles?" And there are still people writing text-games, but it's sort of goes on by samizdat; it's underground. And the thing is that the people playing these games are very literate; they're not unable to read. They don't want to read . . .

Delany: . . . while they're playing games.

Phil: No, the term "game" is perhaps misleading. You can write fiction, you can present many other forms of artistic experience, but what they want to experience are things that are best presented graphically. For instance, I read an interview with John Romero who is the person who designed "Quake," and "Doom," to us, graphical violence games that introduced this concept of running around and killing everything you see and watching its blood spurt. And he commented how he was so addicted to video games that once he was playing an asteroids game and his father came and bashed his head against the machine and took him home and beat him up for playing the games. And I thought, "This is interesting. This is the kind of thing that he wants to do and the kind of game he wants to make."

And so I think the problem is not literacy so much as why our society produces people who don't want to read and don't want that type of experience.

Butler: There is the quotation—I don't recall who said it—"There's not that much difference between a person who doesn't read and the person who can't read."

I wanted to draw a comparison. When I was a kid, I lived on comics. My mother actually went into my room one night or one day when I wasn't home and ripped all my comic books in half. (GROANS) A familiar experience, I suspect, for anybody growing up when I was because they were supposed to rot your mind. When I was reading comics, comics had a lot more language, a lot more words, and a lot more story. It wasn't just Jack Kirbyesque people swatting other people and standing with their legs four feet apart. And gradually, it became just that, so that there were fewer and fewer and fewer words, less and less story, and a lot more people beating each other up or wiping each other out.

And I find it interesting that computer games are going this way. I find this drift toward simplicity, no matter what the genre or venue, scary, frankly.

Reading Hypertext

Burstein: I have a quick question primarily for Samuel Delany. In your other role besides writing science fiction, you're also a professor of literature at UMass-Amherst, and I know that you do write a lot of essays analyzing texts. I've read some of your work in the *New York Review of Science Fiction*, for example. I wonder if you have any comments you might make about the concept of hypertext. A few years ago, people were talking about hypertext as this whole major new thing, the end of the "book." For example, if you're reading something and you don't know a word, you can click on it to get to the definition. Or if you're reading about, let's say, Clinton and Monica Lewinsky, you can click on names and find out more information. You have people who actually were constructing "hypertext novels," where you have a book that is not read linearly and where a different path would give you a different reading experience. I was wondering if you had any opinions on this.

Delany: Some of them are very interesting. Some of the Michael Joyce work is very interesting. One lists the names of people who've done interesting things— Katherine Kramer.

The one thing, however, I think that does need to be pointed out to people when they're talking about interactive art and the notion of something being interactive. The amount of energy that you spend, for instance, to get yourself together to go to a gallery and walk around the gallery from picture to picture is much more than the amount of energy that you spend to click from image to image on a computer screen. So that the energy that you put out to be interactive with classical texts—they are much more interactive—is greater because you have to do things to get to them that involve you in a much larger way than the way you interact with something on a computer screen.

All texts, in a sense, are hypertext. You come to a word you don't understand, so you look it up in the dictionary. You read a passage and you stop and you think about another book; you may even put it down and go get another book off your bookshelf and read something about something else. Texts are not linear. Texts are multiple and for anybody who really reads and enjoys reading, it is an interactive process.

What hypertext and the interactive material do is make that a much less energy-intensive process; as such, on the absolute scale, they are less interactive than the ones we've got now because in order to interact with the ones you've got now, you have to put out more energy. Now I think something is gained by having the interactivity require less energy. It becomes a medium in itself that's interestingly exploitable.

But not only do you limit the amount of interactivity, you also limit the places you can go. So the interactive text is not an expansion of what we've got now; it's a delimitation of what we've got now. If you read, as I was doing a couple of days ago, Walter Pater's *Plato and Platonism*, I stop every two pages or less and have to go read a section from Heidegger or read a section by Derrida where he's talking about Plato. "Is that where this idea came from? Oh! Why is he using this word 'parousia'? Didn't I see this word?"

Just bear in mind that the interactivity in the new different interactive art is less energy-intensive and there are less places that you go within it. It's fascinating, and it's lots of fun, but it's not more interactive than what we had before; it's less interactive.

Butler: I don't have access to this kind of thing on computer but, oddly enough, what you're talking about sounds very much like the way I start looking for ideas when I'm not working on anything. Or when I'm just letting myself drift, relax.

I generally have four or five books open around the house—I live alone; I can do this—and they are not books on the same subject. They don't relate to each other in any particular way, and the ideas they present bounce off one another. And I like this effect. I also listen to audio-books, and I'll go out for my morning walk with tapes from two very different audio-books, and let those ideas bounce off each other, simmer, reproduce in some odd way, so that I come up with ideas that I might not have come up with if I had simply stuck to one book until I was done with it and then gone and picked up another.

So, I guess, in that way, I'm using a kind of primitive hypertext.

Burstein: I find interesting what you say that hypertext is actually limiting. I don't think I've actually run across that opinion before because everybody talks about hypertext being expansive and exploratory. But I think I see your distinction.

Delany: Traditional reading is more interactive in terms of requiring more energy to interact, and there are more possibilities for interaction. I don't know if any of you remember that old, ancient technology called, "the card catalogue." (LAUGHTER/APPLAUSE) I am so happy with the libraries' being on-line. They're great, but we do lose something when we lose the card catalogue because there's a kind of serendipity; there's a kind of propinquity that simply comes from the fact that you stumble over another title of another book and you say, "Oh, that's interesting" because I'm looking up something else.

It's the same thing with the physical books on the shelves. Anybody who does actual research in a library knows that you look on this shelf and then you turn around and you look on this thing, it's not related alphabetically; it's not related subject-wise; it just happens to be the book you need. And if you don't have the physical propinquity of the way the books are arranged, you're going to miss out on this opportunity, and this limits the kinds of research gems that can come up.

I'm not saying we should go back to card catalogues, but I'm just saying, again, the media are not replaceable. If you do replace one medium by another medium, you're going to lose something, and, frequently, this is going to be something that's going to be missed.

The Age of Misinformation

Vicka Khoury: I'm actually a neuro-linguist at the University of Washington. I'm just working in Boston these days. I wanted to respond to the literacy issue in general I think there's something implicit in what you were saying before that equates literacy and things that you read with truth and says that things that you read are or ought to be truer than things that you hear. And while I agree with the irreplaceability of any of the media and with the importance of literacy and the importance of access to information in any medium, I also think that it's as possible to lie in texts as it is to lie verbally.

Butler: I was not, by the way, talking about print-truth being more true than spoken truth. Not at all. One could spend enormous amounts of energy, print, computer time, broadcast time, etc. on garbage. I wouldn't recommend that anybody take something to be true simply because it was written down. As a matter of fact, this is an argument I used to have with people quite a bit. Something was written or on TV, so it must be true. No, the importance of literacy is that you can look around and find out more about what is true, as opposed to being confined to what somebody's willing to tell you.

Delany: We talk about this being the age of information, but this is not the age of information. This is the age of misinformation. And the thing that we have to remember is that misinformation tends to be simpler and more stable than information, kind of like an intellectual Parkinson's law where bad money drives out good. Misinformation tends to drive out information because of the relative simplicity and the stability of misinformation.

One of the things that literacy and texts have going for them is that it stabilizes the argument so that you can look at it long enough to actually do a little analysis of it. A purely verbal interchange about information tends to be a little bit more slippery and harder to analyze because all you end up analyzing is the comparatively simple elements which tend to be the things that are misinformed.

Also what is information in one context becomes misinformation in another context. What the popularizer of science writes in his or her popularized science book is information but if it was given to the specialist, then it becomes wild misinformation. It depends on the context. That is why I think really this is the age of misinformation, par excellence.

Butler: Or it's the age of being snowed with so much stuff that we can't tell the difference.

Who Controls the Web?

Melissa: Basically, I wanted to ask about this idea of literacy on the Web and especially, more specifically, children's education through experience with the Web. I've had this argument before with people, that they feel that you can just put somebody in front of a computer and they'll have access to the Web, and everything will be wonderful. But it's a question of what's there for them to have access to. A lot of people take it for granted that everything that's in the real world, scanning the bookshelves, what not, will eventually find its way into the Web, and eventually find its way to all the children's minds, and we'll live in a happy, joyful place.

But there is a real danger that a certain group will have control of what actually goes onto the Web. As far as science fiction goes, there's a group on the Web now that likes science fiction, so that gets on the Web a lot, but as access widens to the larger population, different things come on. I wondered if you thought that the ideals of freedom through science would get drowned out in the noise.

Delany: Well, I don't think it's any accident that sex plays the part on the Web that it does. And I think that that's fundamentally very healthy because I think desire is a big problem in the human condition.

When new media come along, the first thing they want to deal with is desire, and it's usually the sign that something good is going on rather than something bad is going on.

Butler: What do you think of the efforts at censorship?

Delany: And then you get the efforts of censorship, and I'm not a big fan of censorship, to put it mildly. (LAUGHTER)

Race, Cyberspace and Equality

Teresa: Mr. Delany, I was re-reading your book, *Triton*, and that's always fascinated me. One of the things I noticed was that everything was equal. There was absolutely no distinction as far as race, gender, or what have you, but then, at the same time, everything about a person could be changed; they could change their physical appearance, even their height, and even their skin color or their sex. And I guess my question for you is: Was that actually necessary for that to come about for them to be able to achieve equality?

Delany: First of all, I don't know whether they're really equal. The lines of inequality don't run along the usual crevices. They don't run between genders; they don't run between races. They run in other places, and certainly all the material in the appendices explains how, for instance, one of the places where inequality does run is between the people who have been there for a while and the people who are new to the place.

Triton is a playful attempt to just see what it would look like if things were different, and if things worked in a different way from the way they actually do, and if certain things were more flexible. That's why it's not a utopia; it's a heterotopia. It's not the best of all possible worlds by any means.

Jenkins: One of the conferences we're planning in the future for the Media in Transition series is an event focused around race and cyberspace and the issue of cyberspace poses some parallels to the situation you described. The famous *New Yorker* cartoon that promised, "In cyberspace, nobody knows you're a dog," implies, of course, that you construct your on-line identity or that you give only what information is necessary. In many ways, this parallels the fluidity of identity which science fiction writers imagine in their stories. So one of the questions is: What happens to race in cyberspace? Is it a good thing or a bad thing that people can choose to have a race or make their race disappear when they write in cyberspace? And what are some of the implications of that?

Butler: Well, OK, I'm not on-line—I've got to say that upfront—but it seems to me, we've got this window where we can do that kind of thing and play that way and be whoever we choose to be in cyberspace. But soon, that window will close. With respect to showing people's pictures, at first it will be, "Well, if you want to," and then it will be expected, you know; otherwise, some might wonder, "What are you hiding?" I don't know how it'll work, but I'm wondering if by our pictures' being shown, or videos of us as we are speaking, that we lose the window.

Delany: The problem, of course, is not race, itself. It is all those forces that make certain white people think that somebody black might want to hide their race or that makes people who are black like me say, "That's the last thing in the world I would hide." And it's those forces, per se, that are the problem. And it's the interplay of those forces that creates the problems, and that's a set of material socioeconomic forces that I don't think really go away when you sit in front of a computer.

Science Fiction and the Black Community

Jorge Enteronas: I study literature here at MIT, and I had two quick comments or questions. First, to Mr. Delany. As a black, gay man, I really like to thank you for helping to open up a space for us to write and express ourselves. Literacy has been really important in the African-American tradition—written literacy, especially, writing. *The Talking Book* and slave narratives, equality through literacy in the Harlem Renaissance, the search for a black aesthetic in the '60s. And I was just kind of wondering what you felt your place, as science fiction writers, was within the African-American literary tradition.

Delany: Well, one's own place is something that other people have to tell you. (LAUGHTER/APPLAUSE) You sound kind of like a fool saying, "Well, my place in the tradition is. . . ." because it is something that other people assign to you. So, in a way, my place is whatever place you are kind and generous enough to give me.

Butler: What you said about "place" is probably true in one sense. In another sense, I think my place is wherever I happen to be standing. I don't write just one kind of work, and I used to get criticized for writing science fiction at all back in the community because the idea was "You should be doing something more relevant," which was a big word when I was in college. And I was not behaving properly; I was not contributing. And if that didn't stop me, I don't think worrying about my place now would. (LAUGHTER)

Burstein: Just for your information, if you want to know their place in the science-fiction community, speaking on behalf of the entire science-fiction writing community, I will say that both Samuel Delany and Octavia Butler are very well-respected for what they've been able to do with our genre. The fact that they've been able to transcend it in some ways and yet have both remained extremely loyal to it is something that, at least, pleases every science-fiction writer whom I've ever come across. People in the science fiction field sometimes tend to think we are in our own little ghetto, and the fact that you have literary writers of such caliber who are willing to identify themselves as being science fiction writers is very gratifying. It helps to spread the idea that stories of this sort do not have to just be thought of as, well, like that movie that Octavia was describing before.

Jenkins: Another way to circle around this question is to say, "Are there opportunities which science fiction grants authors for debating issues of identity that more realistic or melodramatic or other forms of narrative don't offer, particularly around issues of race?"

Butler: To me, the attraction of science fiction is just the freedom, that there isn't anything I can't do in it. There isn't any issue that I can't address. I don't know that I can address things better because I'm writing science fiction; it's just that I can address more things.

Delany: I think anything that presents itself as some kind of social debate becomes the kind of thing that science fiction is set up to address. Science fiction has a self-image as an intellectual enterprise and because of that, it welcomes information in a way that I would say that the literary genres tend to be wary of, such as vast amounts of data, vast amounts of information, big debates over abstract questions, like "Well, we don't want it to be propaganda, do we? It's got to be art." (LAUGHTER)

I think science fiction doesn't have the same fear of data that the literary genres have sort of grown up with. This probably has both good and bad sides. The upside is that we rush in blindly where the angels are afraid to go. So often when there are social questions, you'll find them first reflected and talked about in science fiction. I think of the history of feminism. I don't think anybody could really talk about the history of feminism without talking about all the ways in which science fiction has some of the earliest and the most powerful examples of people thinking about this situation. So it welcomes a certain kind of social debate that the literary genres have to wait around until it's all settled before they will go and take it on.

The Ghettoization of Science Fiction

Nick Pappadakis: I'm at the Artificial Intelligence Lab. Very briefly, the ghettoization of science fiction, it seems to me, is due to this anti-intellectual trend that our society has had for many, many years and that, maybe, finally is beginning to abate.

Delany: I don't think the reason science fiction is not accepted is due to just anti-intellectualism. Science fiction is not accepted because it is primarily seen as a working-class kind of art. It's a working-class practice, and it is given the kind of short shrift that working-class practices of art are traditionally given. Movies started out the same way but because their fantasies appeal across class-lines—everybody wants to be rich and beautiful—they somehow managed to escape the limits of being just a working-class art.

Butler: Are you sure it isn't because it's also seen as something terribly juvenile?

Delany: Well, it's seen as juvenile because it's working-class art. (LAUGHTER)

Butler: Well, I mean, literally juvenile. I was at a New Mexico writer's group speaking to them a few years ago, and they told me that a very well-known mystery writer had been there the year before, and one of the women had told him that she wanted to write science fiction. And he said, "Why? Nobody over fourteen will ever read it?"

Delany: And yet, *Alice in Wonderland* is also a juvenile book. It's also for children, and it still makes its way into the literary canon. And the parables in Genesis from the J-writer, according to Harold Bloom, are children's teaching tales, and do we have any other more sacred literature?

Anna Azamson: It seems to me that the point of education is to teach people to think abstractly and especially with science fiction, it seems that you can do so much of that. Could you talk a little bit about how you view science fiction in dealing with problems abstractly?

Delany: May I leap into this? I would actually argue with your initial premise. The point of thinking abstractly is so that you can think concretely. Abstract thinking is a tool to help your concrete thinking, so that the final point of education, I think, is to think concretely, not abstractly. The abstraction is simply a tool to facilitate the concrete thinking.

And, again, if you have the education, then the dangers are less dangerous. If kids are educated properly, I think, then you don't really have to worry about what's on the Internet or what's on anything because they'll know how to deal with it. There is a whole level of the country that believes that the way you keep children safe from sex, as though it is something that they need to be kept safe from, is that you don't let them know that it exists. You don't talk about it, and you don't explore it.

Although I am a black, gay man, I also have a wonderful twenty-four-year old daughter, and there was never any censorship in our house. Some bizarre movie would come along and she'd want to see it, so we'd all go see it. And what we did is we talked about it if it had something sexual in it she didn't understand. And she's a very happy twenty-four-year old at this point, and she hasn't self-destructed. And I don't see her about to do that at any time in the near future. Education is the best way that you deal with all these things that everybody thinks of as so dangerous. Educate people and they're not dangerous anymore if people know how to handle them, and what to do with them.

Butler: I'm not sure how to bring this in. It goes back to the non-literate video games we were talking about earlier. I hit little periods during my writing when I'm overwhelmed by my own writing and by my own problems and whatever and I take a week or so when I read novels, preferably nice trashy ones, and I listen to music. And I wind up generating quite a few ideas doing that; that's my excuse. I don't do it very often, but I do do it.

I went to the grocery store looking for a good novel to read—well, I said "trashy," you know—and what I found was the novel as confession story and the novel as video game where the big deal was to kill the bad guy. And I think that maybe the need for a little abstraction is not that bad a thing, really, when you consider this degree of literal-mindedness.

I don't like it when people talk about my work in terms of good guys and bad guys—this kind of simplicity—because it happens often and I never write that way. I've never written a novel about the good folks and the bad folks. I've always written novels about where all the characters have something to say for their position. And even if they cannot avoid a collision, it's not about the good guys winning or losing. So a little abstraction is probably good for us all.

Carla Johnson: I do want to say "thank you" to both of you for writing because when I was growing up, it was one thing that I could count on to see myself reflected in both your work, and that's why I always stayed with science fiction. It's the only place I can see myself, whether if I'm going to be black or if I'm going to look at myself in the different kinds of sexuality that you might have. I prefer short stories but you're the only two that I actually have full science fiction novels of because I can't stay with the hard science fiction. So, thank you. (APPLAUSE)

Speaker: One of the things that intrigues me about both of your work is that it's science fiction, but one of the things that makes me love it so much and come back and read the same stories over and over again is that it's such incredibly powerful fiction that grapples with complexities. And at the risk of over-generalizing, I say that I read nonfiction for information and read fiction for truth. And so I, too, want to affirm and thank you and just express such gratitude for the work that you've given us, for the opportunities to really grapple with those many truths. And especially a note of thanks for *Bloodchild* for we got a little bit of fiction and nonfiction. The question that was raised earlier about where you sit in the African-American literary tradition, I'm happy to say that you sit firmly in that tradition—especially your stories, Ms. Butler, are virtually all about ordinary black women thrust into extraordinary situations and having to deal. So it's inspirational and affirming.

I'm not a science-fiction writer but I am a writer. And I thank you for being such an incredible role-model. (APPLAUSE)

Nebula Award Nominee Octavia Butler Is Expanding the Universe of Science-Fiction Readers

Jane Burkitt/2000

From *Seattle Times* (9 May 2000). © 2000 Seattle Times Company. Reprinted with permission of the Seattle Times Company.

Perhaps it should not be surprising that Seattle—a city whose most famous structure is a flying saucer-topped homage to the future—has become something of a science-fiction hotbed over the years.

It has Clarion West, the renowned science-fiction writer's workshop. It has many noted authors who call this area home, such as Greg Bear and Terry Brooks. And, as of last November, it has Octavia Butler, the celebrated author and nominee this year for science fiction's coveted Nebula Award, to be announced May 20.

Before she settled here, Butler had never lived anywhere other than Southern California. That region has figured prominently in some of her works, including *Parable of the Talents*, the novel that earned her the Nebula nomination. Still, she says, her move to Seattle had been a long time coming.

"I fell in love with this place way back in '76, when I was roaming around the country," she said. Butler, fifty-two, had been drawn to Seattle before that, though—drawn, in fact, since the city built the Space Needle.

"I wanted to come for the (1962) World's Fair, but my mother said something to the effect of, 'Have you lost your mind?'" she recalls. Travel was a luxury Butler could rarely afford until well into her adulthood.

In fact, though she has long been a critical success—having won a Hugo in 1984 for the short story "Speech Sounds," and both a 1985 Hugo and a 1984 Nebula for the novelette "Bloodchild"—it has only been relatively recently that Butler has been able to support herself through writing.

A $295,000 MacArthur Foundation "genius" grant awarded to her in 1995 helped. With that money, she bought her first house, where she lived with and cared for her elderly mother, who has since passed away.

"My mother was the reason I stayed in L.A. as long as I did," she says. After her death, "I decided it was time to fish or cut bait."

The only child born to a poor family, Butler spent much of her youth at the public library in Pasadena.

"I was a very shy kid, and very tall and awkward, and socially even more awkward," she says. "Nowadays, somebody like me would probably go into computers or something."

Certainly, her literary inclinations were not encouraged.

"Nobody really had high expectations for me," she says. The message conveyed to her throughout her youth, by nearly everyone around her, was that women, and black women in particular, needn't aim too high.

"I remember feeling that I would only be able to be a secretary or teacher or nurse. And then social worker was the next thing; I could be a social worker," she says. "They all sounded like levels of hell to me."

But somehow, the grim picture others painted of her future didn't taint her own aspirations.

"I needed to write," she says. "Writing was literally all I had consistently. People came and went. Most things in your life come and go. Then if you have this one thing . . . I used to give up writing like some people would give up smoking."

Butler started writing science fiction/fantasy at age twelve, and at thirteen, she was sending her stories to publishers. "It didn't occur to me that it was not possible. I just didn't have any sense, as one of my friends told me." She studied at Pasadena City College and California State University, Los Angeles, but her most formative writing education came at the celebrated Clarion Science Fiction and Fantasy Writer's Workshop, in 1970. Science fiction has many more prominent female writers than it did thirty years ago, though it is still a man-heavy genre. Successful black science-fiction writers remain a relative rarity; Butler is, to her knowledge, the only black woman who makes a living at it.

This, compounded with the substance of her work—which addresses issues like slavery, sexism, and environmental destruction—gives Butler more crossover appeal than many authors in the typically insular field.

"There are always young women who come up and talk to me about what they should do, which makes me suspect that someday (the science-fiction community) is going to be a lot different," she says, adding that she goes "out of my way to be encouraging to anyone who seems to be serious about writing."

But she consorts less than she once did with established science-fiction writers, including those in the Northwest. "There are quite a few of us, I guess, but I'm not really entrenched enough to know most of them," she says.

This is partly because she no longer needs to go to conventions to network. Also, she is, by her own description, "basically a hermit."

She does travel a great deal for various speaking engagements, but is happiest when she can stick to her routine: waking between 5:30 and 6:30 A.M., taking care of things around the house, and sitting down at her computer to write by 9 A.M.

She's now working on a story about people who choose to immigrate to another world, but find themselves homesick when they arrive. What's her inspiration in describing this new place? The gray winters of the Northwest.

Octavia Butler

Juan Williams/2000

From *Talk of the Nation* (May 8, 2000). © National Public Radio. Permission granted by NPR.

Juan Williams: This is *Talk of the Nation*. I'm Juan Williams. Octavia Butler has unusual credentials for a science fiction writer. She's won a MacArthur Fellowship, the so-called "genius award," and her stories take the science fiction genre into uncharted realms, even for science fiction or, as it's sometimes now called, fantastic realism. Her works focus on power, gender, family, and race. In fact, Butler's real-world skin color makes her a fantastic story. Female science fiction writers are rare. Black female science fiction writers are so rare as to practically be a category of one and that one is Octavia Butler. But, her work stands out for more than she is black. Her writing has won science fiction's top awards—the Nebula, the Hugo, and the Locus. The power of Ms. Butler's work is in her character development. Her characters are often independent women who use their minds and strength but not their sexuality to win the day. Her first work was *Patternmaster*. It tells the story of a world split between a telepathic ruling class and two other groups: the mute humans who serve them and the clayarks, four-legged creatures from outer space. Then, there is her book *Kindred* in which a modern day black woman travels back in time to save a white slave master who is her ancestor. In *Parable of the Sower*, Butler writes about smart pills, drought, and socio-paths taking over Southern California. Her most recent novel continues that story with her heroine Lauren Olamina, a black woman who must make a future in that terrible landscape. It's called *Parable of the Talents*. Octavia Butler has made a future for a shy, awkward child, herself. She joins me. Octavia Butler, welcome to *Talk of the Nation*.
Octavia Butler: Thank you.

Williams: Ms. Butler, let's begin by asking about that your latest book. The title is *Parable of the Talents*. Is that right?
Butler: That's right. That's right.

Williams: And what is that a reference to?

Butler: Well, it's a reference to the biblical parable—which is really one of the rougher biblical parables—about the fact that we had better, if we are going to have any success at all as Christians or as people, use what talents we have, invest them and make the best of them.

Williams: How does that then play out in the story? What is the story?

Butler: This is the second half of a kind of fictional biography. I have wanted for a long time to write the fictional biography of someone who, after death, might be thought of as a kind of god. And, it would have to be after death because this woman is imperfect enough for no one to make that mistake while she's living. But I wanted her to be a person who begins a new belief system, a new religion, and who does it in response to the times in which she is born, the difficulties and the fact that people are very much without hope—the poor people are anyway— during her lifetime, and what she comes up with is this belief system that she believes will put them on a path to something better.

Williams: Well, then I guess we have to go back and tell the listeners a little bit about the previous book, *Parable of the Sorrows*. Now what was that title about?

Butler: Parable of the Sower.

Williams: Sower.

Butler: Yes.

Williams: What was that title referring to?

Butler: Another biblical parable. The "Parable of the Sower" is the parable of a man who goes out to sow some seed, to plant some seed, and some of it falls onto the rocks and doesn't grow and some of it falls among the weeds and is choked by the weeds and the birds eat some of it, and the rest grows and multiplies a hundredfold, or a thousandfold and that is what my character and her few friends manage to do in a sense. They lose absolutely everything. They very nearly lose their lives, and then they begin to put their lives back together again. And because my character has this belief system, and because she seems to be going somewhere when all the rest of them aren't quite sure where they should go or how they should get there, she is leading them. This doesn't mean that she knows a lot more than they do; it just means that what she does know she believes in.

Williams: Well, you know what strikes me here is that you have your character living in a world where there's smart pills, where—and, in fact, I think, you know, we're on the verge of having smart pills in America today—but you have her living in a world . . .

Butler: That's a little frightening, isn't it?

Williams: But it's true.
Butler: Yeah.

Williams: But you have her living in this world where there are these smart pills. You also have her living in a world where there's drought. And, we know from, you know, the heating up of the world, global warming, that there is increased chance of drought these days. You also have her dealing with an increased number of gangs and sociopaths, and I think there are lots of people who would argue that we are dealing with that in the world today.
Butler: Mm-hmm.

Williams: It sounds almost as if you have simply projected, on the basis of current events, to create your fantasy world.
Butler: I have in a very real sense. And the smart pills, by the way, were not presented as something that people should rush out and get in the book. The way they are presented is that my character's mother was addicted to them, and, as a result, she has a birth defect. So, they're certainly not presented as something that people should be on the lookout for. Although I . . .

Williams: Well, hang on a second. What do you mean a birth defect? I think, in fact, she's very smart.
Butler: Yes. Oh, I didn't say that she wasn't smart, but she has a problem. She has a kind of delusionary defect that causes her to believe that she feels the pain of other people. She feels pain that she sees other people enduring. It is a delusion. It is a dangerous delusion because it prevents her, or could prevent her, from protecting herself in a very violent world. It's a kind of biological conscience on the one hand. You know, she can't give pain without receiving it. But, on the other hand, it means that when she's attacked she's in much more trouble than someone else might be.

Williams: Well, in fact, one of the things that strikes me about the telling of this tale is that you see her as extraordinarily sympathetic, and yet she is viewed as defective by others around her.
Butler: She's viewed as defective by herself, and it really is a defect. She would physically certainly be better off without it. I began writing the book with the thought that maybe what we needed was a biological conscience. It does seem to

me that there are too many people in this world who would just as soon wipe out half their country, if they could rule the other half. We keep running across them, and they keep starting wars.

Williams: Like who are you talking about?

Butler: Oh, I'm thinking of the former Yugoslavia. I'm thinking of several countries in Africa and the former Soviet Union. This kind of thing keeps happening where you have people who . . . They don't have a wonderful new philosophy. What they have is a desire to be immensely rich and powerful.

Williams: Hmm.

Butler: The person who was just killed in Sierra Leone, for instance.

Williams: Right. Well, now in these stories, as you're telling them, as we see science fiction evolving, what's striking to me is that we are seeing more and more biological engineering as a reality. In fact, I think the general consensus is the biological revolution of science is what's coming next. Is that impacting your science fiction writing?

Butler: I have written science fiction that was strictly biological science fiction. As a matter of fact, I have three novels being reprinted soon. *Dawn, Adulthood Rites,* and *Imago* are being reprinted as *Lilith's Brood* and that is biological science fiction because the people in those books use biotechnology instead of other kinds of technology. They don't use machines, except for biological machines.

Williams: And, when they use these biological machines, it's for evil.

Butler: Oh, no! No. No. No. No. I don't write about good and evil with this enormous dichotomy. I write about people. I write about people doing the kinds of things that people do. And, I think even the worst of us doesn't just set out to be evil. People set out to get something. They set out to defend themselves from something. They are frightened, perhaps. They set out because they believe their way is the best way to perhaps enforce their way on other people. But, no, I don't write about good and evil. As a matter of fact, my new book *Parable of the Trickster* that I'm working on now is a little bit about the idea that the whimsical, the different, the "stuff happens" attitude is real, is something that we have to deal with. And, it's not really all that useful to just say, "Well, the devil made me do it."

Williams: Now, what about men and women in science fiction? Your female characters tend to be very strong characters. And, for me, as a casual reader of science fiction, I'm unaccustomed to it.

Butler: Well, there's more of it now than there used to be. There are a lot more women in science fiction, and there are even a few more black women. Would you like some names?

Williams: Sure. Go right ahead.

Butler: Ok. There is Tananarive Due who writes a kind of horror-fantasy, which is a related genre. And, there is Nalo Hopkinson who writes science fiction. And among men there is Steven Barnes who writes science fiction. And, of course, there is Samuel R. Delany who was one of my teachers and who's kind of the grand master.

Williams: Now, when you see women in science fiction—I was saying earlier— especially if you see them like on *Star Trek* or on some of these TV and movie shows—I never see them take the lead role. What's striking about your work is they're in a lead role.

Butler: Mm-hmm. Well, I wrote myself in. This is one of the things that I did without even thinking about it. Now, and by the way, please don't take science fiction to be limited by what you see on television and at the movies, because television and movies are always way behind. For one thing, I suspect that money is very conservative and people want to do with their money what they've seen done successfully before, so what we wind up with in the movies and television is what was done in print many years ago.

Williams: Let's talk about you for just a second.

Butler: Sure.

Williams: When I was reading about you, I was struck by the notion that you said you were a loner and someone who, from the time that you were a child in California, was creating different realities for yourself.

Butler: Mm-hmm.

Williams: Why was that? Tell us about what kind of child you were and what your parents did.

Butler: Well, I was an only child, and my mother was a widow very early on. I don't really have any clear memories of my father. So, I was on my own a lot and I was also . . . Since I was on my own a lot as a very young child, I did not learn to be with other children early and that meant that when I was finally going to school and going to child care after school, I didn't really know how to get along with other kids. But I knew how to make little worlds of my own and that's what I did for my amusement. I told myself stories. I've been telling myself stories since I was four years old. When I was ten, I began writing them down. And when I was thirteen, I discovered how you submit stories for publication, and I began bothering editors with my stories. I got them back by return mail, of course, with rejection slips, but that's how old I was when I knew that this was what I wanted to do for a living.

Williams: But then at some point you were frustrated, and I believe it said that you were working cleaning places when you finally . . .
Butler: Oh, I did all sorts of work. It wasn't a matter of frustration. It was a matter of paying the rent.

Williams: And even, I think, telephone sales, right?
Butler: Yes. Yes. Yes. I make a joke of that. I tell people, you know, I'm that person who called you and tried to sell you what you didn't want, and I really don't appreciate what you said to me when you answered. So . . .

Williams: But then you were fired from that job and that's what forced you to make it or break it in terms of science fiction writing.
Butler: Well, that's what forced me to write the novels. I had been writing short stories and submitting those. I never stopped writing. It's pretty much my religion, I think.

Williams: All right.
Butler: This is probably true of a great many writers, but when I began . . .

Williams: Octavia Butler, we're going to have to take short break. We'll come right back, though.

[Music]

Williams: Octavia Butler, I felt like I interrupted you there. Was there something else that you wanted to add?
Butler: Oh, I think I'd gone on about that enough. I really was just talking about my getting started as a writer.

Williams: Well, you know, I think lots of people would be interested to know that you have been in touch with many other science fiction writers. That, in fact, Harlan Ellison is someone that was very much involved with you. Ray Bradbury is a big fan of yours.
Butler: Oh, that's nice to know.

Williams: Well . . .
Butler: Harlan was one of my teachers. I've only met—I met Bradbury once actu-

ally. But my Ray Bradbury story is actually winding up on my very first speaking engagement following him as a speaker.

Williams: That must have . . .
Butler: A terrible thing to do to some poor kid who's just written her first few books and, you know, it's impossible.

Williams: Well, I read a quote from Ray Bradbury in which he said that he remembered a story about the Egyptians, and it said that when you die and you arrive in heaven the one question you are asked is whether or not in this real-world life you had enthusiasm. And he said of Octavia Butler, "She clearly has enthusiasm for what she does." So I thought that was a very nice compliment.
Butler: It is very nice.

Williams: Yeah. Let's go to the phones. Let's go to Judith, Newport, California. Judith, you're on Talk of the Nation.
Judith: Hi. It's Newport Beach. Anyway, I love the *Parable of the Talent* and the *Parable of the Sower*. And I was going to ask you to explain that, but you already did . . . because no matter how many times I read those—your explanation in the book, I just couldn't get it, but thank you for explaining that. But, what I wanted to tell you is that I drive around Southern California a lot and there are a lot of middle-income housing projects that are getting gates and walls and I just . . . I mean, I just think to myself, "Oh, no. Those walls aren't high enough." And, "Oh, they're going to have to do something about those gates."
Butler: Ah, yes.

Williams: Well, you got to share with the rest of the audience. You're having these thoughts because of what you read in Octavia Butler's book.
Judith: Right. Because Lauren came from one of these . . . a gated community and it wasn't like one of the high-class ones like in Beverly Hills. It was somewhere out here in Orange County. And there's a lot of them being built now, you know, not . . .
Butler: That's right.

Judith: Yeah. A lot. And with gates and walls and, you know, I just really wonder a lot about that. Then I think, "Well, can I plant a vegetable garden in my backyard?" And we don't have any gates in my community. And, you know, I definitely think about your books.
Williams: Judith, why would you have to plant? Because people are hoarding food . . .

Judith: Because you're afraid to go to any stores. Well, especially down here in Los Angeles in Octavia's story. Well, you can't get to Los Angeles without being killed mostly.
Butler: Oh, come on now. Oh, my. I lived there for a while, but I wouldn't say that. But I'll tell you. When . . .

Williams: No. She said in your book, Octavia.
Judith: No. No—right. The book.
Butler: Oh, I see.

Judith: The book.
Butler: I see. When I began working on *Parable of the Sower*, I didn't know anybody who lived in a gated community. By the time I finished the book, at least one of my friends had moved into a gated community. So I know what you mean. And this is just an ordinary middle-class person. She was a teacher.

Judith: Yeah.
Butler: And there are more and more of them, as you say. It's . . .

Judith: There are. But then I sometimes wonder if that is gonna be a cause rather than—well, it turns into a solution in your book of sorts.
Butler: No, it never becomes a solution.

Judith: No, it doesn't. People breach the walls and then Lauren begins her journey. But it seems—you know, then—I don't know. It's just like your book haunts me. I mean, no matter where I go, I see . . .
Butler: I'm glad of that because it is a cautionary tale.

Judith: Definitely.
Butler: It is a book that says, "If we keep doing what we're doing, here's what we might wind up with."

Judith: But you can definitely see it.
Butler: I've heard people call it prophecy, and I generally respond to that with horror because certainly I don't want it to be prophecy. I don't want to live in that world.

Judith: Absolutely not. No. No. We don't want it to be prophecy, but it definitely is a cautionary tale. But it is frightening how accurate a lot of your scenes and ideas are. I mean—and then up in Northern California and all that.
Butler: Thank you.

Judith: I don't know. You know, I'm really glad it finally had a happy-ish ending, but . . .
Butler: Well, my endings are always hopeful.

Judith: Yeah.
Butler: I used to worry that I was a pessimist, but I realized that I couldn't seem to write a story that ended in a pessimistic way.

Williams: Well, Judith, thanks for your call. Let me say for the listeners that in fact the story is set in the year 2032 and it's kind of what . . . I think you refer to it, Ms. Butler, as an installment plan for World War III.
Butler: Well, one of my characters refers to it that way. It is something that—it's a matter of a kind of an avalanche of results. All the things that we ignore—some of them you've mentioned—drugs, global warming becoming more and more of a problem, and it's not just a matter of drought; it's all the effects of global warming all over the world . . .

Williams: Combined with gated communities, race, and murder.
Butler: Yes. Sure, gated communities.

Williams: You have people being taken by the officials. Disappearing.
Butler: Mm-hmm. Yeah.

Williams: You have people hiding food and weapons. There are no public schools.
Butler: Exactly. People just—politicians decide that public schools are an experiment that didn't work so, in many cases, there aren't any more.

Williams: And you have slavery.
Butler: Yes. Well, slavery never really left. It just kind of . . . it quieted down a bit. It went underground. But, in a lot of places—in a lot of countries, for instance, debt slavery is still around and legal.

Williams: But you have slavery in the United States.
Butler: Yes, and there is slavery here now. Every now and then, there's a news story about a new place where slavery has been discovered. But, in this story, slavery becomes almost legal. It becomes not so much slavery as indenture. You can become an indentured person because you're broke.

Williams: And—but—well, I have a number of questions coming about what you just said. You mean—do you mean things like sweatshops and people being brought like you have Chinese immigrants brought in the bowels of some ship and then . . .

Butler: Mm-hmm. Or remember the women from, I believe, Thailand who were discovered working for nothing and being forced to work horrible hours and generally being kept locked up?

Williams: But, in your book what you have is literally collars on people that, you know, administer shocks—pleasure, pain and so they're enslaved in that way.

Butler: Well, when I created the collars, I didn't know about the electronic belts—the prisoner-control devices that were coming into existence. And they were just coming along as I was writing the first of these books. And I realized in the second book, when I intended to introduce collars, that I had to not just introduce the collar but make it a descendant, a kind of technological descendant of the current belts. The belts are pretty basic. I mean, they hurt you, and the collars are more sophisticated. They can even make you feel good. They can play you like an accordion or something so it's a fairly nasty situation, and it's one that some people envy the dead when they find themselves in that situation.

Williams: Mm. Let's go to Rachel in Chapel Hill, North Carolina. Rachel, you're on *Talk of the Nation.*

Rachel: Thank you for having such a wonderful show today, Juan. I really appreciate it.

Williams: Oh, you're welcome.

Rachel: Octavia Butler is, in my humble opinion, the very best fiction writer today.

Butler: My goodness. Thank you.

Rachel: I use her *Parable of the Sower, Parable of the Talents* in my political theory classes, and her work really encourages students to think about political participation and what it means and what realities can happen and might happen. I guess the question I have is: Number one, Octavia, what are some of your favorite political novels and are there any movie deals in the works, and when does *Parable of the Trickster* come out?

Butler: Well, *Parable*—from the last backward. *Parable of the Trickster* is not written yet. I'm working on it. It's doing what all my novels do at the beginning. It's giving me trouble, so it probably will be written either by the end of this year or sometime in the first part of next year.

Rachel: Ok.

Butler: As for movie deals, my book *Kindred* is generally, usually, under option. It is now. My book *Parable of the Sower* is optioned sometimes. As a matter of fact, most of my books have been optioned at one time or another. But you realize that a movie option just means that someone is buying the right to shop it around and see if they can put together a deal to make the movie. So far . . .

Rachel: Have you talked to Spike Lee yet?
Butler: So far, no one's put together the deal.

Rachel: Ok.
Butler: Also, you . . .

Williams: Ms. Butler, I think she asked if you had spoken to Spike Lee or, I guess, she's thinking of black filmmakers.
Butler: Well, I have, but not formally. I mean, we met at an event where we were both doing—we were both talking, but not as a matter of "Oh, is he going to make the movie?" Probably not. I mean, I haven't heard anything.

Rachel: Ok.
Williams: Ok.
Butler: I wouldn't mind, but I haven't heard anything.

Rachel: It's a great idea.
Butler: Oh. And as for novels that I've enjoyed, I mean, the only political novel that comes immediately to mind is the obvious one, *1984*, which I read on my own before it was required reading at school. And, of course, the other, *Animal Farm*. I don't know that political novels have influenced me as much as just being a news junkie has influenced me. I read and hear the news a lot, more than I should, more than is good for me, I suspect. And . . .

Williams: I read about you that you liked to read science fiction magazines when you were a kid.
Butler: Oh, I did. But, I mean, now I don't seem to be able to avoid the news. As a matter of fact, Juan Williams, I listen to your show.

Williams: Well, thanks, Octavia.
Butler: Oh, my.

Rachel: Can I ask another question?
Butler: Sure.

Williams: Sure. Go ahead.
Rachel: Thank you. Do you . . . can you talk about your political agenda that you

may or may not have about . . . that you've used with these two books? I mean, there clearly is a vision that some say we are quickly moving towards.
Butler: No . . .

Rachel: Even if we embrace compassionate conservatism, some can say that we're moving in that direction, and I was wondering if you felt comfortable addressing that.
Butler: I really—my political agenda doesn't quite sound right. It sounds as though I'm trying to, as I've said, put forward prophecy with these novels. These novels are not prophetic. These novels are cautionary tales. These novels are, "If we are not careful" you know, "if we carry on as we have been, this is what we might wind up with." The problems that I write about are problems that we can do something about. That's why I write about them. We don't have to have the educational problem that we have now, and we certainly shouldn't give up on public education, although I've heard surprising numbers of people talk as though that's what we should do. They don't have an alternative; they just think, "Well, public education doesn't work, so why bother paying for it?"

Williams: Well, I think that is increasingly the attitude in this country. But I wanted to challenge you . . .
Butler: That's terrifying.

Williams: Well, that's terrifying as in science fiction, isn't it, in a way?
Butler: Well, it's terrifying in real life.

Williams: Right.
Butler: I mean, you have to think about what kind of world you want to live in, and I don't think there is a person alive who would want to live in the world that I've written about, but we can arrange it.

Williams: Well, in fact, I was gonna challenge you on the notion—you said you didn't really write about power relationships, but I think you do. I think . . .
Butler: Oh . . .

Williams: . . . *Patternmaster*, in which you write about a ruling class that's joined together through telepathy—that's a ruling class. That's a power elite.
Butler: Yes. I said I didn't write prophecy.

Williams: Oh, I'm sorry. Maybe I misunderstood you.
Butler: Mm-hmm. Yeah, I was . . .

Williams: Because I think you definitely write political—there's a strong political slant there.

Butler: Oh, yes, I write quite a bit about power.

Williams: Yeah.

Butler: I hadn't mentioned it until now, but, yes, one of the reasons I got into writing about power was because I grew up feeling that I didn't have any, and, therefore, it was fascinating. I get into all sorts of things. I go to the library and graze. I buy courses on tape so that I can listen to them when I travel. I do all sorts of things. And I have a course that I just recently bought on tape, and I've been listening to it on this particular trip. One of the people spoken about in the course is Hegel, and it was fascinating to hear his ideas of "might makes right"—of course, never put that bluntly. I must have been made to read some Hegel when I was in school, but it's—you know how some of the things you read in school are forgotten as soon as you're out of that particular class.

Williams: True.

Butler: And having it all brought back to me now, you know, how wonderfully cleverly he went about saying that whatever is going on is what's supposed to be going on; whoever's on top, that's who's supposed to be on top—I find myself still interested in power relationships and still writing about them—not so much any longer because I worry about not having power myself but just because they are part of what it means to be human.

Williams: Right.

Butler: And I do write about different ways of being human.

Williams: Let me remind the listeners that they're listening to *Talk of the Nation* from NPR News. Let's go to Angie in Portland, Oregon. Angie, you're on *Talk of the Nation.*

Angie: Hi. How are you?

Williams: Fine, thanks, Angie.

Angie: Octavia, first of all, I just wanted to comment on your use of science fiction to make some commentary on modern society and offer what you see as problems and offer potential solutions. And, I really appreciate your views. I think I share a lot of them. But what, for me, makes a tale like that so effective is its ability to move the reader. I read fiction because I love the tale, I love the story. And I've read a lot of utopian, dystopian novels that certainly are kind of coming from my perspective, but they leave me feeling kind of hollow. And what I appreciate most about your characters, especially the protagonists of the Parable series and *Kindred*, is this incredible affinity I feel for them. I feel about them kind of the way I would an old friend. And my question is, Do you do that on purpose? Do you set out to create that relationship between your character and the reader, or is it just your talent as a writer?

Butler: I do, Angie. I like to read novels that I can get involved in, and I like to write novels that involve other people. We can never know one another as well as we can know a fictional character, because we can get into the fictional character's mind. And I don't like—I don't really enjoy reading the kind of novel that keeps me outside the character. So since I don't enjoy reading it, I don't write it.

Angie: Well, I really appreciate your books. Thank you.

Williams: Thanks for your call, Angie.

Butler: Thank you.

Williams: You know, Ms. Butler, I was thinking to myself that part of this is the idea of, in fact, seeing people who are friends in your real life—black people, Asians, Hispanics—suddenly pop up in science fiction. Why were they absent before?

Butler: They weren't entirely absent. I came along at what was, for me, a very good time. I went to a Clarion science fiction writers' workshop in 1970, a . . .

Williams: We only have about thirty seconds before this break, so if you could be brief, I'd appreciate it.

Butler: Ok. And that's one of the places that we learned to be more inclusive of women and whatever. I can't help being more inclusive myself, just because I have to write myself in.

Williams: Alright. We're gonna take a short break right now . . .

Williams: Welcome back to *Talk of the Nation*. I'm Juan Williams. Ms. Butler, I want to throw a question in there as if I was a caller. I notice that you are very interested in religion, and especially in creating religion, and in fanatics, fanaticism. Is this a concern? Are you worried about fanaticism and about the growth of new religion in American society?

Butler: Oh, well, no, not exactly. These two novels are specifically concerned with religion. They were intended to be. Of course, fanaticism is a problem, especially the kind of scapegoating fanaticism that points out who's responsible for all the trouble and wants to do something about it. In these novels, I think I take advantage of the reality that there are no human communities without religion. I mean, there may be human communities that don't acknowledge a specific god, but they've found some way of creating religion, either secular or sacred. And in this case, my character looks around and says, "Well, why shouldn't religion be used for something? Why shouldn't it be a tool? Why shouldn't religion take us where, perhaps, other things can't take us?" The religion that she creates is called Earthseed, and she says the destiny of Earthseed is to take root among the stars. She gives people a goal. It is a difficult goal; it's a long-term goal. It's like during the Middle Ages, you know, the goal of building a cathedral. You could begin a cathedral, but surely you wouldn't live to see its end.

Williams: Well, what's the difference between that religion and, let's say, Judaism or Catholicism or any of the Protestant religions?
Butler: Well, basically, her people get to go to heaven while they're alive, the ones who go. She does feel that the destiny of Earthseed is to take root among the stars, that if we are to be anything other than smooth dinosaurs we'd better get out there. And the best way for us to get out there is to create the huge family of projects that it will take to get us out there. She is not about colonialism or anything like that; she's just about sort of taking out some human insurance. The . . .

Williams: And what's the difference between what she's doing and a cult?
Butler: Well, any religion, I would suppose, could be called a cult when it gets going.

Williams: But the degree of intensity, I suspect, is different—you know, Jim Jones is a little different than the pope.
Butler: Ah, I see what you're saying—although the pope didn't begin as the pope. I mean, that began as a small cult among the Jews. Christianity began as a small cult among the Jews. So, I mean, most religions begin as cults, just because they're small—few adherents, not a great deal of understanding from the outside world, that kind of thing. My character begins with a few people, some of whom believe in what she's saying and some of whom just want to be warm and well-fed.

Williams: Ok. Let me go to Michael in St. Louis. Michael, you're on *Talk of the Nation.*
Butler: Ok.

Michael: Hello.
Williams: Hi.
Michael: How you doing, Juan?
Williams: Fine, thanks, Michael.

Michael: Hello, Ms. Butler. I really appreciate the opportunity to speak with you on the show.
Butler: Thank you, Michael.

Michael: I've read of all your books twice over. And I wanted to speak to that in terms of the realism and the sort of compellingness of the books, that once you start reading them you can't put them down. And I was wondering . . .
Butler: Thank you.

Michael: . . . because of the fact that, like, there's so much unrealistic views of the future in science and it's been glamorized so much in movies and TV: Do you think the people have a total misconcept of how things may be in the future and how they're gonna be involved?
Butler: I don't think any of us can know how things will be in the future. We're creating the future, but we can't see it clearly. We can only try to make it better.

Michael: I understand that. And one of the points I wanted to try and comment on was, like, because of the fact that so many in the media, and the way the future's depicted in movies and so forth, a lot of people are excluded, and, like I said, a limited sort of view. And your writing sort of includes everybody and all situations and everything social. And maybe—would you say that that's one of the reasons why, like, the lady earlier referred to some of your writing as almost like prophecy?
Butler: Oh, I'm not sure she put it that way, but my writing is inclusive. I write about people, and, I mean, the differences fascinate me as much as the similarities. I come from Southern California and I've never lived in a segregated community, and I think that helped me to recognize that everybody's out there.

Williams: You know, but one of the descriptions . . .
Butler: And I . . .

Williams: . . . that I . . . oh, sure.
Butler: Oh, one thing more. I don't know whether I'd said this before, but in my writing, when I began writing science fiction back when I was twelve years old, everybody I read about in science fiction was white, and most of the people I read about in science fiction were male. So, I really did have to write myself in.

Williams: What I was . . .
Butler: And once I—I'm sorry.

Williams: No, what I was gonna say to you was that, in reading about you, your personal biography as opposed to your works, I noticed that you said oftentimes you personally feel like an outsider and that as a child you were tall; you were six feet tall and that you felt, even though you were living in an integrated community, as if you were off to the side.

Butler: I was off to the side. I was as socially awkward as they come. A lot of science fiction writers come from socially awkward, physically unusual young people who grow into their physical presence but who, by then, have been hooked by writing science fiction. And I was definitely one of those. When I went to a science fiction writers workshop, I found that the people that I met there, even though they came in different races and sexes, were very much like me in that one respect. They were outcasts, too.

Williams: All right. Let's take a bunch of calls here. Let's go to Elizabeth in Minneapolis. Elizabeth, you're on *Talk of the Nation.*

Elizabeth: Hello. I had the opportunity to meet Octavia Butler in Minneapolis, during the convention. However, I was blind at the time, and I couldn't find anyone to take me to you.

Butler: Oh.

Elizabeth: However, I do have a question about your insight into the people in the *Patternmaster* series who are latents, and they act in such a way that makes them look as if they're mentally ill. And I gleaned from that that they were just so sensitive that they had to maybe abuse alcohol and drugs in order to dampen the hurt. That's my insight.

Butler: Exactly.

Elizabeth: If you have a different insight, I'll listen to it off the air.

Williams: Well, Elizabeth, hang on. Before you go—you said you were blind at the time?

Elizabeth: I had eye surgery, and I couldn't find anyone to take me to Octavia Butler to ask her this exact question.

Butler: I wish I had known. My goodness.

Williams: But you've recovered?

Elizabeth: Oh, yes.

Williams: Oh, good. Well, OK. Thanks for your call, Elizabeth. Octavia?

Elizabeth: I'll take it off the air. Thank you.

Williams: Yeah.

Butler: OK. The latents in, for the most part, *Mind of My Mind*, are people who have telepathic abilities or other abilities and are not in control of them, don't necessarily understand them, and are suffering from them very much as though they were mentally ill. What's the difference, after all, from somebody who has real telepathic ability and hears the thoughts of others, and someone who's schizophrenic and hears voices? They don't know, and they suffer, and they do abuse alcohol and drugs because they're just trying to quiet the voices.

Williams: Hmm. Let's go to Bill in Somerville, Massachusetts. Bill, you're on *Talk of the Nation.*
Bill: Hi, Juan. Hi, Octavia.
Williams: Hi.
Butler: Hi there.

Bill: A comment and then a question. The comment is that so often science fiction writers never challenge the potential of the discipline. They simply project the dominant culture that we're in, in this historical moment, with more gadgets. And what I love about Octavia's writing is she looks at the full human potential so that her science fiction isn't just technical science, but it's social science fiction, too.
Butler: Thank you.

Bill: Thank you. Here's the question. In your Lilith trilogy, the folks that you call the Oankali tell Lilith that humans have an inherent conflict in them which, if they had not intervened, would have led to human extinction. And I'm wondering if you believe that that—if in fact, that's your voice speaking. Do you believe that conflict exists, and do you see a means of managing it?
Williams: Bill, thanks for your call.
Butler: The conflict, by the way, or the contradiction is that human beings are intelligent but also that they are hierarchical and that their hierarchical tendencies are a lot older than their intelligence, and the hierarchical tendencies are sometimes in charge. And I emphasize this by having the story begin after a terrible war that has wiped out a good portion of humanity. The hierarchical tendencies have obviously been in charge at that point, and we've just about one-upped ourselves to death. Do I think that's true? I suspect that it might be. Not necessarily exactly like that but that we do seem sometimes much more interested in one-upping each other—one-upping one country over the other—than in doing ourselves some long-term good.

Williams: Ms. Butler, it does sound as though you believe in sort of a genetic destiny. There are certain things in our genes, such as a love of hierarchies, that we can't get away from.
Butler: Not a love of hierarchies; hierarchical tendencies, the kinds of things that

you can find in the lowest kinds of plants and animals. I remember one of the things that inspired that particular description of the problem, watching a nature show on PBS in which a clone of algae—two clones of algae grew on a rock, and as they grew round the rock, they met. And it wasn't a matter of, "Oh, pardon me. Now I'll grow upward," but it was a matter of one poisoning the other—one-upsmanship. So I'm not talking about anything organized and I'm not talking about anything evil; I'm just talking about a tendency.

Williams: All right. Let's to go Neecie in Seattle, Washington. Neecie, you're on *Talk of the Nation.*
Neecie: Hi, there. Hi, Octavia. How you doing?
Butler: Hi, there.

Neecie: Good show. I wanted to ask you—I know that you've been a student at Clarion, the writer's workshop, and an instructor. I wanted you to talk about the value of critique groups after workshops, and I wondered why you'd never belonged to one.
Butler: Ah, that's probably not a good question to ask me, Neecie, because I reached a point of not—well, I reached a point of not needing critique groups but needing instead to focus on doing my own work and getting it out, mailing it out.

Neecie: But . . .
Butler: Sometimes you do reach that point, where your career is getting critiqued instead of getting the work out.

Neecie: Did you actually belong to a critique group at one point and found that it was less valuable as your career went on?
Butler: Two or three of them, yes, I did. And it wasn't a matter of as my career went on; it was a matter of, if I was going to have a career, I had better go home and write.

Williams: Neecie, thanks for your call. Ms. Butler, is science fiction moving in new directions?
Butler: I think it usually is. I mean, by nature—not necessarily new prophecies or brand-new—for instance, the more we learn about, oh, just about anything—nanotechnology—the more we can write about it.

Williams: Just briefly, because we have to go. Alright . . .
Butler: Ok. The more we learn about anything, the more we can write about it and the more we can consider what will happen if we keep doing what we're doing.

Williams: Thank you so much. That's all the time we have for today. I'd like to thank all of you who called this hour, and especially my guest, Ms. Octavia Butler.

Butler: Thank you.

Williams: Her newest book is *Parable of the Talents*. She joined us from NPR's New York bureau. Thanks for being with us. In Washington, I'm Juan Williams, NPR News.

Octavia E. Butler: Persistence

Charles Brown/2000

From *Locus Magazine* (June 2000). © Locus Magazine. Reprinted with permission.

"*Devil Girl from Mars* is the movie that got me writing science fiction when I was twelve years old. I had already been writing for two years. I began with horse stories, because I was crazy over horses, even though I never got near one. At eleven, I was writing romances, and I'm happy to say I didn't know any more about romance than I did about horses. When I was twelve, I had this big brown three-ring binder notebook that somebody had thrown away, and I was watching this godawful movie on television. (I wasn't allowed to go to the movies, because movies were wicked and sinful, but somehow when they came to the television they were okay.) It was one of those where the beautiful Martian arrives on Earth and announces that all the men on Mars have died and they need more men. None of the Earthmen want to go! And I thought, 'Geez, I can write a better story than that.' I got busy writing what I thought of as science fiction.

"I thought if you wrote science fiction, it has to take place on other worlds, so these were all Martians, and that's why they had their powers. They were busy fighting with each other, acting like good human beings. And I really enjoyed it. The first book I ever bought new was about horses, when I was ten. When I was twelve, I saved my pennies and bought another book new, and that was about the planets and the stars. I read about Mars and I was very put out to discover it was unlike the kind of civilization I had imagined could possibly be there. So that's how they became the people they became in *Patternmaster, Mind of My Mind*, and *Wild Seed*.

"I just kept taking them back in time, after wondering, 'How'd they get like that?' And that's how the various novels got plugged into wherever they are on that timeline. Those were all the novels that were 'in my trunk,' and I could write them very quickly. I had a novel a year out—to me, that's quick. But since I ran out of 'trunk' ideas, I've written much more slowly. I have to live in the book's world a bit, understand it, get to know the people. I need the people to be real, and their situation to mean something to me. I need to understand the world enough to live there in their skins. So it takes me a while to get a new book out now. It's very frustrating, but it's just the process of writing a novel, now that my old trunk is empty.

"When I was in college, I began *Kindred*, and that was the first one that I began, knowing what I wanted to do. The others, I was really too young to think about them in terms of 'What do you have to say in this novel?' I just knew there were stories I wanted to tell. But when I did *Kindred*, I really had had this experience in college that I talk about all the time, of this Black guy saying, 'I wish I could kill all these old Black people that have been holding us back for so long, but I can't because I have to start with my own parents.' That was a friend of mine. And I realized that, even though he knew a *lot* more than I did about Black history, it was all cerebral. He wasn't feeling any of it. He was the kind that would have killed and died, as opposed to surviving and hanging on and hoping and working for change. And I thought about my mother, because she used to take me to work with her when she couldn't get a baby sitter and I was too young to be left alone, and I saw her going in the back door, and I saw people saying things to her that she didn't like but couldn't respond to. I heard people say in her hearing, 'Well, I don't really like colored people.' And she kept working, and she put me through school, she bought her house—all the stuff she did. I realized that he didn't understand what heroism was. That's what I want to write about: when you are *aware* of what it means to be an adult and what choices you have to make, the fact that maybe you're afraid, but you still have to act.

"In my fiction, I put my subconscious to work a lot of the time. I will ask myself questions that I think are important, then sleep on them, and get up the next morning and write about them. Sometimes my subconscious has sorted things out very nicely, and sometimes it hasn't. When I was writing *Parable of the Sower*, I went on walks all around Pasadena, because the story was going to take place in that general area. I wanted to know what grew well, when it came to flower, when it came to fruit—I needed to know everything about these plants that my characters were going to be using. And just walking every day, in the same general area, was an education. But I think that's the only time walking has been an answer to questions.

"In Xenogenesis, I bring in the aliens, but in the Parable books I wanted to keep everything as realistic as I could. I didn't want any powers, any kind of magic or fantastical elements. Even the empathy is not real—it's delusional. I wanted to have human beings in that one book find their own way clear. And I used religion because it seems to me it's something we can never get away from. I've met science fiction people who say, 'Oh, well, we're going to outgrow it,' and I don't believe that for one moment. It seems that religion has kept us focused and helped us to do any number of very difficult things, from building pyramids and cathedrals to holding together countries, in some instances. I'm not saying it's a force for *good*—it's just a force. So why not use it to get ourselves to the stars?

"It seems to me we're not going to do that for any logical reason. It's not going to happen because it's profitable—it may not be. The going certainly won't be. The people who work on it will probably not live to see whether or not they've been successful. It's not like, 'In ten years we'll go to the moon'—which, unfortunately for us, we did. It might have been better if we had almost made it, but then the Russians did ahead of us. If we had lost the race to the Russians, we would be farther along in space travel. One of the reasons going to the moon was a big thing to do was Sputnik. The Russians were sending up their satellites, and ours were crashing and burning. I was a kid with her eyes glued to the television set back then in the fifties.

"In the Parable books we have one person who decides this is what religion should be doing, and she uses religion to get us into interstellar space. *Sower* and *Talents* were the fictional autobiography of Lauren Olamina, though *Talents* turned out to be a mother/daughter story. There are no more books about *her*, but I am working on a book (which may or may not come off, and may be called *Parable of the Trickster*) about people who go, who *do* fulfill that destiny and go to this other world.

"I'm not interested in confronting them with natives. I've done that elsewhere. What I'm going to confront them with is just a nasty world. It's not violent, just nasty and dull and awful, and what they're going to have to deal with is themselves. There's no going home. Nobody will follow within their lifetimes. They will have a particular medical problem that comes up—I do tend to create 'particular medical problems'!—that's a killer. But the real problem is dealing with themselves, surviving their promised land.

"I was pretty despairing when I began the Xenogenesis books. This was back during the first Reagan administration, when the guy was talking about 'winnable' nuclear wars, 'limited' nuclear wars, and all that. It scared me that we were electing someone who was talking that way. What if he meant it? But with the Parable books, it was more like, 'We really *are* going to have to get ourselves out.' We probably are due for something fairly nasty, something alongside which the Depression would look good. We build ourselves up, and then we crash, and then we build ourselves back up again. It's not a matter of pessimism; it's just the cycles humanity has gone through since there's been humanity.

"I'm not talking about the Stock Market. I'm thinking about things like

Global Warming, which will probably have a great deal more effect than some science fiction people seem to think. What we feel now is a lot of things that can be taken individually. 'Oh, it's the flood of the century,' 'Oh, it's the stormy season of the century,' 'Oh gee, how odd that this disease should appear in New York,' or 'The coastline seems to be crumbling away more than it used to.' And most of us refuse to recognize these as symptoms of a single problem. It's not just about things getting warm. If you're forced to change what you grow and where you grow it, and maybe food prices are going up, and we've got tropical diseases coming north, sea level rise, coastline being inundated. . . .

"Obviously we're going to have to endure these effects. There's no sense figuring that we can push a button or make a magic wish and it will all go away. Even if we stopped *now* with the internal combustion engine and other forms of carbon dioxide-producing or methane-producing industries, it wouldn't do any good, because the system is just too big. It's not just that something is going to happen, but a lot of things are going to happen, and more and more they're going to happen all at the same time, and not just in this country. And that's what people who brush off the idea of Global Warming refuse to understand. They're capable of understanding it, but I think they dislike it so much, they just brush it off.

"Global Warming is a character in *Parable of the Sower*. That's why they're having so difficulty with water. When I went to Peru, on the coast where Lima is, the mountains are memorable because they're so utterly barren, like the moon. I thought, 'Is this what Southern California could look like after a few decades of Global Warming?' That's what I pictured: a place where they're really enthusiastic because it's raining, and it hasn't rained for five years, where there are water stations the way there are now gas stations—because if you're out away from home, you need to buy water, so there are water sellers like in a desert country. I don't go on and on about it, just let my characters feel the effects of it. It's the reason for the terrible storms and the disease, and a lot of what's going on that has just overwhelmed people because the economic difficulties have already made so much trouble that the government is really in no shape to do anything about it.

"Race was not my characters' huge problem: because they had so many other problems, racial problems were just a kind of subset! I don't think we will get over racial problems, because they're just one more version of dominance games, and human beings unfortunately spend enormous amounts of time playing dominance games. When they don't have race, they divide themselves in other ways, like a small Texas town where the teenagers are either Freaks or Jocks. Here are these people who all come from the same beckground, they're all the same color, probably all the same religion—but they still found a way to divide themselves, fight each other, and kill each other.

"One of the reasons my character Lauren opts for interstellar travel is, it's a major distraction. And when the kid just absolutely wants to run in the streets, you've got to find a way to distract him. Which is, I guess, the female way of looking at the human species. The lack of empathy—or worse, the trivialization of empathy—is a real problem. The idea that you're some sort of bleeding-heart idiot because you worry about another person's feelings, or you're just trying to be politically correct. Why *not* come down hard on them just because you can?

"That's why, at the end of *Talents*, my character says, 'I know what I've done.' She does not feel that she's set everything right and they are going to some paradise in the sky. She recognizes that probably a lot of them are going to die, and they're taking their problems with them, but she hopes the distraction of surviving on another world will enable them, slowly, to grow into something better. *Can* we grow into something better? Probably not while the worst behavior is rewarded. And here on Earth, the worst behavior is rewarded. In a world where, if you really behave badly, take over, and make everybody miserable, you'll probably kill off the whole colony, they'll either manage not to do things like that and survive, or they won't and they'll die.

"I consider writing a book about some of this an act of hope. About Global Warming, about racial relations, about human relations, sexual interaction. But we are humans. I've talked to high school kids who are thinking about trying to become a writer and asking, 'What should I major in?' and I tell them, 'History. Anthropology. Something where you get to know the human species a little better, as opposed to something where you learn to arrange words.' I don't know whether that's good advice or not, but it feels right to me. You don't start out writing good stuff. You start out writing crap and *thinking* it's good stuff, and then gradually you get better at it. That's why I say one of the most valuable traits is persistence. It's just so easy to give up!

"I feel hopeful about the human race. I know we can kill ourselves, but I think that if we're not OK, if we don't make it this time, it will be a lot like me climbing a rope. We've gotten a lot farther this time than we ever had in the past before we knock ourselves down, and go for another 'age of chaos.' I remember saying at a science fiction convention that it seemed to me we were doing just what every other animal species does: turning our environment into ourselves, just as quickly as we could. And we were better at it than most species because we had technology. This upset and annoyed some people. They wanted to opt us out of any natural cycle—'We're beyond that.' Well, we're *not* beyond it!

"We can still wipe ourselves out if we insist. We are wiping out a lot of other species, just casually doing it, and afterwards we realize they were canaries in the coalmine and they were telling us something that we weren't listening to. I don't despair, but I recognize that. I have the horrible feeling the Amazon may be a desert in my lifetime. And all of a sudden, people will realize they've gone that one step too far, and what they have left is not the Amazon anymore. I think of it as 'Easter Island Syndrome.' Although I don't expect them to go as far as the Easter Islanders who cut down every tree to use it to placate the gods, we do a lot of harm placating our gods, whatever they happen to be. In this case, perhaps the God of Money.

"There are a number of myths we live by. For instance, the myth of 'away,' as in 'I'll throw it away.' Where's that? There's no such place. It's going *somewhere.* Or the myth of 'my little bit won't hurt, or obvious myths of 'bigger is better' and 'more is better.' We have all these myths, and we believe in them without even recognizing that they're there. We just act on them—and that's liable to be our downfall.

"When I was at Contact, the NASA/Ames conference on science/SF, I heard about a wonderful way of educating teenagers. The ones on this particular track learn in a kind of interconnected, interdisciplinary way, even in high school, so everything's linked together as what makes a whole planet work. At the end of it, they create a species, a world on which that species can live. So they've got their biology, their math, geology, geography—you name it!—and they're putting it all together to figure out how a world works. I think we could use a lot more of that kind of thing. And the fact that they use it creatively means that it's got to be of more interest to *them* because they're going to be using it. Let's face it, we are a competitive species. We have characteristics that can be very nasty but can be put to good use.

"I don't think of religion as nasty. Religion kept some of my relatives alive, because it was all they had. If they hadn't had some hope of heaven, some companionship in Jesus, they probably would have committed suicide, their lives were so hellish. But they could go to church and have that exuberance together, and that was good, the community of it. When they were in pain, when they had to go to work even though they were in terrible pain, they had God to fall back on, and I think that's what religion does for the majority of the people. I don't think most people intellectualize about religion. They use it to keep themselves alive. I'm not talking about most Americans. We don't need it that way, most of us, now. But there was certainly a time when many of us did, maybe most of us.

"The religion in the Parable books would probably change over time to make it a more comforting religion. For instance, Lauren doesn't believe in life after death, but that's one of the hopes people have. They know they're going to die, so they have to believe, a lot of them, that there's something else. An interviewer I mentioned this to said she didn't feel she needed her religion to be comforting, and I said, 'Well, that's because you're already comfortable.' It's those people who have so little, and who suffer so much, who need at least for religion to comfort them. Nothing else is. Once you grow past Mommy and Daddy coming running when you're hurt, you're really on your own. You're alone, and there's no one to help you.

"I used to despise religion. I have not become religious, but I think I've become more understanding of religion. And I'm glad I was raised as a Baptist, because I got my conscience installed early. I've been around people who don't have one, and they're damned scary. And I think a lot of them are out there running major corporations! How can you do some of the things these people do if you have a conscience? So I think it might be better if there were a little *more* religion, in that sense. My mother didn't just say, 'Go to church, go to Sunday school.' I did all that, but I could see *her* struggling to live according to the religion the believed in. My mother worked every day, sometimes on Sundays, and I didn't have a father, and she still managed to install all this.

"Religion is really a part of human nature. We never grow out of that need to call 'Mama!' and have somebody come running to make it OK. And once *we*'re old, 'God help me!' serves the same function. The sower in the original biblical parable of the sower is despairing. The sower goes out to sow his seed, and the birds eat some of it, some falls on rocks and doesn't germinate, some falls in very shallow soil and dies soon after germination. But a little bit of it falls on good ground, and reproduces a hundredfold. That's why I used it as the title—I *did* see some significance to it! What really bothers me with *Parable of the Sower* is, some reviewers just passed it off as one more *Mad Max*-type story. Sometimes when reviewers hear the term 'science fiction,' they immediately think they know what you're all about—and they know nothing.

"What winning the MacArthur Grant did for me that I didn't expect or understand at the time—it was a great confidence-builder. And one can always use confidence. I always had ego as far as my writing was concerned, but an award like that gives you confidence that maybe you're doing something right. It was also very nice knowing that a certain amount of money was coming in, because freelancing is catch-as-catch-can. You might know what you're *owed*, but you don't know what you're gonna get. And I think it helped the sales of my books a lot. It caused people to take another look—'Oh, it's not just that sci-fi stuff.' This is the only time I've said 'sci-fi' in an interview, I'll have you know!

"And I was able to move to Seattle. I'd gotten burglarized a few times in L.A.. and that was really horrible. They'd come and get my typewriter and then, as soon as I'd buy another, they'd come and get that. I lost three of them like that. *Parable of the Trickster*—if that's what the next one ends up being called—will be the Seattle novel, because I have removed myself to a place that is different from where I've spent most of my life. I remember saying to Vonda McIntyre, 'Part of this move is research,' and it is—it's just that Seattle is where I've wanted to move since I visited there the first time in 1976. I really like the city, but it is not yet home. As they tell writers to do, I'll take any small example of something and build it into a larger example. I've moved to Seattle; my characters have moved to Alpha Centauri, or whatever. (That was not literal.) But they suffer and learn about the situation there a little bit because of what I learn about from my move to Seattle. Writers use everything. If it doesn't kill you, you probably wind up using it in your writing."

Essay on Racism

Scott Simon/2001

Simon: As it begins this weekend in Durban, South Africa, the UN racism conference got us thinking, how would human beings know where they stood if racism just vanished? In short, imagine a world without racism. We took this notion to writer Octavia Butler. She has spent her career speculating about the future of the human species and our possible counterparts elsewhere in this universe. She has won every major science fiction award, as well as a MacArthur Fellowship, what they call the "genius" grant. We asked Octavia Butler to imagine a world without racism, and like her stories, the results both surprised and disturbed us. Her essay is posted on our website at npr.org. Octavia Butler joins us from the studios of member station KUOW in Seattle, Washington. Thanks very much for being with us.

Butler: Thank you.

Simon: And you concluded that utter, absolute empathy might be something to try, but your conclusions about how that would work were surprising.

Butler: I think sometimes we'll get an idea and think how wonderful it is until we begin to try to live with it for a while, and that's the way I write. I try to live in the worlds I create for a little while, and I think that would be a very difficult world to live in.

Simon: Maybe we should get you to explain how absolute empathy would work in the world.

Butler: Well, everyone would feel everyone else's pain and everyone else's pleasure, so it would be very difficult for you to hurt someone unless you were willing to accept that pain yourself

Simon: Maybe I can get you to read a few lines from the essay now; you wound up thinking that there are some practical drawbacks to what sounds like an awfully beguiling proposition.

Butler: "In my novel, unavoidable empathy worked fine as an affliction, but popular, painful sports like boxing and football convinced me that the thread of shared pain wouldn't necessarily make people behave better toward one another, and it might cause trouble. For instance, it might stop people from entering the health-care professions. Nursing could become very unpopular, and who would want to be a dentist in such a society?"

Simon: A journalist? Well, that's something we think about here. What is hypothetically removed if we could somehow remove at least a racist and xenophobic tint from our eyes?
Butler: A lot of our competitiveness might be removed, and that would make us a very different people.

Simon: You said at one point that you reluctantly concluded that we as a species kind of enjoy feeling superior to somebody for some reason.
Butler: There was even a commercial about that recently, that has someone saying "I'm better than you are."

Simon: I think it was a car commercial or something, if I'm not mistaken. Cars might be a commodity that is particularly vulnerable to that, aren't they?
Butler: I think anything that's for public display as well as private use can be vulnerable to that.

Simon: Such as?
Butler: Oh, well a house for instance. Where you live and how your house looks, whether your lawn is greener than your neighbor's; I mean, we actually compete in that ridiculous way. It's probably one of the safer competitions; at least we don't hurt each other.

Simon: From the artist's point of view, would a world without this kind of racial division be a little bit more challenging to write about?
Butler: Yes, it would be boring.

Simon: I guess we found that out through modern literature.
Butler: If it's possible.

Simon: Correct me if I'm wrong, but so many portrayals we see in literature of some kind of utopia, you spend the first 25 percent of the book thinking, well this is nice. But then the rest is the protagonist realizing that this is not utopia, this is some kind of happy, benign tyranny, and there's nothing fun about this at all.
Butler: I think the problem with utopian literature is that in literature there needs to be conflict, and in utopia, there shouldn't be. I don't think human beings can

live without some sort of conflict. Not that we enjoy it particularly, but I think it is inevitable.

Simon: Does your study of our species suggest that if we weren't rivalrous about ethnicity and skin color, we would choose something else?
Butler: We always have. In areas where everyone is the same color, the same religion, the same language, whatever, they find other things to beat each other up about.

Simon: What does that say about us?
Butler: That we are a sadly hierarchical species, and the hierarchical tendencies that we have do seem to be old and more likely to dominate our intelligence, so that we use our intelligence for silly purposes sometimes, or dangerous purposes.

Simon: Is there something we can concentrate on that makes this a less ugly place?
Butler: I think this conference in South Africa is certainly headed in the right direction. I think as long as we can talk about it, negotiate about it, we will be less likely to fight about it.

Simon: I notice in your essay you use a word which kind of surprised me, tolerance.
Butler: I used to dislike it very much, because I thought, how terrible that we should only tolerate each other. Finally I realized that to tolerate someone is basically to let them alone, and to let them live their own lives, and that is a very precious commodity, the right to be let alone, the right to be allowed to live your own life, worship your own god, just basically be who you are.

Simon: There are a lot of people I think who would like to think that tolerance is a self-rewarding virtue, that the motive to be tolerant is that in the end we will deliver ourselves a better society. You seem to suggest that the moral math is not that easy.
Butler: It isn't, just because we can't depend on other people to be equally tolerant. My example was way back in the schoolyards, school bullies. No matter how tolerant you may be, they aren't, and your being tolerant won't stop them from tackling you if that's what they want to do. I think most people can get along together by being tolerant.

Simon: Is there another part of the essay you'd like to read for us?
Butler: Well maybe the last bit. "Back in the early 1960s, there was a United Nations television commercial, the audio portion of which went something like this:

ignorance, fear, disease, hunger, suspicion, hatred, war—that was it, although I would have added greed and vengeance to the list—all or any of these can be the catalysts that turn hierarchical thinking into hierarchical behavior. Amid all this, does tolerance have a chance? Only if we want it to; only when we want it to. Tolerance, like any aspect of peace, is forever a work in progress, never complete, and if we're as intelligent as we think, never abandoned."

Big Thinker

Susan Stamberg/2001

From *Weekend Edition* (December 29, 2001) © National Public Radio. Permission granted by NPR.

Stamberg: Another conversation on the year 2001, this time with science fiction writer Octavia Butler. She has won every award in her genre, plus a MacArthur fellowship. Ms. Butler spends much of her time thinking about the future of the human species and what life could be like on other planets. Octavia Butler joins us from member station KUOW in Seattle. Welcome and thanks for joining us.
Butler: Thank you.

Stamberg: We're asking people to think back on 2001 for us. Do you think this is a year that has changed us as a nation?
Butler: I think every year changes us as a nation, and it's really only a question of how much. This one may have changed us a little more than others, or in a direction that we didn't expect, but change is inevitable.

Stamberg: Tell me something, Octavia Butler; there you are out in Seattle, we here on the other coast, particularly in New York and Washington find ourselves talking about the eleventh of September obsessively and far more than any other events that took place in this year. Is that your experience there?
Butler: Yes. When I was asked to do this, I started writing—the way I think is to write, just scribble—and that was what I wrote the most about. I found myself thinking back also to the tax cut, and the environmental issues, global warming, ANWR, that kind of thing, and they're all there, they're still there, they haven't gone anyplace. It disturbs me that we've forgotten them because that means that some time in the future we're going to be in trouble, and we won't have seen that coming either. It won't be terrorism; it will just be our negligence.

Stamberg: We find ourselves engaged in a war at this moment. Is this one different?
Butler: I think it is, just because we don't really have an enemy who is a country. In spite of our efforts in Afghanistan, the enemy is, I think, a lot of mainly young men who don't know what to do with themselves and who have very little hope.

I think there's probably nothing more dangerous than a person who imagines that he has nothing to lose, and that's the kind of people that we're really at war against.

Stamberg: What about in science fiction, is there terrorism there?
Butler: Probably there is, but I don't know about it, I can't claim to have read anything recently that involved terrorism, but I'm sure there is terrorism in some of the stories and novels.

Stamberg: What I wonder, Ms. Butler, has happened to you as a writer since the eleventh of September? Have you shifted?
Butler: I killed off a novel. It was my frivolous novel; I was writing a fantasy that I thought was going to be kind of a rest-stop because I had done *Parable of the Sower* and *Parable of the Talents*, and I had in mind another novel that was equally grim, and I needed a break, so I was writing a frivolous novel that I somehow couldn't go on with after 9/11. I wound up writing a short story that made the same point and that way ridding myself of the need to write the novel.

Stamberg: So you wrote, you got it out, but you did it shorter, feeling in some way that you didn't want to spend a whole lot of time in a world that bubbly?
Butler: Yes.

Stamberg: Has that ever happened to you?
Butler: I don't think it has. I've written bad novels and then published them, but I've never had a novel just kind of fall away like that.

Stamberg: What are you working on right now?
Butler: I've gone back to the grim one. But writing the short story was fun.

Stamberg: So if you don't see 2001 as a major turning point in history but simply another turning point through which we are passing, what has it meant, do you think?
Butler: I guess on the personal level, because I write science fiction, it's interesting to see it come and go, and realize that we hadn't gotten as far as another science fiction writer thought we might have. Arthur Clarke I mean.

Stamberg: The author of *2001: A Space Odyssey.*
Butler: I was sort of rooting for what he had in mind, the good parts of it anyway.

Stamberg: What was that?
Butler: The idea of greater space travel and almost casual space travel. I grew up

during the Space Race, during the sixties, and it was a wonderful way of sort of having a way without having one. We could get the technological push, and we could get the combat with the Soviet Union, but we never quite had that nuclear war. Instead we raced each other to the moon, and I guess I see space still as a way to achieve a lot of technological efforts without necessarily hurting anybody.

The Lit Interview: Octavia Butler

Daniel Burton-Rose/2003

From *San Francisco Bay Guardian* (December 2005). © Daniel Burton-Rose.
Permission granted by author.

The following interview was conducted on two separate occasions: in the winter
of 2003, just after Octavia Butler completed a tour celebrating the publication of
a twenty-fifth anniversary edition of her first successful novel, *Kindred* (1979),
and in the fall of 2005, coinciding with the publication of *Fledgling* and the first
expanded edition of *Bloodchild and Other Stories*. At Ms. Butler's request, both
interviews were supplemented by portions of public lectures. The first of these
took place in the Morrison Reading Room on the Berkeley campus of the University of California. It was organized by the African-American Studies Department
and Africana Studies Program. The second was at Marcus Books, an Afro-centric
bookstore in Oakland. The interviews thus benefit from the profound relationship of mutual devotion between Ms. Butler and her audience. Approved of by
Ms. Butler, I believe that the following accurately represents her thoughts on a
wide range of her work at what tragically turned out to be the end of her life.

Interviewer: How did you come up with the idea for *Kindred*?
Octavia Butler: I got the idea for *Kindred* while I was in college. I got the idea
from a classmate, someone who was sort of our scholar. He had made himself our
best resource on black history because he'd read more of it than any of us. If you
wanted to know something and you didn't understand it, you could talk about it
with him and get some idea.

But one day he said something that made me realize that even though he had
a vast collection of facts, a seriously detailed outline of history in his head, he
didn't necessarily understand it in one specific way. We were arguing and he said
something like this, "I wish I could kill all these old black people who've been
holding us back for so long, but I can't because I'd have to start with my own parents." I realized that part of my research went back into my own life. Not that I
knew I was doing research at the time—this goes under the heading "writers use
everything."

My mother was taken out of school when she was ten and set to work. As a result she basically knew how to clean houses and not much else. That's what she did for a living for most of my childhood. She would take me with her sometimes, when she didn't have a babysitter, and I would get to see her going in back doors, and I'd get to see her not pay attention, not hearing when things were said that ordinarily she'd respond to very vehemently. And I was embarrassed, I was ashamed. I remember saying to her, "I will never do what *you* do. What *you* do is *terrible*." And my mother was not a person to take sass from me. Normally if I got sassy I learned about it right away, I learned I shouldn't do that. But in this case she just looked at me, and she looked kinda hurt, and didn't say anything.

I carried that look for a number of years before I understood it, and before I understood what my friend had failed to understand. I didn't have to leave school when I was ten, I never missed a meal, always had a roof over my head, *because* my mother was willing to do demeaning work and accept humiliation. What I wanted to teach in writing *Kindred* was that the people who did what my mother did were not frightened or timid or cowards, they were heroes. I wanted to make that clear to people like my friend. I wanted to reach people emotionally in a way that history tends not to.

Int: How did you research the book?
OB: One of the things that I did was read a lot of slave narratives. One of them was *To Be a Slave* by Julius Lester. It was intended for high school kids. He took bits of slave narratives and showed them to you. One line stayed with me. The line was this: "They whipped my father because he looked at a slave they killed and he cried." Sometimes one line can mean so much and tell you about the whole institution of slavery.

I also looked at slavemasters' wives' journals. My favorite was Frannie Kimball's journal. It's still available in a more abbreviated version, but I was lucky enough to get hold of the long version in the library. I read bits of *The Underground Railroad* by William Still, because it's important to know a lot of slaves did get away, even in impossible situations where they were very far south; you wouldn't imagine they could but they did. I read a book called *Cotton Kingdom* by Frederick Law Olmstead. Olmstead is the man who designed Central Park in New York City. He got on a horse and began to ride through the South. He discovered he didn't much like the slaves and didn't much like the slavemasters. But he had a good eye. He looked around, he noticed things, so his book was interesting for me to read. He was also an alien wandering through a strange land, and for that reason it was valuable.

My favorite collection of slave narratives was a nineteen-volume set called *The American Slave: A Composite Autobiography*. It was assembled in the 1930s by the Writer's Project [of the Works Progress Administration], and these people interviewed the slaves who were left, the very last ones. It was depressing reading not only because bad things happened to slaves, but because slavery could become so pedestrian when you read enough of it, so ordinary. I remember someone telling me that they'd read the Harriet Jacobs narrative, and they said it was mild compared to other slave narratives. And, horribly enough, it was, but that doesn't make her any less a slave. It wasn't something you'd want to undergo.

Int: Reading *Parable of the Talents*, I imagined you being inspired by news accounts of modern-day slavery in the Sudan, or the kind of disintegration taking place in Colombia or Somalia.

OB: No, what I did was I looked at our own country. I also looked at Nazi Germany. I was interested to see how a country goes fascist. Because it concerned me that in some ways we could head down that pathway. And I was also interested in all the things we weren't paying attention to in a useful way. These things are used to play politics but they're not really used in any useful way most of the time. I was thinking of education and the economy and the ecology, and the various things that, if we don't pay attention to, are going to lead us to living in a world that we really don't want to live in. This is not about the past. This is about the present and the future.

Int: What were some of the common themes in the sci-fi genre when you grew up? Did you immerse yourself in those books?

OB: I used to have a teacher who said "the problem with would-be science fiction writers is that they read too much science fiction." I was certainly in that category. For quite a while it was all I read.

When I was very young, I read whatever was out there, but I found great fun in reading fairy tales, and I discovered mythology and comic books, and loved both. I got into science fiction by way of a bad movie, but I had been reading science fiction novels without really recognizing them as a separate genre. But once I got into it—especially when I got into the adult section of the library, when I was fourteen, I had a whole [wall] of science fiction. I read my way through it. I got to read a lot of hard science fiction and a lot of fantasy, and a lot of soft science fiction dealing with anthropology, sociology. I read Heinlein and Asimov and Clarke and J. T. Macintosh and any number of others. Whoever was there.

During the period between twelve and fourteen when I wasn't allowed in the adult section of the library, I read magazines a lot. At that time it was *Analog*, *Worlds of If*, and *Galaxy*, those. I thoroughly enjoyed myself. I knew nothing about fandom and I never went to a science fiction convention until I was in my mid-twenties.

Int: The majority of your writings at this point are deeply integrated into Los Angeles and its environs; no less of an L.A. *cognoscenti* than Mike Davis credits you with qualitatively updating the city's probable dystopian development. How do you characterize your relationship with the city?

OB: At that time the L.A. area, which is a pretty big area, was the only place I'd ever lived. So when I thought about the future, and the future we're bringing upon ourselves if we're not careful, of course I thought about how it would affect us where I was living. I thought about other places too, but I thought about that place first because it was my home.

Int: Was Lauren Olamina's trek north in *Parable of the Sower* a foreshadowing of your own?

OB: No. I live in Seattle, and believe me, I didn't walk here! I have wanted to live in Seattle for quite a long time. I couldn't leave while my mother was elderly and a widow, and in '96 she passed away. I was able to begin, after I got her affairs straightened out, to think about what I might want to do with myself. I figured I'd better move up here before I felt myself to be too old.

Int: Do you see the change in locale influencing your writing?

OB: No, not the change in locale so much. Of course I will be writing more about up here. As a matter of fact in my story "The Book of Martha" the character does live up here.

Int: Your work reflects many of the concerns and considerations of politically aware people, but you also maintain a critical distance from social movements. In the *Parable of Talents*, for example, the journals of Lauren Olamina, who's promoting one of these movements, are framed by a critical voice.

OB: By her daughter, yes. It wasn't so much maintaining a critical perspective. Her daughter, coming in as she did, was almost a direct result of my mother passing away. When she died, I had to clear up her affairs and get myself back together. I'd just bought a house in the expectation that she was going to come live with me. I had this big pause in writing the novel. When I got back to it, it had suddenly become a mother-daughter story without my ever having really planned for it to be.

Int: Certainly a difficult one, and very painful for the mother.

OB: I didn't understand that for a long time. It was something that seemed to be working and I let it happen, but I think I realized later that it was mainly me missing my mother and being a little annoyed that she was gone. Which is not logical, but people do things like that.

Int: Are there social movements that you identify with or are inspired by?
OB: Not terribly. Not in the sense of joining something. I'm with the ABB—"Anybody But Bush"—movement right now [winter 2003]. For the first time in my life I was sending campaign donations to a political candidate—Dean, as a matter of fact, before he fell out.

There are a lot of things that I care about, and I mention some of them with relation to the two *Parable* books. I belong to a lot of environmentalist organizations. I really feel that it's important we stop playing games, and the idea that we're somehow going to improve the forests by having people go in and chop down the most valuable trees is just obscene, and the idea that we are going to lose environmental legislation for clean air and clean water that earlier groups worked really hard for is obscene. I mean we're doing such unutterably stupid things that I can't not pay attention to it.

Then there are things like war and peace, of course. I found the war [in Iraq] to be totally unnecessary, and I said so before we got into it. We're going down a lot of wrong paths. The books are warnings, they're "If this goes on . . ." novels.

Nobody really needed warning, everybody could see that we're sliding in the wrong directions, especially with regard to things like global warming. But nothing is being done, at least on the part of our national government.

Int: One thing I had difficulty understanding in the *Parable of the Sower* is pushing for the fulfillment of human destiny in the stars.
OB: The destiny of Earthseed. Why was that a problem?

Int: It's difficult to separate space exploration from a massive concentration of wealth diverting from pressing needs at home. These funds are then used by people intent on a militaristic conquest of whatever they may encounter.
OB: I don't think that extra-solar worlds would be a militaristic conquest. There's just the distance alone [to prevent it]. What I saw was the possibility of a huge family of difficult long-term projects as something that would perhaps divert our attention from tearing at each other. We'd also have the benefit of a little species insurance. If we did manage to destroy ourselves, we probably wouldn't destroy ourselves everywhere.

Part of the reason I came up with that as [Olamina's] goal is because I was a kid during the space race. I used to get up early in the morning and watch as the preparations were made and the Mercury capsules and then the Gemini and the Apollo went off. It was riveting. It seemed important.

Later I thought this was our way of having a nuclear war with the Russians without having one. You had the kind of fallout that you get from war, the technological fallout, and you had the competition. And yet massive numbers of people were not dying. We had wars of course, with Vietnam being the nastiest of them, but we didn't have that nuclear war. This was one of the reasons. People have often used religious mandates to work on very long-term difficult projects, from the pyramids to the cathedrals of the Middle Ages. And why not give them a long-term difficult project that, if they actually manage to complete, would actually do some good for the human species?

Int: In the Xenogenesis series you have the Oankali, the aliens, identify two characteristics of our species, intelligence and hierarchy, the latter of which is our critical problem.
OB: Yes, two characteristics. And unfortunately, the older one is in charge.

Int: The hierarchical. Is an empathy that's so strong that you can't control it, as presented in *Parables*, the antidote you propose for this characteristic?
OB: The hyper-empathy syndrome is by no means a solution to anything in *Parables*. It's a problem! It's something that almost prevents my character from surviving.

Int: But it also prevents her from attacking. It makes aggression intensely unpleasant. Is it intended as a safeguard against people's propensity for violence?
OB: I think so, when I came up with the idea I actually thought I might write a book about a time when everybody has this. Somehow everyone is affected with it. I realized after a little bit of writing that if that's the only change, it wouldn't be nearly enough. It's always possible, for instance, to pay people to take more pain than you're willing to take. And it is, after all, delusional. These are not powers that somebody has. These are delusions that my characters, and those others who are damaged by the drug, have. I wanted to write a book—it wound up being two books—in which everything that happened *could* actually happen. I wasn't writing about any newly developed powers. I was writing about somebody having a certain kind of delusion that she *couldn't* shake, and it didn't do any good to have somebody say "it's all in your head"—of course it was. So what, it still hurts! That's why I emphasize that she can be tricked. And others can be who have the same problem. They can be tricked by someone who isn't in pain but who pretends to be. They can be tricked by someone who is stoical about pain and simply

doesn't let on. There's the pleasure angle, which is a nice thing, but turns out to be grotesque when my character is raped.

Int: You mentioned wanting to do a book where everything that takes place could. For someone identified with the sci-fi genre, it seems like you have absolutely no infatuation with technology in and of itself.

OB: Not infatuation perhaps, but interest. In the Xenogenesis books, the technology is almost entirely biological. I find that I am much more fascinated by the biological sciences. But that's just personal interest.

Int: How did you come to write *Fledgling*?

OB: I began working on *Fledgling* for very much the same reason that I wrote *Wild Seed*. I wrote *Wild Seed* as a reward for having written *Kindred*. *Kindred* was *depressing*. I had to go to places that I didn't enjoy going, in my own mind and in history. Also, my characters in *Kindred* couldn't really win. I couldn't change history and make them win. The closest they could come to winning was to survive. They lived. They didn't live *whole*, but they lived.

When I finished *Kindred*, I needed to do something that was fun. *Wild Seed* was fun. Which is odd because it was also one of the most difficult novels I've ever written. But I thoroughly enjoyed writing it.

I did the two Parable books, and I wanted to do a third but I realized I was kind of written out for a while. The Parable books came out of reading the news. They're books that warn us that if we're not careful, we're going to end up living in a fairly nasty world in the not-too-distant future. This meant that I had to think up the nastiest. If we keep doing what we're doing, what's likely to become of us? I've done a lot of that, and I didn't want to live in that world anymore.

I kept trying. I tried to write a third Parable book, and nothing came of it. I tried to write a couple other books that were fairly serious, and nothing came of them. And finally, for my sins, somebody gave me a vampire book. I read it, and I had such a good time that I went out and bought some more vampire books. After a while, I wanted to write one. So that's what [I did].

Int: Are you a long time devotee of the vampire novel or are you a recent convert?

OB: It's not something I paid a lot of attention to. I read Bram Stoker's *Dracula* ages ago. It was on my mother's bookshelf. It was nice—I read whatever was on her bookshelf, grazing and finding what I could. Later on I heard about Anne Rice. I read her first book and found it interesting but I didn't pay that much attention.

What caught my attention is that you can write a vampire novel as a historical novel, as a mystery, as a romance, as science fiction. The variety amazed me. I thought, "There are all these different kinds of vampires. I'm going to make my own."

Int: I've seen *Fledgling* classified in bookstores under "Horror," but it could just as easily be under "Erotica."
OB: I am surprised. I didn't realize that there was this division. I thought it was all just fantasy. I realize now that the division exists, but I didn't know before.

Int: You've always caused difficulties for people who would like to pin you in one genre.
OB: I don't worry about it because it's not something that I can control.

Int: In our imaginations, vampires stand-in for our uncontrollable desires. Usually these are understood as injuring others, but the "Ina" community you've imagined anticipates and channels its members' desires in a mutually satisfying way.
OB: This is what a culture is for: looking after its members in one way or another. It's a matriarchal culture. Chemically, people get along together reasonably well most of the time. Unfortunately, every now and then, something goes wrong, just like in any culture.

Int: In your previous work—particularly the Patternist and Xenogenesis series— there was a disturbing power dynamic in the genetic selection process between immortals and mortals, and aliens and humans, respectively. In *Fledgling*, it's the progressive female elders who experiment with genetic engineering and irrational conservatives who attack them.
OB: There's going to be a power dynamic no matter what. The position of Wright [one of the protagonist Shiori's "symbionts," or human lovers] is an interesting one. He's not that unhappy about where he ends up, but it's not something he chose. It's a group marriage.

Int: Can you unpack the racial dynamics of *Fledgling?* There's an apparent parallel between the way in which the African-American protagonist suffered a violence-induced cultural amnesia at the hands of European-Americans and the African-American experience in the United States as a whole.
OB: If Shiori did not have amnesia she would probably have more in common with the people who raised her than with, say, just an ordinary African-American. But because she has the amnesia, she doesn't have that much in common with *anybody.*

Int: You've referred to most of your previous work as your "world-saving" novels and *Fledgling* as your "fun" one. Is there any fun way to save the world?

OB: "The Book of Martha" was a fun way to save the world. "The Book of Martha" is a short story that appears in the second edition of *Bloodchild and Other Stories*. Martha is going along with her life when suddenly she is practically kidnapped by God. God tells her that she is to figure out a way to make the human species less suicidal. What she comes up with, she will live at the bottom of; she has to come up with something where, even if you're at the bottom, you're still okay. It's like: "Here's the pie. You cut it and your brother gets first pick."

Int: God offers constructive criticism on her proposals.

OB: She doesn't want to make a mistake and accidentally wipe out the species!

Int: Martha decides to make peoples' dreams more powerful and satisfying.

OB: Their dreams are utopian for them in particular. They get to live in their own utopia for the period of their dreaming.

Int: Can you discuss the genesis of "Amnesty," the other new inclusion in *Bloodchild*?

OB: "Amnesty" is a story in which aliens arrive and they're not that interested in us. They're not even interested in taking anything from us that we value all that much; they like nice, hot deserts, like Death Valley. They run some of us through mazes as lab rats, but mostly they ignore us.

They take a few people in, then make them do things to find out what the heck we are. Then they let them go. My character is one of the first people let go, but she's been a prisoner for years. The human police agency that picks her up when she's released decides that she must know secrets and that if she's not telling the secrets that she knows, it must be because she's siding with the aliens. They arrest her and lock her up and treat her rather badly.

This whole thing was inspired by what happened to Dr. Wen Ho Lee in the late 1990s. He is a Chinese-American who worked at Los Alamos [National Laboratory] and was suddenly accused of spying for Red China—which was interesting because he was actually from Taiwan!

His career was pretty much ruined because of the accusation and he was locked up for a while. He didn't know when he would get out again, *whether* he would get out again, what might happen to him while he was inside. That's truly the terrifying part: if you're innocent and you're locked up and you have no information to trade for your freedom. I had no idea how popular this behavior was about to become.

Int: There's already speculation that *Fledgling* is the beginning of a series. Can you comment?

OB: I have bits that would relate to another book, but that always happens when I finish a book.

I've wanted so much, for so long, to write the *Trickster* book, which follows *Parable of the Sower* and *Parable of the Talents.* In those two books a new religion is created. One of the verses describes God this way: "God is trickster, teacher, chaos, clay . . ." I would like to write the story of the people who leave Earth following the mandate of their new religion, Earthseed, which says: "The destiny of Earthseed is to take root among the stars." I don't know if it's going to happen. I don't dare tell anybody I am definitely doing it!

A Conversation with Octavia Butler

Nick DiChario/2004

From *Writers and Books*, www.wab.org, (February 2004) © Nick DiChario.
Permission granted by author.

W&B: In writing *Kindred*, what were you trying to say about slavery?
Butler: The idea really was to make people feel the book. That's the point of taking a modern day black person and making her experience slavery, not as just a matter of one-on-one but going back and being part of the whole system.

W&B: Is this something that you felt other authors had not covered?
Butler: Actually, I had never seen it done.

W&B: Is there something that you would like to have readers know about this edition of *Kindred*?
Butler: There is that introduction, not written by me. I think that if people haven't read the book yet, it would be a good idea for them to read the introduction at the end. I actually tried to have it put there, but nothing happened. Otherwise it blows the book a bit. It should be an afterword instead of what it is.

W&B: Why did you pick that particular period of the 1800s to write about? Was there anything that drew you to that time?
Butler: No, I wanted to begin early enough so that the Civil War didn't become part of the story. I wanted the Rufus character to have time to grow up. I also was aware of the two particularly famous Marylanders who had been slaves, Frederick Douglass and Harriet Tubman. There are places where my characters actually mention Tubman. They were there then. That was a time I felt a little bit familiar with.

W&B: Why did you set the book in a border state like Maryland instead of setting it down in the deep south?
Butler: Because I wanted my character to have a legitimate hope of escape. A stranger plopped down in the middle of Mississippi was pretty much going to stay there. People who were born there [in Maryland] did escape. There were a

number of escapes in a book that was one of my sources. In Maryland [Dana] was less than two miles from freedom.

W&B: How much do you think the slaves of that era really knew about escape routes?

Butler: It would depend on the slaves, really. Some knew nothing. That's why some of them, even in their effort to escape in Maryland, wound up starving to death or getting caught, because they didn't know which way they were going. They might be able to find the North Star and all that, but if they didn't know what to eat or what not to eat . . . that's one of the advantages that Harriet Tubman had. Her father had taught her how to live off the woods. She escaped and that's one of the reasons she survived. But other people did not—either didn't survive or just didn't succeed.

W&B: Do you have any ideas about the numbers of people who did make it to freedom from Maryland at that time?

Butler: I know that Harriet Tubman is credited with bringing about three hundred out of Maryland, but I don't know how many apart from that. Probably quite a number. It's not the sort of thing that the slavemaster structure in Maryland would have wanted to have widely known, of course.

W&B: You said that *Kindred* was the first novel that you knew of that tried to make readers understand what it felt like to be a slave.

Butler: Not so much make a person understand, but confront a modern person with that reality of history. It's one thing to read about it and cringe that something horrible is happening. I sent somebody into it who is a person of now, of today, and that means I kind of take the reader along and expose them in a way that the average historic novel doesn't intend to, can't.

W&B: Is that one of the reasons you kept her in modern dress throughout the book?

Butler: That, and the reality that nobody would be giving her new clothes. They might find something for her, but what she was wearing worked, and there were slaves who were close to naked. The dressing of slaves was not high on anybody's agenda.

W&B: I've read that you did quite a bit of research into slave narratives for this book.

Butler: It was the first time I ever specifically took off and went somewhere, went to Maryland to do research. As a result, later, I was less intimidated when I had to go to South America to the Peruvian Amazon to research another trilogy of novels. The whole thing was a learning experience for me. I didn't know how to research such a novel and everything I did was kind of learning on the job.

W&B: Would you do anything differently today, now that you have more experience?

Butler: Going the way I did . . . I don't think I would have done that again. I think I would have been able to get more information before I went. The library in Los Angeles, which is where I lived then, was pretty good. It's just that Maryland is such a small state, I really felt that I had better go there and use their libraries as I would be more likely to find information that I could use.

W&B: Does the book as a whole have a different meaning for you now that you look at it over the quarter of a century since you wrote it?

Butler: It still means pretty much what I wanted it to. If you mean do I feel any different for having written it, no. Like most of my books, I say what I have to say and then I move on. I'm doing something else right now. I'm pretty happy with the way *Kindred* turned out.

W&B: Some people have commented on Dana having a white husband and having to deal with a white master and the interracial slave children of the time. I assume this was a deliberate device to show how some attitudes have changed over the years.

Butler: Certainly . . . in this country there is a great deal more kindred than we have always chosen to recognize. When I wrote *Kindred*, interracial marriage was less prevalent than it is now. Now it's a shrug; then it was a bit more unusual. I think I had one set of friends—actually, they were triplets—in school who had a white father and a black mother. That's going all the way from K through 12.

W&B: Could you say a bit more about how there were so many children born to slaves by their masters and the fact that so many blacks today do have white ancestry as their heritage.

Butler: It works the other way too, you know. That quite a few whites are surprised to find that they have black ancestry. Because it was very inconvenient to be black and if you could pass, well, there was a time when that was a good idea.

W&B: Until this century, I'm sure.

Butler: As a matter of fact, when I was traveling with [my novel] *Parable of the Sower*, one person I kept running into was the woman who wrote *The Sweeter the Juice* [*The Sweeter the Juice: A Family Memoir in Black and White* by Shirlee Taylor

Haizlip]. It's about her family and the fact that one day the lighter-skinned portion of her family just disappeared. They left the area and went off to Michigan, I believe, and became white. Her mother was the darkest member of that branch of the family so her mother got left behind.

When she was researching the book, she found some members of her family who had not known about this connection, because of course nothing would be said: it would be very carefully kept from the children as time went on. She found some members of her family in Orange County and the older ones were still touchy about it and the younger ones were kind of enthusiastic about it. "Really? How interesting! Tell us how that worked!" It was really interesting to hear about the differences. The times have changed, at least a little. When I first wrote the book, I got a little bit of criticism for trivializing slavery. You know, writing what they thought of as a science fiction novel about it.

W&B: Do you consider yourself a science fiction writer?
Butler: I consider myself a writer. As you probably are aware, it's unbelievably boring to have people continually trying to get you to define, oh, are you writing speculative fiction or science fiction or . . . You know, is it a good story? And if so, then accept it as that.

W&B: You don't consider that just the use of time travel makes a book science fiction?
Butler: It would be science fiction if I had presented a mechanism, maybe some phony physics. But no, I didn't do any of that—it's a grim fantasy.

W&B: Did your parents encourage you to read? Or were they bothered by your reading science fiction, especially?
Butler: Well, my father was dead. I don't think my mother had any awareness of science fiction or any other genre really. She only had three years of education; she was pulled out of school early to be put to work. My grandmother was widowed about the time the Depression started. This meant that a lot of her older children—they were poor anyway—didn't get to get an education. She was glad I was [inside] reading because if I was in the house reading I wasn't out getting into trouble, and maybe I might survive. I think the reading was not nearly as suspect as the writing. I think the family that I know as her family—her and my aunts and uncles—were alarmed that I actually imagined I could earn a living writing stories.

W&B: It's been suspect for a long, long time. Almost more now than ever before. Easy to understand how they might think that.

Butler: It's interesting how many science fiction writers get going when they are very young. I was on a program with Greg Bear, and he mentioned that he had gotten started writing when he was eight. And I began writing when I was ten. I think we're influenced by the stuff, we find it and we love it and we're influenced by it.... I know I collected my first rejection slip when I was thirteen, and I went on collecting them for a long time after that.

W&B: You're not especially prolific.
Butler: I wish I were, but I'm not. I used to worry that I would never be able to earn a living writing because I wrote so slowly.

W&B: But you have been doing this for quite some time.
Butler: The good thing is that if you last long enough and enough of your work is in print, you do survive. Especially if Hollywood every now and then throws a few thousand at you. It's nothing to get excited about, I just mean options.

W&B: I was just going to ask if anything is currently optioned.
Butler: *Kindred* is generally under option. It is now. Unfortunately, people have not been able to find the money to make the movie.

W&B: I suppose it doesn't have enough special effects in it.
Butler: [Laughter] Oh, my—people do have their ideas about science fiction and what it's supposed to be like.

W&B: Are there other science fiction writers that you particularly admire?
Butler: I went through a Sheri Tepper phase for a while. Someone introduced me to her work and I got busy and I read a lot of her novels. There are a lot of classics, as I think of them, books like *Perfume* by Patrick Suskind, that don't sound as though they're science fiction but seem to me to be exactly that. I think the most interesting thing about looking back now at the 1950s is how familiar things would be.

W&B: Could you expand on that?
Butler: We can do a lot of things faster, bigger, higher, that sort of thing, but they're essentially the same things. We're talking on the telephone. Now of course we could be going on computers, but even so we would be typing and looking at a screen and in those days we had typing and we had screens. We're connected. The cars might look different but they're still internal combustion engine cars for the most part. All the things that we thought, the flying cars, and buildings a mile high . . .

W&B: The Jetson's future.

Butler: The nonsense, I like to call it. The things that would make our era un-recognizable are mainly the social things. Imagine going back to the fifties and explaining that we're now discussing homosexual marriage. In the fifties, you didn't even hear the word homosexual, let alone that they might get married. I mean, black and white was illegal, forget two people of the same sex. And it was still OK to lynch people in different parts of our country. It was still OK to expect people to be openly racist in all parts of our country. Interesting how that goes in and out of fashion.

W&B: On another point, I just finished reading *Lilith's Brood* and I was very struck by . . .

Butler: Now *that's* science fiction.

W&B: Yes, that is definitely science fiction. But the themes of it seem to be al-most the inverse of the themes in *Kindred*. In *Lilith's Brood*, your alien race is non-hierarchical, nonviolent, very cooperative, unable to make small distinguishing characteristics based just on appearance. It seems you went very much in the op-posite direction after *Kindred*, approaching those themes from a positive angle instead of a negative angle.

Butler: I was doing something else that I had not seen done. I was writing about an alien species that was xenophilic. And when I began working on the novels, I thought "xenophilic" must be a word, it's a perfectly good word, there must be such a word. But in the dictionaries that I had, which were a few years old, I couldn't find it. And I didn't find it until I went to the library and looked in the *OED*. And some of the newer dictionaries out now, well, most of the bigger dic-tionaries, do have it. What I found instead was "xenophobic," a fear of strang-ers, and "xenomaniac," a person who has an unnatural liking for strangers. That's probably because my dictionaries were written in the shadow of the fifties, and xenophobia was rather popular back then.

W&B: Well, xenophobia runs deep throughout American history, well, all of his-tory, unfortunately.

Butler: I'm afraid that that's liable to get going again with all the problems we've been having.

W&B: What do you appreciate most about doing public appearances around *Kindred*?

Butler: I had a very good experience not long ago at Pomona College. The freshman class had read *Kindred* and the nice thing was that they came up with questions I hadn't heard before and provoked me to say things or think about things that I hadn't put into words before. I'm hoping that will happen in Rochester as well.

Interview: Octavia E. Butler

John C. Snider/2004

From *SciFiDimensions*, http://www.scifidimensions.com/jun04/octaviaebutler .htm (site accessed in 2006). Reprinted with permission of John C. Snider.

Octavia E. Butler has been an inspiration to a new generation of writers for the last quarter century. In the mid-1970s, at a time when few women—and even fewer blacks—were writing science fiction, Butler persisted, publishing the first three novels (*Patternmaster, Mind of My Mind,* and *Survivor*) in her Patternist series. Then, in 1979, she published *Kindred,* a dark fantasy novel that drills down into the prickly core of American history: slavery. This novel, in which a young middle-class black woman finds herself shuttled between 1976 California and antebellum Maryland, has become a classic of SF&F and required reading in both women's and African-American studies. But don't be fooled—while Butler's fiction appeals to feminist and minority demographics, it's not propped up by that appeal. To read Octavia Butler is to read good literature—period.

Although she has written a dozen or so novels and numerous short stories (and won two Hugos and a Nebula), she is still most celebrated for *Kindred.* Now, Beacon Press has published a special twenty-fifth anniversary edition of *Kindred,* which includes a critical essay and discussion questions.

scifidimensions: Congratulations on the twenty-fifth anniversary of *Kindred.*
Octavia E. Butler: Thank you.

sfd: Did you have any idea when this book was first published, or when you were writing it, that it would have the impact that it's had?
OEB: Of course not. What I write gets called "science fiction" a lot, but I don't have any particular ability to see the future [laughs]. I knew it [*Kindred*] was something that I had not done before, and that it was going to be especially difficult. I didn't know how to write it. I got going with it after I'd done three other books, because at least by then I knew how to write a novel. I didn't really know how to write or research this novel. That's what I had to learn as I went along.

sfd: What kind of research goes into creating a book like *Kindred*?

OEB: Well, of course I did a lot of library research, and I went off to Maryland and did some on-the-spot research. I talked to members of my family, and did some personal research that didn't really have anything to do with the time and place I was writing about, but that gave me a *feeling* of the experience of being black in a time and place where it was very difficult to be black.

sfd: Is the book's location in Maryland a real place, or based on a real place?

OEB: Well, the eastern shore of Maryland is a real place. I didn't really make up any locations—except that particular plantation.

sfd: If my memory is correct, Alex Haley's *Roots* (at least the mini-series) came out about the time you were writing *Kindred* . . .

OEB: Actually, I don't think the mini-series had come out yet, but the book had come out and was a bestseller. When I was traveling around in Maryland, I kept running across little "Alex Haley was here" signs; you know, advertising that he had done research at that particular place. I was writing a completely different kind of book, so it didn't bother me. It at least let me know that I was in the right place to do research.

sfd: So it didn't have any specific influence on you?

OEB: I hadn't read it, no, because I really was doing a completely different kind of book. I wasn't trying to work out my own ancestry. I was trying to get people to *feel* slavery. I was trying to get across the kind of emotional and psychological stones that slavery threw at people.

sfd: It's interesting to look at the different venues in which *Kindred* is studied. Science fiction fans read it. It's used in women's studies, as well as courses about African-American history.

OEB: I tried to convince my original publishers of this but I don't think they ever quite believed me. I knew that I had at least three audiences. My work before this had been all science fiction, and even then I felt that I had three audiences, but I couldn't get anyone to really pay attention.

sfd: Having multiple audiences is a good thing, isn't it?

OEB: It was especially good back then, because there were a lot more independent book stores: science fiction, women's studies, and black studies. It was wonderful. I always hoped they would carry my work, but usually when I went in, the moment I said "science fiction" I should have just turned around and gone home [laughs].

sfd: Does the label "African-American woman writer" bother you at all?
OEB: It's silly because it puts me in a weird corner. It puts me in such a strange corner that a lot of people don't want to look at what I've done—either because they think they know what it is, or they're afraid of what it might be. I've gone to interviews where that's all anybody wanted to talk about. "What do you think of yourself as . . . How do you define this . . . How do you define that . . ." It's very tiresome.

sfd: What do you think, in general, of the phenomenon of hyphenated-Americanism?
OEB: People have the right to call themselves whatever they like. That doesn't bother me. It's *other* people doing the calling that bothers me.

sfd: I also wanted to talk a little bit about your Parable series, and specifically its religious aspects. For those that aren't familiar with it, can you give us a quick summary of the Earthseed religion and its basic tenets?
OEB: Well, the character [Lauren Olamina] who comes up with the religion is living during a near-future time that's gotten very nasty; the U.S. has collapsed economically and ecologically, and things are going very badly. People, if they're surviving with any degree of comfort, are living in walled communities. Her father is a Baptist minister, and she feels that he's a good man in his religion. There's nothing wrong with it, except that it isn't really preparing people for what they have to deal with today. What she comes up with is a religion that gives people a goal. It helps them deal with what's going on in their day, but it also gives them a future goal. Actually, the goal is to go to heaven, but she means it literally. She says the destiny of Earthseed is to take root among the stars. She helps people deal with the changes that have happened and the changes that will happen. She kind of points the way as she sees it, and describes things as she sees them. It's a fairly harsh religion, because there's no one to worship, and there's no one who's going to pull you out of hot water if you get into it.

sfd: Could Earthseed become a real religion?
OEB: Oh, it wouldn't work as a real religion. There's not enough of it. It's not comforting enough, really. When I was doing a tour for *The Parable of the Sower*, some asked something similar to that, adding that Earthseed was "a series of good rules to live by." I said, "Well, yes—but it's not very comforting." And she said, "But I don't really need comfort from my religion." And I said, "Well, that's because you are comfortable." And most of us are. I don't mean we're rich, but

we're not starving in the gutter. Most of us don't have to worry about being shot if we poke our noses outside. So we are comfortable, but the people I'm writing about are definitely *not* comfortable, and being shot while they're still *inside* is a good possibility. Considering that they are eventually burned out of their homes, this brings it home even more. She [Lauren] is living in a time when people need to be told, okay, you're in trouble and you're going to have to save yourself, because you're the only person you can depend on to do it—you and those with whom you bond.

sfd: So what would the ideal religion be? Maybe you've already found one for yourself?
OEB: Goodness, I wouldn't even want to say what the ideal religion would be! I was raised Baptist, and I like the fact that I got my conscience installed early. I have a huge and savage conscience that won't let me get away with things. I think if there were more of those around, we'd be better off.

sfd: Do you feel external pressure to write more in the universes you've created? To write a sequel to *Kindred*, or another Patternist book, or another Parable book?
OEB: No . . . a novel is a long business. I'm a slow writer, even when I'm doing very well I write slowly. For me, a novel has to be something I'm going to be interested in for the duration. If it's something I'm trying to write for any reason other than interest, it's probably not going to do very well.

sfd: Why did you get into writing science fiction, as opposed to some other genre of literature?
OEB: I guess it goes back to what I just said, really—it has to hold my interest. What held my interest early on was fantasy. But my problem with fantasy, and horror, and related genres, is that sometimes the problems are illogical. I have the kind of mind that demands that I work things out, to see how they would really work if they were real. I have to be able to do that. So fantasy was fine early on, and when I discovered science fiction, I was very happy with it, because my first interest in science fiction came with an interest in astronomy. That meant I got to read about the stars and the planets and everything—that was very exciting, even though they were duller than I expected. I thought there'd be Martians and Venusians and all that, and then I began to read and realized . . . well, no. But still, it was more interesting than anything I had to deal with in my day-to-day life. I think part of it was that I was an only child, and my day-to-day life was fairly dull. So I reached out for something that was more interesting. On the other hand, I was very much interested in the way people behaved, the human dance,

how they seemed to move around each other. I wanted to play around with that. Science fiction let me do both. It let me look into science and stick my nose in everywhere. I would never have been a good scientist—my attention span was too short for that. Here I was into astronomy, and here into anthropology, and there I go into geology. It was much more fun to be able to research and write about whatever I wanted to. So, I was writing and sending stuff out when I was thirteen. No one was going to stop me from writing and no one had to really guide me towards science fiction. It was natural, really, that I would take that interest.

sfd: What role did Harlan Ellison play in your early career?
OEB: Harlan was a big help in making my writing more publishable. He was one of my teachers. He was a teacher at a workshop in Los Angeles called the Writers Guild of America West Open Door Workshop, back around 1969. What he introduced me to was Clarion Science Fiction Writers Workshop. Clarion is a six-week writer's workshop. Each week is taught by a different publishing writer or editor, or occasionally someone else in the field. When I went, it was in Clarion, Pennsylvania, which is where the name comes from. It still exists, but now it's at Michigan State University in East Lansing, and there's a Clarion West in Seattle.

sfd: What kind of advice do you have for up-and-coming writers?
OEB: I know a lot of people are where I was several years ago, when I was getting started with writing, wondering how they might get started as writers. And I have this little litany of things they can do. And the first one, of course, is to write—every day, no excuses. It's so easy to make excuses. Even professional writers have days when they'd rather clean the toilet than do the writing. Second, read every day. Read voraciously and omnivorously, whatever's out there. You never know what's gonna grab you. Third, for people who aren't doing it already, take classes—they're worthwhile. Workshops or classes—a workshop is where you do actually get feedback on your work, not just something where you go and sit for a day. A workshop is a way of renting an audience, and making sure you're communicating what you think you're communicating. It's so easy as a young writer to think you're been very clear when in fact you haven't. Those are some of the suggestions I give to my young writers.

sfd: Is there anything lacking in today's science fiction? Any themes that aren't being explored?
OEB: The thing about science fiction is that it's totally wide open. But it's wide open in a conditional way. Fantasy is totally wide open; all you really have to do is follow the rules you've set. But if you're writing about science, you have to first

learn what you're writing about. There are no walls apart from that. There's no subject you can't discuss. And by the way, I wanted to point out that *Kindred* is *not* science fiction. You'll note there's no science in it. It's a kind of grim fantasy.

sfd: I've heard you're working on a new installment in the Parable series?
OEB: No . . . I tried, but I had some health problems and some very damping medication that kind of stopped me from doing anything worth publishing for a long time. That was one of the things I tried to do that didn't work out. So I'm doing something completely different right now.

sfd: But there's still a possibility you might come back to it at some point?
OEB: Probably, yes. Not something about the two characters you meet in the previous books, because, of course, most of them are dead by the end of the second book. But it would be about people who tried to follow the Destinies.

sfd: Are there any other new projects you're working on that we ought to know about?
OEB: There are a couple of short stories, one called "The Book of Martha" and one called "Amnesty." These are stories people might not have seen because they're published online at *SciFiction*. They're from last year (2003), but they're my most recently published stuff. What I'm working on now—I'm back to fantasy, although considering that it's me, I'm turning it into a kind of science fantasy. It's a vampire story—but my vampires are biological vampires. They didn't become vampires because someone bit them; they were born that way. That's the novel I'm working on right now. I tend to write a lot stimulated by what's going on in the world—the news, history—plus I think I got a little depressed from my medication. And I realized the way out was to write something fairly lightweight, but still reasonably logical, so I'm writing this little science fantasy.

sfd: Any idea when that'll get published?
OEB: No, it's not something anyone has seen yet. I'm just over halfway done with it, and I'm hoping to finish somewhere around the middle of this year [2004].

sfd: Congratulations once again on the success of *Kindred*, and thanks for your time.
OEB: Thank you.

Octavia Butler's *Kindred*
Turns Twenty-five

Allison Keyes/2004

From *The Tavis Smiley Show* (March 4, 2004). © National Public Radio. Permission granted by NPR.

AK: The story about the African-American woman married to a white man who keeps getting sucked back in time to save her white slave-owning ancestor has always blown me away. How did you come up with that concept?

OB: It's something that I got an idea for when I was in college. A friend who was kind of our historian because he knew so much about black history said something that I thought indicated that he didn't know as much as I had believed. He said, "I wish I could kill all these old black people who have held us back for so long but I can't because I'd have to start with my own parents."

AK: Oh my goodness.

OB: I thought, he knows a lot of facts and figures, but he doesn't really understand or feel the realities of history, and I wanted to write something that would enable people, not just him, but anybody, to feel this particular bit of history. I wound up writing *Kindred* many years later after I had learned to write a novel.

AK: You are a science fiction writer, but is *Kindred* a science fiction story?

OB: *Kindred* is not science fiction. The only reason I'm called a science fiction writer is because that's the reputation I got early on. It's like people have to have a label for you or they're just not happy, and when I tried to sell *Kindred* that really gave me trouble, because nobody wanted to buy it. I had about fifteen rejections; fortunately with an agent so that it didn't take fifteen or more years, which it could have I suppose if I not had an agent. People kept rejecting it because they said, "Well, gee, we like this, it's well written, but we don't know what it is. What they were really saying was "We don't know how to sell it."

AK: Among the many themes you deal with in this novel are interracial relationships, both in the past and in the present—or 1976 I guess, and the importance of preserving family heritage. What made you want to deal with both of those issues and do you view them differently than you did when you wrote the book?

OB: I didn't really set out to deal with issues, I set out to make people feel history, and the story grew from that. I mean I never set out to deal with issues, I set out to tell a story about something or other. For instance with my book *Parable of the Sower*, and its sequel *Parable of the Talents*, I want to talk about what's going to happen if we keep doing what we've been doing, if we keep recklessly endangering the environment, if we keep paying no attention to economic realities, if we keep paying no attention to educational needs, if we keep doing a lot of the things that are hurting us now, and that's what I wound up writing about, and everything else just kind of fell into it, fell into place.

AK: I have read many critics who seem to feel that if you are a black fantasy/ science fiction writer, you must deal with race issues. Do you feel obligated at all to do that in your work?

OB: I don't feel obligated to do anything that doesn't seem to me to help the story, and I haven't really run into anybody like that since the sixties, so if they're still around I've happily avoided them. Back in the sixties I know I had friends who said, "You shouldn't be writing that, that's nonsense. You should be doing something to help the struggle." I listened, and I wondered what they had in mind, but meanwhile I have to do the thing that it's important for me to do. I am basically a storyteller, and I have things that seem important to me; I mentioned the emotional reality of history, I mentioned the news items that we seem to be ignoring so completely—

AK: The degradation of society continuing—

OB: These are the things that reach me, and whatever else happens, happens.

AK: Do you think that people in this country are doing any better with interracial relationships than they were then?

OB: I think they are. There are people who would argue with me about that, but I think they are, mainly because I can remember what it was like back when I was in college, for instance, or even when *Kindred* was written. I think, however, that it's not exactly progress because it can be snatched away so quickly. All sorts of social changes can be snatched away quickly. I remember I was traveling and talking about *Parable of the Talents*, and I ran into a young woman in Chicago who told me that she had come from the former Yugoslavia, and her parents had emigrated because one was Moslem and one was Christian. Now, these people lived together for a long time, and here was a case where a couple of them fell in love and got married and produced a family, but all of a sudden everything changed, and they had to run for it. So I don't have a lot of faith in the changes, I'm glad to see them, I just don't mistake them for permanent.

AK: The character of Dana really fascinated me. How much of yourself is there?
OB: A lot of personal history. I used to work in all those jobs that she had, for instance. I was the struggling writer who worked out of what we called the Slave Market, but of course it was just a blue-collar temporary agency, and I found that I preferred blue-collar work because with white-collar work you had to pretend you were enjoying it, and I wasn't. I was getting up at around two in the morning to do my writing, so I figured if I'm already tired and I come in crabby, I might as well be with a lot of other crabby people who are not having fun either. I used to go work with this agency and I did a lot of warehouse work, and cleaning, and factory work, food preparation; all tiresome stuff but things that people need done.

AK: So what are you working on now?
OB: I'm working on a vampire story.

AK: Really? A vampire story with black people?
OB: Well, I thought about it, and I thought, "What do vampires really need?" and I tried that on a few people and they said, "Blood." And I said, "No, no, you know, they need something else that they can't have," and finally somebody got it; "Well, gee, walk during the day?" And I said, "If vampires were a separate species, and they were into genetic engineering, what would they engineer for to be able to walk during the day, and what would they need to be able to do that?"

AK: Well, if you read Anne Rice they would need the blood of extremely strong vampires.
OB: Well, I figured melanin might help.

AK: Yeah, that's fabulous.
OB: So that's why my story is from the point of view of the first black female vampire.

AK: From Egypt?
OB: No, she's from Seattle.

Science Fiction Writer Octavia Butler
on Race, Global Warming, and Religion
Juan Gonzalez and Amy Goodman/2005

From *Democracy Now!*, http://www.democracynow.org/2005/11/11/science_
fiction_writer_octavia_butler_on. © *Democracy Now!* Reprinted with permission of *Democracy Now!*

Juan Gonzalez: Well, normally we don't spend a lot of time talking about science fiction on *Democracy Now!*, but today we're joined by one of the preeminent
voices writing in the genre today. Octavia Butler is one of the few well-known African American women science fiction writers. For the past thirty years her work
has tackled subjects not normally seen in that genre. The *Washington Post* has
called her "one of the finest voices in fiction, period. A master storyteller who
casts an unflinching eye on racism, sexism, poverty, and ignorance and lets the
reader see the terror and the beauty of human nature." Octavia has described herself as an outsider, a "pessimist, a feminist always, a Black, a quiet egoist, a former
Baptist, and an oil-and-water combination of ambition, laziness, insecurity, certainty, and drive."

Amy Goodman: Octavia Butler wrote her first story when she was ten years
old, and she has said she's been writing ever since. Race and slavery is a recurring theme in her work. Her first novel *Kindred* was published in 1979. It's a story
of a black woman who is transported back in time to the antebellum South. The
woman has been summoned there to save the life of a white son of a slave owner,
who turns out to be the woman's ancestor. Octavia Butler is the author of ten
other novels, including *Parable of the Sower* series. She's the recipient of many
awards, including the MacArthur Genius Award. Her latest book is called *Fledgling.* Welcome to *Democracy Now!*

Octavia Butler: Thank you.

AG: About a vampire?

OB: Yeah, it was kind of an effort to do something that was more lightweight
than what I had been doing. I had been doing the two Parable books—*Parable of
the Sower* and *Parable the Talents*—and they were what I call cautionary tales: If

we keep misbehaving ourselves, ignoring what we've been ignoring, doing what we've been doing to the environment, for instance, here's what we're liable to wind up with. And I found that I was kind of overwhelmed by what I had done, what I had had to comb through to do it. So eventually I wound up writing a fantasy, a vampire novel.

JG: But you also tell a lot about vampires themselves. The Ina people? Could you talk a little about that?

OB: Well, of course, I made them up. But one of the things I discovered when I decided to write a vampire novel was that most writers these days who write about vampires make up their own, and it really is a kind of a fantasy matter. You make up the rules and then you follow them.

AG: Tell us about your protagonist in *Fledging*, who this vampire is.
OB: Okay, she is a—

AG: "She" is an operative word, I think, to begin with.
OB: Oh, okay. She is a young girl. You're right. Most vampires I have discovered are men for some reason. I guess it's because of Dracula; people are kind of feeding off that. She has amnesia, she's been badly injured, she's been orphaned. And she has no idea what she is or who she is. It turns out she's the first black vampire because of her people's desire for a twenty-four-hour day and her female ancestor's discovery that one of the secrets of the twenty-four-hour day is melanin.

AG: What do you mean?
OB: It helps to have some protection from the sun, so her people managed to genetically engineer her. These vampires are a different species. They are not vampires because somebody bit them, so they—she is genetically engineered to be quite different from her own people. On the other hand, she's not human. So she's kind of alone to begin with. It's just that by the time we meet her she is very much alone, because she knows nothing. She's fifty-three years old, and all those fifty-three years have been taken from her.

JG: How did you first start writing science fiction? You grew up in Pasadena—
OB: Uh huh.

JG: —and how did you first become attracted to that type of writing?
OB: Oh, I think I loved it because, well, I fell into writing it because I saw a bad movie—a movie called *Devil Girl from Mars*—and went into competition with it. But I think I stayed with it because it was so wide open, it gave me the chance to

comment on every aspect of humanity. People tend to think of science fiction as, oh, *Star Wars* or *Star Trek*, and the truth is there are no closed doors, and there are no required formulas. You can go anywhere with it.

AG: We're talking to Octavia Butler, her latest book is *Fledgling*; she wrote the Parable series. As Katrina was happening, in the aftermath of Katrina, a lot of people were talking about Octavia Butler and how the *Parable* series made them think about that. Explain.

OB: I wrote the two *Parable* books back in the 1990s. And they are books about, as I said, what happens because we don't trouble to correct some of the problems that we're brewing for ourselves right now. Global warming is one of those problems. And I was aware of it back in the 1980s. I was reading books about it. And a lot of people were seeing it as politics, as something very iffy, as something they could ignore because nothing was going to come of it tomorrow.

That, and the fact that I think I was paying a lot of attention to education because a lot of my friends were teachers, and the politics of education was getting scarier, it seemed, to me. We were getting to that point where we were thinking more about the building of prisons than of schools and libraries. And I remember while I was working on the novels, my hometown, Pasadena, had a bond issue that they passed to aid libraries, and I was so happy that it passed because so often these things don't. And they had closed a lot of branch libraries and were able to reopen them. So not everybody was going in the wrong direction, but a lot of the country still was. And what I wanted to write was a novel of someone who was coming up with solutions of a sort.

My main character's solution is—well, grows from another religion that she comes up with. Religion is everywhere. There are no human societies without it, whether they acknowledge it as a religion or not. So I thought religion might be an answer, as well as, in some cases, a problem. And in, for instance, *Parable of the Sower* and *Parable of the Talents*, it's both. So I have people who are bringing America to a kind of fascism, because their religion is the only one they're willing to tolerate. On the other hand, I have people who are saying, well, here is another religion, and here are some verses that can help us think in a different way, and here is a destination that isn't something that we have to wait for after we die.

AG: Octavia Butler, could you read a little from *Parable of the Talents*.

OB: I'm going to read a verse or two. And keep in mind these were written early in the 1990s. But I think they apply forever, actually. This first one, I have a character in the books who is, well, someone who is taking the country fascist and who manages to get elected President and, who oddly enough, comes from Texas.

And here is one of the things that my character is inspired to write about, this sort of situation. She says:

> Choose your leaders with wisdom and forethought. To be led by a coward is to be controlled by all that the coward fears. To be led by a fool is to be led by the opportunists who control the fool. To be led by a thief is to offer up your most precious treasures to be stolen. To be led by a liar is to ask to be lied to. To be led by a tyrant is to sell yourself and those you love into slavery.

And there's one other that I thought I should read, because I see it happening so much. I got the idea for it when I heard someone answer a political question with a political slogan. And he didn't seem to realize that he was quoting somebody. He seemed to have thought that he had a creative thought there. And I wrote this verse:

> Beware, all too often we say what we hear others say. We think what we are told that we think. We see what we are permitted to see. Worse, we see what we are told that we see. Repetition and pride are the keys to this. To hear and to see even an obvious lie again and again and again, maybe to say it almost by reflex, and then to defend it because we have said it, and at last to embrace it because we've defended it.

AG: On that note we'll have to leave it there, but we'll continue it online at Democracynow.org. Octavia Butler.

Interviewing the Oracle:
Octavia Butler
Kazembe Balagun/2006

Octavia Butler's conversation style is like her prose: lean and to the point. Not that she does not have a lot to talk about. She has written eleven novels including *Kindred*, whose heroine keeps falling back in time to save her white slavemaster ancestor, and *Parable of the Sower*, a richly imagined tale of a small band of survivors founding a new earth-centered religion in the midst of a post-apocalyptic America.

"You can call it save the world fiction, but it clearly doesn't save anything," she says. "It just calls people's attention to the fact that so much needs to be done and obviously there are people who are running this country who don't care."

Winner of the Hugo Award for science fiction and a MacArthur Genius Fellowship, Butler's fiction bends the boundaries of race and gender, while focusing on the problems of pollution, the legacy of slavery, and racism. *The Indypendent* spoke with Butler while she was on tour promoting *Fledgling*, her first novel in nearly a decade.

Q: What were some of your major influences in terms of the decision to start writing science fiction?
A: I began reading science fiction before I was twelve and started writing science fiction around the same time. I was attracted to science fiction because it was so wide open. I was able to do anything and there were no walls to hem you in and there was no human condition that you were stopped from examining. Well, writing was what I wanted to do, it was always what I wanted to do. I had novels to write so I wrote them.

Q: You mention wide openness and I noticed in *Lilith's Brood* and your most recent novel, *Fledgling*, there is a great concern with bending the constraints of gender, race, and sexuality, as well as open relationships. Do you think polygamy is the future of humanity?

226

A: No, I think the future of humanity will be like the past, we'll do what we've always done, and there will still be human beings. Granted, there will always be people doing something different and there are a lot of possibilities. I think my characters [Lauren in *Parable of the Sower* and Shori Matthews in *Fledgling*] have communities that are important in their lives or build communities around themselves.

Q: Your novels deal with the past, future, and present as one. Some have compared it to the concept of Sankofa: "We look to the past to understand the present and prepare for the future." How do you see the concept of Sankofa playing in your work?

A: Well there's only one novel that remotely deals with that concept and that's *Kindred*. I was trying to make real the emotional reality of slavery. I was trying make people feel more about the data they had learned. I wanted to make the past real and [show] how it scars the present.

Q: What's interesting to you on the literary scene at the moment?

A: I've been on the book tour for a few weeks, which means I haven't read anything more difficult than a newspaper (laughs) so I can't recommend anything in good conscience. One of my favorite books is *Issac's Storm* by Erik Larson. It gives us a picture of the great storm that hit Galveston, Texas, and gives us a picture of 1900. Also a book called *T-Rex and the Crater of Doom* by Walter Alvarez. It's a history of the finding of the asteroid that killed off the dinosaurs. I like it because it shows more about how science is done than most books that you read about the subject. It talks about how the way we think about science can become religious if we are not careful. There were people who were firmly entrenched in the belief that things can only happen one way, they found it difficult that it could happen another way.

Q: Do you see a tension between writing save the world type of fiction and the artistic impulses of the writer?

A: No, not at all. I have written books about making the world a better place and how to make humanity more survivable. While *Fledging* is a different type of book, the Parable series serve as cautionary tales. I wrote the Parable books because of the direction of the country. You can call it save the world fiction, but it clearly doesn't save anything. It just calls people's attention to the fact that so much needs to be done and obviously they are people who are running this country who don't care. I mean look at what the Congress is doing in terms of taking money away from every cause that is helping people who aren't very rich.

Especially making it harder for people to get an education. Who would want to live in a world where there were fewer educated people?

Q: We're speaking at a time of crisis in the country between the Iraq war and Katrina. As a writer what makes you hopeful for the future?
A: At the present, I feel so unhopeful. I recognize we will pay more attention when we have different leadership.

I'm not exactly sure where that leadership will come from. But that doesn't mean I think we're all going down the toilet. I just don't see where that hope will come from. I think we need people with stronger ideals than John Kerry or Bill Clinton. I think we need people with more courage and vision. It's a shame we have had people who are so damn weak.

Index

Lightning Source UK Ltd.
Milton Keynes UK
UKOW01f2223261016
286242UK00001B/281/P